# L'HVOMO
## DI
# LETTERE.

# Daniello Bartoli

# *The Man of Letters*

## *Defended and Emended*

### *in two parts*

An annotated translation from Italian and Latin of

*L'Huomo di Lettere difeso et emendato*

1645

by

Gregory Woods,

*laureato in lettere italiane*, PhD.

Gregory Woods
609 Columbus Ave. 4Q
New York, New York 10024
*gregorywoods90@hotmail.com*

# Translator's Note

At the University of Rome, La Sapienza, my professor in the Faculty of Letters was Alberto Asor Rosa, a foremost Italian critic and author, between 1973 and 1977. This was after I graduated from Trinity College at University of Toronto (Honours BA, MHML, 7T0) and before getting my doctorate in Italian literature at Columbia University (PhD, 1990). Asor Rosa's seminal work on *La cultura della Controriforma* (1974) and on *Daniello Bartoli e la prosa gesuitica* (1975)[1] helped me to focus a growing interest in the Jesuits and the Baroque on the writings of Daniello Bartoli. Under his direction I wrote a study of the Jesuit writer's *L'huomo di lettere difeso et emendato* (1645) for a *laurea in lettere italiane* in 1977. My *tesi di laurea* was a critical review of the dauntingly erudite treatise, followed by a listing of the multiple editions and translations that disseminated this bestselling work internationally as a central work, indeed, a classic, inaugurating the High Baroque. Thereafter, at Columbia, I began my graduate researches with Bartoli's *History of the Society of Jesus* (1650-1673), a monument of Jesuit historiography and a masterpiece of Italian prose. In this context I went back to the roots of Jesuit humanist historical writing in the sixteenth century and followed the formative role of Antonio Possevino (1533-1611) —attempting to illustrate how, out of the contemporary *ars historica* literature of the Late Renaissance, he formulated a Jesuit *ars historica* out of which he articulated the idea and the program of his epochal *Bibliotheca selecta in Historia* (1593).[2]

At Columbia I taught excellent students as an Italian preceptor over the years of my extended doctoral researches. Then I worked as a USIA escort interpreter for professional visitors from Italy. This interesting international work proved fortuitous for me as a passport for decades of extensive travels around America and as a premise for my work as a tour guide for the United States and Canada, especially in and out of New York City, for foreign language groups. Over the years of these professional activities I have been able to continue with my studies and have had the satisfaction of contributing a dozen Wikipedia entries

---

[1] Letteratura Italiana Laterza, volumes 26 & 30.
[2] "Antonio Possevino and the Erasmian sources of the Jesuit *Ars Historica*: From the Perna *Methodus historica* (Basel, 1576) to the *Bibliotheca selecta in Historia* (Rome, 1593) and the *Apparatus ad omnium gentium historiam* (1597)." PhD thesis, Columbia University, 1990.

relating to them since 2006. Thanks to the contemporary bibliographic revolution on the internet, the *seicento* library of Bartoli's editions and much recent scholarship dedicated to them have become available online, and this tremendous boon has facilitated my long-standing intention to present Bartoli's book to a contemporary audience. My translation also provides the original Latin texts, along with many other sources, in the footnotes, as well as pertinent comments and observations to help orient the non-specialized reader. Despite the remarkable celebrity it once enjoyed, Bartoli's *Huomo di lettere* has only become more widely available through its recent reappearance online and through digital reprints. Significantly and most recently, it has generated considerable interest among art historians, particularly for its influence on the work of Salvator Rosa (1615-72). In the context of my presentation in English, I have attempted to participate in and contribute to this interesting discussion in the preface, in some footnotes and through apposite illustrations.

I want to make grateful mention of a few friends who have collaborated with me since the project began in earnest a few years ago. Beth Green, my dear friend and Central Park walking partner, has been a valuable sounding board and a constant confidante. Another great friend, the venerable sage and polymath, David Sprecher, introduced me to self-publishing and schooled me in the procedure involved. Also, he kindly and expertly helped me with the graphics and the design of the cover of this book. Journalist and editor, and friend, Michael Marciano made a careful review of my text suggesting improvements and correcting punctuation, an indispensable professional contribution. In a broader context I am beholden to the Jesuits who taught me, among other things, enough Greek and Latin letters to make it possible for me to undertake this work, and I say in sincere gratitude: *Esto perpetua*. Finally, as "Uncle Grandpa" — and as Bartoli would have me do (pp. 71/2) — I am immensely grateful to my New York ancestors and family of four dozen characters: siblings, spouses, nieces, nephews and all their children. I congratulate and cherish them across the generations for the delight of their abundant humanity and I thank them for their love and support, *sine qua non*.

# CONTENTS

DELL'

# HVOMO
# DI LETTERE

DIFESO
ET EMENDATO
*Parti due*.

DEL
P. DANIELLO BARTOLI
della Compagnia di GIESV.

IN ROMA,
Per gli Heredi di Francefco Corbelletti,
M. DC. XLV.

_____

*Con licenza de' Superiori.*

# PREFACE

## *A Jesuit Vocation to Sanctity and Letters*

Daniello Bartoli was thirty-six when he wrote his *Man of Letters defended and emended.*[1] In his introduction he states that it was composed in the two hottest months of a summer respite from his priestly duties. This was in 1644, the year after his completion of the twenty years of study and training to become a Jesuit professed of four vows in the Society of Jesus. The immediate and resounding success of the book when it appeared in 1645 confirmed to his superiors that the young priest was a prodigy of learning with a great future as a writer. Born in Ferrara in 1608 to a family of professionals and letterati, Daniello was the third son of Tiburzio Bartoli who, like his own father, served at the Renaissance court of Duke Alfonso II Este, (1533-1598)[2] Tiburzio sent his youngest boy to the neighboring school of the Jesuits. It was known not only for the expert teaching of classical humanities, but for its cultivation of science. Clearly the collegio was an intellectual milieu congenial to the talents and interests of the brilliant youth. Following his vocation, the fifteen- year old Daniello entered the Society of Jesus in 1623 at the height of its remarkable ascendancy within Roman Catholicism.[3] The boy was inspired by the missionary apostolate of Francis Xavier (1507-1553) in India and Japan, who, together with the order's founder, Ignatius Loyola (1491-1556), were then canonized as the first Jesuit saints. In the steady stream of the *Indipetae* that the novice and scholastic addressed to Jesuit General Muzio Vitelleschi he requested assignment to the Jesuit foreign missions, declaring his vocation to apostolic service and even to martyrdom. But his repeated urgings were denied by superiors who were more committed to fostering his manifest intellectual and literary talents and protective of his less than robust health.[4]

While Bartoli's mastery of classical learning was prodigious, he was also deeply emersed in the scientific culture of the age of Galileo (1564-1642) and

---

1 *L'Huomo di lettere difeso et emendato, Parti due del p. Daniello Bartoli della Compagnia di Gesu, in Roma, per gli Heredi di Francesco Corbelletti* MDCXLV.

2 The narrator of Robert Browning's *My Last Duchess* (1842).

3 Alberto Asor Rosa presents Bartoli's work and importance, *DBI, Dizionario Biografico degli Italiani*, (Volume 6, 1964), in an excellent biographical article. In English, see Mattia Begala, "Daniello Bartoli" in *Encyclopedia of Italian Literary Studies*, 1, (2007) 133/6. See the entry in Wikipedia as well.

4 Marc Fumaroli connects these with the "grand desires" envisioned in the *Spiritual Exercises* of Ignatius Loyola, in discussing Bartoli's literary vocation, 'The Fertility and Shortcomings of Renaissance Rhetoric; The Jesuit Case," *The Jesuits, Cultures, Sciences and the Arts*, 1540-1773, (1999), pp. 90-106.

became adept in the use of telescope.[5] Indeed, at the age of twenty-two, in 1630, he used the improved telescope of his teacher, Jesuit astronomer Niccolò Zucchi (1586-1670), to record the first observations of the cloud belts of Jupiter. For this his name, as **Bartolus,** was assigned to a lunar crater, (see p.20). marked at the bottom of the famous moon map printed by Jesuits Riccioli and Grimaldi in their *Almagestum Novum* (Bologna, 1651) (see pp.20 & 247).

The era of Galileo was that of Bartoli's youth, from the success of his *Siderius Nuntius* (1610), to the tragedy of his trial for disputing Biblical cosmology (1633), to his retirement and death at Arcetri in 1642. In a sense the clamorous response to *The Man of Letters* three years later heralded the advent of a new cultural age, the Baroque. The book gave eloquent expression in literary Italian, not in the official Latin of ecclesiastical culture, to a contemporary doctrine of classicism. It spoke a contemporary language that was modern in its world view and adroit in its command of the vast heritage of traditional learning. *The Man of Letters* expressed, to the wonderment of his mid-century generation, the *zeitgeist* of the Baroque. From its Rome headquarters the powerful Jesuit order was at work formulating a fusion of Catholic teaching with the newly global world view of its missions to the four corners of the earth.

Before his book's appearance Bartoli was already engaged in a successful career as a preacher which began after he was ordained to the priesthood in 1637 at the age of 29. Among the cities he visited, his preaching brought him home to Ferrara. It was likely there, where he was stationed in 1640 and 1641 that he composed a set of moral poems envisaged with musical accompaniment.[6] Printed under his nephew's name, a revealing amount of its poetry is cited without attribution in *The Man of Letters*. During the 1640s the young Jesuit's popularity in the pulpit led him beyond the Northern Italian confines of his life at the Jesuit houses of his region, Parma, Piacenza, Milan, and Bologna, where he pursued his studies and became an experienced Jesuit master of Letters. After his book was published Bartoli began to head farther afield to Naples and Palermo and Malta for seasons of Advent and Lenten sermons. In 1646, however, setting out for Palermo, he was shipwrecked in a tempest off Capri. The young preacher made it to shore with his life, but the bulk of his homiletical writings was lost to the storm. This life or death moment would be Bartoli's only personal encounter with the type of adventure he became a master at dramatizing in his *Istoria della Compagnia di Gesù*.

The *burrasca* off Capri eventually put an end to his travels preaching and his decade of itineracy closed permanently in 1648. In that year his gifts as an

---

5 Eric Flint's 1632 series, particularly *The Galileo Affair* (2004) invents an alternate history with many of the particulars of the clash between science and religion of Bartoli's formative years, dictating his cultural agenda.

[6] *Saggio delle poesie morali di Gio. Battista Bartoli, All'ilustrissiimo Sig. Alessandro Canani, Ambasciatore a N. Sig. Urbano VIII per la Città di Ferrara* (Benacci: Bologna, 1642.)

Italian writer were placed by Jesuit General Vincenzo Caraffa at the service of Jesuit history. And so, from the age of forty on, Bartoli dutifully stayed in Rome where he became a literary *primum mobile* of the High Baroque. As such he appears in Robert Browning's *Parleyings with Certain People of Importance in their Day* (1887). Bartoli the writer was indefatigable and produced a whole library of literary, moral, spiritual and scientific works, along with the monumental *Istoria della Compagnia di Gesù,* including volumes on the founder, Ignatius Loyola (1650), Asia (1653), Japan (1660), China (1663), England (1667) and Italy (1673). The excellent *ottocento* Turin edition of the *Istoria* by Giacinto Marietti presents this *magnum opus* in 39 octavo volumes that together run to more than 10,000 pages making it, sizewise, the greatest work of Italian literature.[7]

### Daniello Bartoli and Salvator Rosa

The author of *The Man of Letters* was older at the time than the cleric looking pensively away from his manuscript painted by Salvator Rosa in his *Allegory of Study*. Rosa's work, in closeup, also serves to represent, if not Bartoli himself, then Bartoli's *Man of Letters* on the cover of this book. The image is taken from an etching of Rosa's painting done in 1807 and the full etching serves as the frontispiece for my translation. The original portrait, contemporary with the celebrity of *The Man of Letters* (1645), is now in the Ringling Museum, Sarasota, Florida, whereas the etching of it was published in London as the portrait of the young Rosa himself. This was during the Regency period when the adventurous Neapolitan reigned as the favorite painter-protagonist of the Romantics, especially for the British.[8] The sitter is portrayed dressed in a luxuriously highlighted clerical cassock and wearing his *zucchetto*, a clerical skull cap. He pauses at his writing table, pen in one hand above the inkwell and writing board in the other as it holds his manuscript propped on a pile of folio tomes. He has a manly head turned away in three quarters to a point outside the canvas, but away from the viewer. His fixed gaze of reverie catches our attention and invites us into his moment of reflection. But who is this personification of the scholar-writer, if it is not the painter himself, as was once thought? Salvator Rosa (1615-1673), born in Naples, then active in Rome until 1639, was thirty when in Florence he came under the influence of *The Man of Letters*. He had left Rome and settled there under the patronage of Cardinal Giovanni Carlo de' Medici (1611-1663) and was soon a leading figure as a painter and a man of the theatre, particularly attracting attention for his satires on Music, Poetry, Painting, and War. Rosa's

---

7 For a summary of Bartoli's vast historical production, see the entry on *Istoria della Compagnia di Gesu* in Wikipedia.
8 Engraver James Neagle's work is poorly reproduced as the mistaken portrait frontispiece of Lady Sydney Morgan's popular portrayal of *the Life and Times of Salvator Rosa* (1823).

circle of young artists and literary figures gathered around him as the prince of his *Academia dei Percossi, (Academy of the Shaken Up).*[9]

In another of Rosa's works of this period, the *Allegory of Falsehood (Allegoria della Menzogna)* his subject is dressed as an actor in a white surplus, holding up the mask of a comic *persona* in his right hand and pointing dramatically to it with the classically posed forefinger of his left hand.[10] In both paintings— the face and facial air, the hands and eyebrows and hair of this intense young man, also in three quarters— seem identical. This painting, which has also been named *Plautus and Terence,* hangs in Palazzo Pitti in Florence and, though I am not an art historian, I would venture to identify Rosa's sitter as Giovanni Battista Ricciardi (1623-1686), in his early twenties, fifteen years younger than Bartoli and eight years younger than Rosa.[11] In Florence he and Rosa both fell under the influence of the new book.

---

9 The source work of art historian and contemporary Filippo Baldinucci (1624-1697) on Rosa appeared as a *Vita* in 1822, just before Lady Morgan's *Life and Times*. Besides the uptodate online entry in the *Dizionario Biografico degli Italiani* (2017) there is Helen Langdon's *Salvator Rosa* (2010).

[10] In *Salvator Rosa,* (Hayward Gallery, London, 1973), Helen Langdon discusses these two paintings (*La Menzogna* and *Portrait of a Poet*), their dating and classical style, with a reference to Raphael and describes them as companion pieces, p.26.

[11] Both paintings have received only limited critical attention. I am unaware that their identification with Ricciardi has been previously proposed.

Ricciardi was noble but illegitimate, the son of a wealthy Florentine *marchese*. His mother was a noble, but married lady of Pisa where he was raised and studied at the university. Thereafter he went to Florence, where he emerged as a brilliant and erudite youth— a talented fellow actor with Rosa, a comic playwright, and in time, a professor of moral philosophy.[12] He became close friends with the entertaining, brilliant and somewhat vainglorious painter from Naples. Rosa was in Florence from 1640 after he left Rome as the result of an altercation with the also Naples-born Gian Lorenzo Bernini, his senior by 17 years. Rosa would sojourn regularly at Ricciardi's villa, Strozzavolpe in Chianti, and at other country seats of his patrician colleagues, members of his *Percossi*. In discourse with the erudite Ricciardi, he deepened his reading of Seneca and his familiarity with the ancient Greek philosophers.[13] His young circle in the Florence of the 1640s included painters, men of science, and men of letters such as poet-satirist Antonio Abati and the preacher and playright Reginaldo Sgambati, this last— like Rosa, a transplanted Neapolitan. The *Lives and Opinions of the Eminent Philosophers* of Diogenes Laertius. (3rd century AD) covers 83 Greek philosophers, was an important source for Renaissance scholars, in the original Greek, and in the Latin and Italian translations that became available. It serves as Bartoli's main reference for the lives of the sages in *The Man of Letters*. The ten books of the work divide the Ionian tradition (1-7) beginning with Thales, from the Italian schools beginning with Pythagoras (8-10). This work particularly drew Rosa's attention and became a principal source over his career for the classically inspired subjects of his paintings and etchings. It consists of anecdotes and sayings of the sages including Socrates and Plato, Diogenes and Democritus, Zeno, Aristotle and Crato. Partially due to Bartoli they became the cult figures of Rosa and his contemporaries. Therefore, while the *Allegory of Study* does not depict Bartoli in the flesh, Rosa's portrayal is clearly shaped by the model he articulates in the *Man of Letters*. Both Bartoli's book and Rosa's painting depict the life of study, reflection and writing that the painter aspired to embody in his art.[14]

Recent articles and scholarly research over the last decade have brought new attention to this important relationship, most notably the penetrating studies of English art historian, Helen Langdon, which document the *Man of Letters* as

---

[12] The recent (2016) entry on Ricciardi in the *DBI* is detailed and well-documented.

13 It would be interesting to know more about Ricciardi's classical formation. As they read *The Man of Letters* together, Rosa was encouraged in his desire to don the philosopher's mantle prescribed by Bartoli. Their shared love of antiquity cemented a lifelong friendship and correspondence between the two, even after Rosa moved permanently to Rome in 1650.

14 This is also expressively rendered in the meditative *Self Portrait* the painter dedicated to Ricciardi in the Metropolitan Museum of New York. The same book of Seneca's *Epistulae* may also be in the earlier, Bartoli-inspired, painting.

an influential source for Rosa's work.[15] At the same time her Italian colleague, Floriana Conte, has focused in a number of recent articles on the relationship between Rosa and Bartoli and her findings have now been brought together in an important monograph on Rosa.[16] Most relevant in this connection is in the Florentine edition of the work is the letter of dedication she reprints addressed to none other than Salvator Rosa. Florentine printer, Girolamo Signoretti, friend, admirer and collector of the magnetic painter, addresses him in the letter as the "principe" of his "*Percossi*" and mentions fellow members Abati and Sgambati as promoters of this new edition. He pays tribute to Rosa's entrepreneurship in championing the new book within the younger milieu of his group, rivaling with the more established academies of Florence, like the *Crusca.* His letter also makes the direct connection between *The Man of Letters* and Rosa's *Allegory of Study* as Signoretti tries to suggest the type of painting that the *Man of Letters* might inspire in the artist. *"Who better than you could portray a Man of Letters? Indeed, your canvases have already demonstrated your ability to do so. You might paint a philosopher holding a book, and rather than painting him as a baby, as nature would, you would paint him with the manly aspect of a Prometheus."*

### L'Huomo di Lettere difeso et emendato, parti due.

Bartoli presents his *Man of Letters* in two parts, a defense and an emendation.[17] His defense in **Part One** exalts the Stoic virtue preached by Seneca as the path to overcoming the vicissitudes of the examined life. The **Introduction** features the classical tableau of the exemplary Anaxagoras and adds the writer himself to the list of the champions of Letters.**1**. *Men of Letters Neglected* serves as the premise of his defense and depicts his protagonist at the mercy of the unsupportive, even hostile world of neglectful rulers and scorned by their uncaring inferiors. **2**. *The Taste of Understanding* is the nucleus of his defense. He argues for the transcendent superiority of his letterato through his neo-

---

15 Helen Langdon, *The Representation of Philosophers in the Art of Salvator Rosa,* (2011), Online; "The Demosthenes of painting, Salvator Rosa and the 17th Century Sublime" in *Translations of the Sublime,* ed. Caroline Van Eyk, (2012); "Relics of the Golden Age'' in *Others and Outcasts in Early Modern Europe,* ed. Tom Nichols, 2017.
16 *Tra Napoli e Milano. Viaggi di artisti nell'Italia del Seicento II. Salvator Rosa* (2014). Thus far she has not connected it with Bartoli's spirited repudiation of this printing, *alla fiorentina,* which sparked his later treatise, *Il torto ed il diritto del non si può,* (1655) written under the pointedly anti-Florentine pseudonym, Ferrante Longobardi.
[17] Recently, a discerning presentation of several of the book's main headings is offered by Sari Kivistö, *The Vices of Learning: Morality and Learning at Early Modern Universities,* (Leiden: Brill, 2014) based on a Latin edition (Cologne, 1674) and the English translation (1660), mistakenly attributed to Thomas Snowden, rather than Thomas Salubury.

platonic, almost brahmanic access to a higher state of consciousness to which he is led by his growing enlightenment. With his premise set and the superiority of his protagonist established, he further pursues his defense of the Man of Letters in two mirrored chapters. The first, **3**. *The Felicity of the Sages*, shows them stoically impervious to a series of miseries. The second series, **4**. *The Infelicity of the Ignorant*, demonstrates how true fulfillment is beyond the reach of the uneducated. They both offer an ingenious series of vignettes as illustrations. First, in the *Felicity of the Sage*, Sapience is still happy in poverty (3.1), exile (3.2), prison (3.3) and sickness (3.4). Next, in *The Infelicity of Ignorant* Ignorance continues to be miserable, even despite sanctity (4.1) or the enjoyment of high rank (4.2), or the advantages of arms (4.3), and riches (4.4.), because forlorn of Letters a man lacks the integrity of being and personality (4.5). **Part Two,** presented under nine different headings, is Bartoli's emendation, an exercise in ethical deontology for the profession of Letters, the *"do"*s and *"don't"*'s of the writer's life. It runs through the list of moral and practical failings that he must recognize, avoid, emend, a catalogue reviewing different aspects of failings in Letters subject to correction: **5**. *Plagiary,* **6**. *Lasciviousness,* **7**. *Slander,* **8**. *Haughtiness,* **9**. *Laziness,* **10**. *Imprudence,* **11**. *Ambition,* **12**. *Avarice.* Finally, there is an extended chapter of knowing instruction under the rubric, **13**. *Obscurity,* articulated in nine separate sections (13.1-9). It is a *How to* of starting the work of writing and in it Bartoli follows Cicero and Quintilian as a master of rhetoric and demonstrates his talent and experience as a teacher.[18]

### *The International Fortune of Bartoli's "Happy Pen"*

In a few years every major Italian center had produced editions of Bartoli's book after the first two in Rome and Florence, including Bologna, Milan and the capital of the printing industry, Venice, where a steady stream of editions and reprints appeared over the following decades. At the same time, the work also began to attract international attention. *L'huomo di lettere* was at the height of its fashion in the early 1650s when the cultivated Queen Christina of Sweden in Stockholm asked her Jesuit visitors for a copy.[19] During Bartoli's lifetime translations in five different languages were added to the host of Italian editions of this contemporary *vademecum* for letterati. Translations appeared in French

---

18 For the purposes of organization and reference I have grouped and numbered Bartoli's forty odd sections under 13 main chapter titles and under them the headings he uses are articulated as numbered subsections. In this I am following the final translation into Dutch (Amsterdam, 1722) by the eighty- year old Mennonite apothecary, Lambert Bidloo. He provides Roman numerals for the separate headings of Part One (I-XI) and Part Two (I-XXVIII).
19 John J. Renaldo, *Daniello Bartoli, a Letterato of the Seicento*, (Naples, 1979), p.41. This was during the process of her conversion to Rome.where a few years later she would meet the author along with Athanasius Kircher at the ceremonies of welcome offered to her at the Jesuit Collegio Romano.

(1651), German (1654), English (1660), Latin (1672) and Spanish (1678). Among the illustrations I have used many of their interesting frontispieces and titlepages, as listed on pp. 245-6. Dutch was added to the catalogue as the last of six translations in 1722.[20] In addition to the Italian editions, these vernacularizations gave Bartoli's book a certain prominence in the Letters of the international Baroque

The Welsh Thomas Salusbury (c.1625-1665) celebrating what he features as "*the happy pen*" of Bartoli, brought out his translation as *The Learned Man Defended and Reform'd* in 1660, (pp.78-79).[21] He begins by hailing George Monk and William Prinne as the leaders responsible for the Restoration of Charles II.[22] Salusbury had spent several years in Italy after the decapitation of Charles I and during the interregnum of Cromwell. He was a companion and perhaps the secretary of Sir Kenelm Digby (1603-1665), a Catholic representative of the exiled English Queen, Henrietta Maria (1609-1669) whom he served as the ambassador for interests of the English Catholics in Italy. The preface of the London book relates that Digby had actively promoted the work and planned a translation that never materialized.[23] Salusbury's own energetic and literate translation was printed by William Leybourn (1626-1716), a publisher of scientific works with connections to the Royal Society. Leybourn also printed Salusbury's interesting *Mathematical Collections and Translations* (1661).[24] His translation of Bartoli speaks the flavorful language of his times, though occasionally he is hard put to render correctly the work's elaborately construed style and sense.[25]

---

20 All of them, and some later versions are detailed and discussed with online links to the originals in the article on *L'huomo di lettere* in Wikipedia.

21 Now available in recent reprints of 2013 and 2017. It seems that through this translation Bartoli travelled to America in the library of the Virginia planter, diarist and man of letters, William Byrd II, (1674-1744).

22 The cover illustration copied from a Venetian edition inserts the Salusburty coat of arms, relating him, likely from the wrong side of the bed, to the noble Welsh family of that name, baronets of Lleweni Hall.

23 "*such is its esteem in the Italian Tongue, that several promised it in ours, more especially one, a Gentleman of Known Parts, who at the recreative hours, during his residence with the character of an Publick minister in Italy, had taught it English.*"

24 In two volumes. Works by Descartes, Tartaglia, Castelli and Torricelli as well as Salusbury's translation of Galileo's *Dialogue on the Great World Systems*, edited and published by Giorgio de Santillana at the University of Chicago Press, 1953 The second volume, the first printed life of Galileo, was lost in the Fire of London and only recently rediscovered.

25 The meaning, if not the style, of Bartoli's text I have endeavored to disentangle from the labyrinth of his relative clauses and to clarify what they have to say by breaking his bravura periodic sentences into shorter cumulative units, from hypotaxis to parataxis.

Bartoli's store of myriad quotations in Latin are transcribed by Salusbury accurately, but with no translation. As to the present value of Salusbury's *Learned Man,* drawbacks are its quaint but antiquated English and the obstacle of the untranslated Latin quotes. Both factors contribute to keep contact with the discourse of *The Man of Letters* at arms length. Such impediments and my affinity for Baroque culture have motivated me in this enterprise and I present this new annotated edition to offer a translation of the texts in Latin and Italian through the American medium of a not antiquated, but not thoroughly contemporary, English. Twenty-first century readers and researchers cannot be expected to savor the treasury of carefully chosen citations from the ancients, as were the readers of Bartoli's and Salusbury's time. The *Anatomy of Melancholy* and *Religio Medici* are steeped in the same Latin literacy and their authors, Richard Burton (1577-1640) and Sir Thomas Browne (1605-1682), are prose masters on a par with Bartoli in their Baroque style and erudition. These writers represent the contemporary *"rhetoric of quotations"* studded with the original Latin of the classical authors or the Latin rendering of Greek texts. This grandiloquent style is pivotally important in the shift from the Latin of the *res publica litterarum* of the Late Renaissance to vernacular languages of the separate national literatures in which Bartoli's work plays a transitional role. It serves as the hybrid of a bilingual classicism that the seventeenth century prose masters so energetically marshalled and personalized to their expressive purposes.[26]

## *Theatrum mundi and* Coincidentia oppositorum

Bartoli's work may no longer transport, but it still reflects the cultural milieu and aspirations of the Baroque— classicism with a twist, if you will. The Baroque perceived the world as the theatre of a cosmic drama. This is both a standard classical theme as well as a *leitmotif* of Bartoli's writing. His world is a spectacle grand enough to stage contrasting scenes and metamorphoses where contradictory streams of information alternate. So, for example, the traditional scientific precepts of Ptolemy and the Aristotelians share company with the innovative experimental science of the telescope and the microscope. In frequent passages Bartoli uses the familiar language of astrology to ornament his presentation, (*Imprudence*, 10.1) but he also mockingly negates its validity (*Ambition*, 11.2). He employs the full baggage of Ptolemaic cosmology in support of his discourse, while he regularly dismisses it as fanciful. He does so repeatedly, as in the exordium to Part Two with an analogy on planetary movement that he confesses to be untrue. He investigates confidently the semiotic pretensions of conjectural physiognomy popularized by Giacomo Della Porta and then

---

26 This significant chapter in the evolution of modern style is elucidated in the writings of Marc Fumaroli, most notably, *L'Âge de l'Éloquence: rhétorique et «res literaria» de la Renaissance au seuil de l'Époque Classique* (3rd ed., 2009).

bemusedly dismisses them as totally bogus (*Imprudence*, 10.2). He discourses interersting ly on the optimal balance between Wit (*ingegno*) and judgement (*giudizio*) in the innate genius (*genio*) of the individual, but his artful deployment of the component four humors constructs a fanciful chart that undercuts acute observations with pseudo-scientific embellishments (*Ambition*, 11.2). On one hand (*Imprudence*, 10.2) he extols Plato and the philosopher-sages of antiquity for laying the foundations of human understanding, on the other (*Haughtiness*, 8.2) he rigidly consigns them to the hell of pagans and non-believers. You might say that his rhetoric wants it both ways. In the central encounter between empire and philosophy, it is not so much either Alexander or Diogenes, rather more Alexander and Diogenes. Bartoli presents and develops a sequence of shifting and, at times, contradictory thoughts with the energy and enthusiasm of a rhetorically empowered prose master. His eloquence is parenetic, persuasive and personable. To carry his argument, he employs oratory in a variety of registers. As the Jesuit dictum teaches, *Fortiter in re, suaviter in modo.* (vigorously in execution, gently in manner). For the readers of his day the ancient wisdom he held forth in his *prosa d'arte* never spoke in a language so contemporary. The time-honored quarrel about the advancement of learning between the ancients and the moderns was a standard theme of literary discussion. Between the fundamental wisdom of the ancients and the compelling discoveries of moderns like Columbus and Galileo (*Plagiary*, 5.2), Bartoli holds to the *via media* .in the contest between the primacy of classical tradition and the promise of modern innovation.

## *The Baroque Plethora and The Taste of Understanding*

Bartoli's writing was deeply rooted in the world of sensation. He lives the life of letters as the communication of a transcendental world and of its revealing inklings. Within the horizons of his empyrean inner world, he experiences the sublime to such a degree that he can taste it, to employ a descriptive current metaphor which speaks directly to Bartoli's central conceit. The ideal of consummate eloquence that enchanted Italian letters, especially after Tasso, finds a unique voice in him. His mastery of expression has the capacity to weave together language and erudition into a kind of verbal incantation. Bartoli's **Taste of Understanding** (*il Gusto dell'intendere*) is the title for his second discourse, aimed at transporting awareness from the temporal to the eternal. His word for Understanding is *Intendere* and this expresses a far more direct physical experience of intellection than English renders with *Understanding*. Following behind his sage philosophers he guides his would-be man of letters along the great chain of being in a continuum of experience where man and art, nature and divinity are perceptibly intertwined.

For his Man of Letters **Taste** serves as an important conceptual link between the sensual and the intellectual spheres of perception and understanding. In a way it is the supreme Baroque conceit, a symbol of the interrelationship of the physical and the supernatural reflecting the sensibility of his time. The link between the originally physical experience of Taste transported to the metaphysical experience of Understanding is a startling connection. It symbolizes the characteristic synesthesia of the Baroque in the multiplicity of its cultural manifestations. And it is at the heart of Bartoli's artistic vision and his unique *prosa d'arte*.[27] As an oxymoron, expressing the coincidence of antithetical realities, it represents a characteristic stylistic feature of Bartoli's writing, heightening perception by articulating its apparently contradictory nature.[28] His Baroque mixture of the sensory and the spiritual also represents a much commented on aspect of the spirituality of the Jesuits, grounded as it is in the technique of sensory imagination developed by Ignatius Loyola in his *Spiritual Exercises*. To underscore these themes, I have capitalized the word **Taste** in my translation, along with other key terms I highlight here.

### Res Publica Literarum: Letters

Additionally, I have emphasized the role of **Letters** in my translation by retaining and capitalizing the term to underscore the lineage and the currency of the phrase, *"man of letters."*[29] The expression championed by Bartoli is still in modern usage, particularly in the Romance languages, though perhaps with less frequency in our own. Originally it meant a man of learning equipped by the study of the Greek and Latin classics in the original as a humanist. Now it is less restrictive as applied to practitioners of the literary arts. In its simplicity, letter denotes the alphabetical grapheme, *littera*, from the proto-European *"leyt"* (to scratch), the writing of human speech that has shaped the character and art of civilized communication. In the plural, Letters becomes a synecdoche, the single part that signifies the whole character of written language from letters, to literacy to literature, etc. It is the element of literacy in *Lettere* that conveys its dominion over education, literature, philosophy and culture at large. *Literatus* (man of letters) and *sapientis* (sage) are both terms frequent in the letters of Seneca, his

---

27 In *Del Bene* (Rome: Corbelletti,1644), Jesuit Sforza Pallavicino (1607-1667) investigates the epistemology of sensory perception as a *prima apprensione* and develops *diletto* (delight), an aesthetic equivalent to the *gusto* (taste) of Bartoli. Another interesting connection and possible influence, based on common Stoic sources and the intermittency of his ex-Jesuit teacher, Franciscus Van den Enden (1602-1674), might be established between Bartoli's motivating *gusto* and the similar impulse toward divinity, the *conatus* subsequently elaborated in the *Ethica* of Benedict de Spinoza (1632-1677).

28 Bice Mortara Garavelli places Bartoli's use of oxymoron at the center of his Baroque universe of opposition and harmonization, of interchangeability and unity. See the Introduction to her 1992 edition of *La Ricreazione del Savio* (1659).

29 On Bartoli's formative role in this context, see Raymond Chartier, "The Man ol Letters," in *Enlightenment Portraits*, ed. Michel Vovelle, (Chicago, 1997), pp.169/70.

guiding text. In Bartoli's world, these Letters were of the essence, the passport to all the higher professions. Leonardo Da Vinci, despite his confident technical curiosity, famously and somewhat ruefully described himself as *"omo sanza lettere"* for lacking classical letters. The Renaissance encouraged its artists and scientists to claim this privileged status, on the order of the great Galileo, and this was Salvator Rosa's grand desire.

## *Cultura Ingeniorum, and the Engine of Wit*

*Ingenium, ingegno* or the word I use for it, **Wit**, is another essential component of the *Man of Letters*. For Bartoli, as for the Jesuit pedagogues who developed the *Ratio studiorum* (1599), Wit's creative intellectual energy or *ingegno* was paramount. It dictated their agenda as pedagogical systematizers and masters of letters.[30] One founder of this systematic approach to schooling in the classics, Antonio Possevino (1533-1611) was an accomplished man of letters before joining the Jesuit order in 1559. In his *Bibliotheca selecta* (1593), an official bibliography of Catholic learning, he enunciated the Jesuit pedagogical principles as the program of the *cultura ingeniorum (cultivation of the Wit)*.[31] The divine gift of intelligence required such cultivation as a humanist education could provide. Consequently, the discernment of Wit was essential to their success and made their methods and pedagogy greatly admired.[32] Bartoli discussed the key role of discernment of Wit for school masters at the end of his clever dismissal of conjectural psychology (Imprudence, 10.2).[33] **Wit** is another capitalization. Salusbury's word renders the intellectual vibrancy of *ingegno,* as Wit or Wits. It is a fundamental concept, essential to the mental creativity Bartoli theorizes and celebrates.

## *Sapience and Quotes*

To the list of capitalized words after Taste, Letters and Wit I add **Sapience** and **Sage** as a fourth. The now unfamiliar term **Sapience** I retain rather than wisdom, for its ability to indicate an accumulation of knowledge rather than a level of philosophical understanding. **Sage** is taken from Seneca's *sapientis*. I do not uniformly capitalize sage, but hope it conveys the philosophical dignity due to Bartoli's *savio* as it conveys a more engaged intellectuality than the "wise man" used by Salusbury.

---

[30] For some of the history of Jesuit humanism's *ars rhetortca,* see Robert Maryk, *Saint Cicero and the Jesuits,* (Ashgate, 2008).
31 For Possevino and the *Bibliotheca selecta,* and other links, see the summary entries in Wikipedia.
[32] *"For education, consult the schools of the Jesuits. Nothing hitherto in practice surpasses this."* Francis Bacon, *The Advancement of Learning* (1605).
33 The contemporary Spanish Jesuit, Balthasar Gracián (1601-1658) wrote discerningly on the use of Wit in his *Agudeza y arte de ingenio* (Huesca, 1648).

## Preface

There is much that can be said about the timeliness and untimeliness of this Baroque classic which has lately sparked critical attention. The classical rhetorical ideal of the *vir bonus dicendi peritus* has its Baroque incarnation in Bartoli's *huomo di lettere*. One is hard put to characterize the prodigious erudition the author so skillfully displays as more distinctive for its depth of learning, the universality of its information or the fluidity of its stylistic range. Bartoli's engagement with the early modern age of discovery, and with natural philosophy and contemporary science in general, speaks for both the transitional understandings and the enduring achievements of his age. On the negative side, the traditions of sexism and misogynism Bartoli reflects and propagates are wrong beyond historicizing and blatantly objectionable. The celibate Bartoli is self-censuring and diffident on this score. He has little understanding or no interest in women. For him they are definitely from another planet at a farther remove from divine intelligence  Also, Bartoli's *procul harum* élitism limits the human dimensions of his spokesmanship for learning. For Bartoli there is no easy access to the cult of his ancient household gods. But his "happy pen" does cover a universe of marvels as he describes them. His moral judgements and advice are thoughtful and engagingly presented, with a characteristic Wit and sacerdotal good humor. Consequently, and furthermore, in the context of critical evaluation, I have provided related information and comments in the footnotes. My principal commitment in the footnotes is to preserve the original text of Bartoli's Latin borrowings, the sources, classical, Christian and poetic, decorating his discourse. As an Italianist rather than a Latinist, I can say that the choice excerpts he takes from Italian poetry corroborate the impeccable good taste of his classical florilegium in Latin.

The quotations from the Latin poets that one was expected as a *letterato* to know, like Bartoli, by heart, I have identified. They are generally from the *Aenied* and the *Eclogues* and *Georgics* of Virgil and from the *Metamorphoses* of Ovid, from the *Ars Poetica* of Horace, and from the poetry of Seneca, Lucan, etc. Along with other modern critcs, Ezio Raimondi, an important voice in reviving interest in Bartoli's writing, has written on the unreliability of many of the author's citations and marginal source references.[34] My experience is that his sourcing is good over all, though in cases where he has used or provided an alternate reading of the text I have tried to include the original text in parentheses.

### Daniello Bartoli, Defended and Emended

Bartoli's idiosyncratic *Man of Letters* is a cultural polyhedron that reflects the dynamic and contradictory impulses of the Baroque *theatrum mundi* in the seventeenth century drama between the poles of faith and science.[35] It

---

34 "Daniello Bartoli e la Ricreazione del Savio" *in Letteratura barocca. Studi sul Seicento italiano.* 1961.
35 *"Do I contradict myself? Very well, I contradict myself. I am large, I contain multitudes."* For me Bartoli and Whitman share a poetic consciousness of

assumes a spokesmanship that gives the collective memory of classical tradition its say in a modern language. Affirming that the *magisterium* of this tradition still holds, the book engages the reader in a logic energetically sculpted by Baroque Wit. It uses language and learning to harmonize a variety of opposite truths in a sonorous composition of thematic counterpoints. This peregrination of Wit through space and time invites the reader to follow his *Taste of Understanding* into a world of knowledge where research into unfamiliar sources and authors is part of its instruction, its pleasure and its interest. Following the labyrinthine ways of Bartoli's classical wisdom and sparkling erudition is like a moonlit amble along the statued terraces and Baroque fountains of a garden setting in silhouette illuminated by the heavenly spectacle of the stellar universe, by those *cose belle* that spark the cosmic inspiration of Bartoli and of his poet Dante.[36]

*The Man of Letters defended and emended* is an adventure of the mind that harmonizes with revolutionary movement of our own cybercentury which has quite miraculously revived its consummate spokesmanship for the consciousness of the life of the mind. Whatsmore, we are living through the second four century cycle established for 1600 and 2000 by the Gregorian calendar. This repetition makes every date on our calendar the same weekday it was four hundred years ago. For example, Daniello Bartoli's Aquarius birthday on February 12, 1608 was on on a Tuesday and was again a Tuesday in 2008. The year of this writing, 2018, his birthday was a Monday, as it was in 1618 when Danny boy was ten and talented in Ferrara. And so I offer my rendering of his *Man of Letters* as a second-cycle, neo-Baroque work in progress, a mission back in time to the early modern world moving, *nolens, volens*, willy-nilly, toward our own. Eternity occupies three dimensions— past, present and future— but only in the record of the past has eternity achieved the immortality not found in the eternal present or in the eternal future. Aristotle in his *Nichomachean Ethics* quotes what Agathon has to say about the historical past, that even the gods cannot undo it. History, according to Thucydides, transcends mortality as an eternal possession. Just as he experienced this though the immortal classics, to read Bartoli is to live in an immortal past embraced by eternity. His *Taste of Understanding* offers us a sublime nourishment in the marvelous banquet of knowledge he has set for his *Man of Letters*.

New York City                                                    Gregory Woods

---

creation, infinite in its particularity and infinite in its unity. Whitman's poetry glories in the cosmic "taste of understanding." celebrated in Bartoli's prose. But while his Christian faith moved Bartoli to spiritualize the mystery of suffering and the problem of evil, Whitman, the pantheist, though compassionate, is agnostic.

# REFERENCES and ABBREVATIONS

Here is a list of source texts and abbreviations that are used in the notes:

Diogenes Laertius, *Lives and Opinions of Eminent Philosophers*, Books 1-10 and numbered paragraphs:
**Laertius, *Speusippus*, 4.1**.

Aulus Gellius, *Noctes Atticae*, 1-20:
**Gellius,**

Claudius Aelianus, *Varia historia*, 1-14:
**Aelian,**
Seneca the Younger,
*Epistulae morales ad Licilius* 1-124:
**Seneca, *Letter***

His *Quaestiones Naturales*, 1-7:
**Seneca, *QN*,**

Pliny the Elder, *Historia naturalis*, 1-38:
**Pliny,**

Virgil, *Aeneid* 1-12:      ***Aenied***

Ovid, *Metamorphoses*, Books 1-15:
**Ovid, *Met.*,**

Lucan, *Pharsalia* (*De Bello Civili*) 1-10:
**Lucan, *Pharsalia***

For Plutarch, Bartoli quotes the Latin titles for the 78 sections of his *Moralia*, I give the title in Latin or English, e.g. *On the Fortune or the Virtue of Alexander*.

For Plutarch's *Lives* and *The Twelve Caesars* of Suetonius I cite the eponymous biographical section, viz. *Theseus* and *Vespasian*.

The careful reader has enough to do in the ancient world of philosophy, science, poetry and Letters for his or her information. I have attempted to reward interest and diligence and provide relief from the scruples of chronology by providing the dates of some of those mentioned and quoted.

The translations of the Latin and of the Italian texts, after consulting with others, are my own. Otherwise, I cite the translator I use, for example, John Dryden for the *Aeneid* and Thomas Salusbury for the *Divina Commedia*.

The original authors and works cited by Bartoli in his margins and in his text are printed in **bold: Vegetius, *De re militare*, 1, preface.**

Other sources that I have identified and added are given in normal typeface: Ariosto, *Orlando Furioso*, 35.35.2/4.

When I have added to or updated Bartoli's references, there is a mixture of bold and normal, e.g. **Juvenal,** *Satire* 7. 75/78.

Some critics have commented on the unreliable nature of Bartoli's source citations. At times, he has no issue with tailoring his erudtion to his presentation. Generally, I have been able to locate and confirm his texts ---- with occasional variations, but not in all instances---in which case the Latin is simply noted with no reference.

Most of the editions I have consulted are online. At this point, aside from the table of contents, I have not equipped the text of my translation with the thorough index of subjects and persons that Bartoli presents in alphabetical order in his original twelve-page **Tavola**. This appears at the end of his first edition, but in several later editions it comes before the text. Forty years later the elderly Bartoli integrated and amplified this youthful material in the *Indice delle Materie* of the final, definitive edition he supervised for the collection of this and four other titles in the folio volume, *Opere, Le Morali* (Rome, 1684). Therein, *L'Huomo di Lettere* fits in the first 90 double columned pages provided with markers down the folio from A to E for closer section references. Unfortunatley, in this folio edition, a binding error after page 42 has pp.75-78 replace pp.43-46. This mistake in pagination is corrected in a second posthumous reprint, *Le Opere Morali del p. Daniello Bartoli con un indice copioso* done in Venice in 1687, dedicated to Maximillian Emanuele of Bavaria (1662-1726).

# INTRODUCTION

The calumnies of the ignorant, and the vices of men of Letters, these are the two nodes that eclipse the glory of Letters and diminish the splendor of this bright Sun of the world. The ignorant hate Letters and they cannot see them, and because they cannot see them they hate them. If bats had eyes to stare fixedly at the Sun they would be bats no longer, but eagles. Letterati misuse Letters the way certain malignant stars use light as the vehicle of deadly influences. The most goodly and innocent thing in the world they make hateful to it. Thus, while the integrity of Letters makes them unloved, the judgements of the injudicious make them hateful, while the vices of the letterati, for the ignorant, prove their guilt.

So why should not someone step forward to defend innocent Letters? If he has not the gift of Wit, as that is not required, then let him be endowed with reason, so that he can take up the role of that great philosopher, Anaxagoras who championed the honor of the Sun, and was learned in its ways, so that when it fell into eclipse he inveighed loudly against the ignorant crowd pointing scornfully at the sun to chide it for going dark. He explained that that unforeseen symptom of sudden obscurity was not the Sun in eclipse, as they thought. It was their eyes in the Moon's shadow, as in a miniature night, that were in the dark. For the sun contains the source of all the world's light, so its light can never be diminished, never be lost, as it is not its vehicle, but its embodiment. *"For, if there any obscurity cast on Letters,"* said that brave orator, *"is it the criticisms of the untutored or the vices of those who abuse them that are responsible for any diminuition of their splendor?"*[1]

---

1 *Unde vero si quae obscuritas literarum, nisi quia vel obtrectationibus imperitorum, vel abutentium vitio splendor eis intercipitur?* I have been unable to find these words, despite their vocabulary and style, in Cicero or Quintillian. As to this lapidary statement of his theme, I would surmise that Bartoli, for whom a Latin authority was fundamental, himself invents, with a rhetorical flourish, *"that brave orator"* to furnish one.

,

On this subject, (as it is its own defense,) what there needs to be said is little more than nothing— while of what can be said there is a copious store. But, for my part, my role as been more governed more by the constraints of time than by the material available, and I have only said as much as the time I had would allow which was little more than two of the hottest months of one summer. I had this time free from other responsibilities and I wrote more as an entertainment for myself, than as instruction for others. In any case, may God grant that this little work be short enough, for when writing is not good, even a little is too much.

# PART ONE

## 1 *Men of Letters Neglected by the Powerful, but Happy Nonetheless*[1]

The misfortune, not to say with others, the fate, of unhappy virtue, proven and bemoaned in all ages, is that she cannot find in this great theatre of the world a place worthy of her merit, or a niche fit for her statue. Gone are those golden ages when royal crowns would take the measure of the heads that claimed them: when the fillets of imperial diadems did not yet serve to bind the brains of fools (as often happens today) but to honor the merit and crown the prudence of the wise. The walls and the foundations, remnants of the ruins of that famous Temple of Honor, with the portal of merit as its only entrance, are today so decayed and buried that we have neither the memory of where it stood, nor the hope of seeing rise from the decay of its present ruins to the glory of its past grandeur. However much virtue may now struggle to ascend, it is seen to make no progress. Certain stars near the Antarctic pole have had sixty centuries to rotate around night and day, with so little to show for their efforts, that never have they appeared on our horizon, nor ever once been seen. Mountains rich with gold have no woodlands for glades, nor grass for pasture. There is nothing to see but cinder and sand and on top the bones of their massive stones. They display a certain shameful nudity and, next to other mountains dressed in trees and grass, they are shamed by the comparison. Such is the miserable lot of virtue in the world. With veins of gold hidden in its breast, it looks as poor on the outside, as it is rich on the inside. And so, the truth of it holds, that virtue and nakedness were born together in earthly paradise, never to be separated or split to this day. The attire of the body is honored more than the habit of a virtuous mind. No use having knowledge and goodness, as pearls of the Orient, concealed inside. If your ragged garments make you look like the lowly veneer of mother of pearl, no one will look at you, much less care about you.

---

1 In 1684 Bartoli changed *non curati* to *non istimati.* As a traditional mainstay of Letters, Renaissance court patronage was eclipsed.

All this holds true as well for Letters as for virtue. Born alike under the same ascendant, they are fated never to rise. For them, all features are retrograde, with no good signs in their houses, disrespect in every aspect, and where Fortune has no aspects, but those of misfortune.

Today it seems a miracle, that Dionysius played the coachman of his royal chariot to drive Plato through the streets of Syracuse and he basked in the glory of the deed, as if he were driving the chariot of light, or the Sun in triumph.[2] Alexander Severus covered Ulpian the jurist with his royal mantle to make his imperial purple a robe to honor and a shield to defend him. There were Justinian, and Sigismond emperors, and numerous others like them, who made their courts the home for Men of Letters and attended the homes of Men of Letters as their courts. At a huge profit, they shielded the mortal life of those from whom, as recompense, they received, for their name and their glory, life immortal for posterity. These once fruitful laurels have now grown barren. They give neither fruit for food, nor even shade for protection. The fathers of fecundity, the Zephyrs, blowing during the Golden Age, now are kept under lock and key in the courts of princes, not in the grotto of Aeolus. Lost is the custom that held that **Penes sapientes regnum sit** *(the kingdom should be ruled by the sages,)* which Posidonius said was followed **in illo saeculo quod aureum perhibetur** *(in that era, they called the Golden Age),*[3] and that **penes reges sint sapientes** *(Kings should be surrounded by the sages).* Sometimes, the books of Men of Letters may chance to be read by the powerful who give them praise and commendations. But it does not follow that the plaudits and honors that their books receive redound to the benefit of the authors. This is just what Lactantius said in another instance: They adore the images of the gods, but care not for the artificers who engraved them, they offer gifts to the statues, and exact tribute from their makers, they honor the stones as divinities, and trample on those who made them, as if they were stones: *"They venerate the images of the gods, the artists who made them they scorn. What a contradiction to despise the sculptor and adore the statue, to ban from your table the man who makes you your gods?"*[4]

---

2 **Aelian** 4.18.
3 **Seneca,** *Letter* 90.5
4 **Lactantius, ex Seneca, De origine errorum,** 2.14/5: *Simulacra Deorum venerantur, fabros qui illa facere contemnunt. Quid inter se tam contrarium,*

4

Fortunate are the princes (said a Grand Duke of Milan) who have nets of gold and purple with which to fish for men of great wisdom and worth. These are the most precious pearls that Heaven can bestow on mortals, they have the riches to buy men of Wit, outstanding in every profession of Letters, a merchandise worthy of princes alone.

Famous is the foolishness of a poor rich man. Seeing he was an ox and wanting to be an eagle, he paid a great sum of money for the lantern by whose paltry light Epictetus in his nighttime vigils became a sun of moral prudence.[5] A lantern might well illuminate the parchment, but not the understanding; might give light to the eyes, but what good is it for learning, if the mind is blind? Living scholars are living lanterns. In the beams of their radiant luster are discovered the features of Pallas, conservatrix of states and patroness of princes. Theirs are in truth the authentic eyes, once falsely identified with the eyes of the Gorgons, that can be lent from one to another. With these a blind prince may become a hundred-eyed Argos, all-seeing. Nor should the aphorism concerning warfare, found in Vegetius, be less true for peacetime: "*It behooves none more than the prince to have a thorough knowledge of many things, for his learning benefits all of his subjects.*"[6]

Before Dionysius could grasp this, more out of mockery than curiosity he wanted to know from Aristippus why, if philosophers go to the houses of the rich to beg for sustenance, the rich don't go to the houses of the philosophers to look for wisdom. In reply the reponse was no less true, than quick: Because poor philosophers know what they need, while the ignorant rich do not.[7]

Men of great learning are not born only as the phoenix, once every five hundred years. The reason we have none around studying to enrich the world with new discoveries in Letters and in the Arts is not because the ages have grown sterile, or the nations grown barren of Wits. It is the fault, in great part, of those who give them no port

---

*quàm statuarium despicere, statuam adorare? et eum ne in convivium quidem admittere qui tibi Deos faciat?*
5 **Lucian, *Adversus Indoctum*** (*The Ignorant Book Collector*), 13.
6 **Vegetius, *De re militare*, 1, preface**: *Neque quemquam magis decet, vel meliora scire, vel plura quam principem, cujus doctrina omnibus potest prodesse subjectis.*
7 **Laertius, *Aristippus*, 2.8.69

for their sea voyage, who dangle no bait for them to fly. Minds with great wings and Wits with great sails are not wanting. Aptly on this issue spoke the man who said,

*The Poets and the Studious are few;*
*And when they both food and cover lack*
*Even wild animals will look for somewhere new.*[8]

If we lack men celebrated for their great knowledge to leave the world in speechless amazement, it is the fault of those in power who neglect to build their theatres according to the advice of Vitruvius,[9] who emphasized it to be of primary importance for a theatre, where plays are performed and music is played, to have good acoustics so that the performers do not waste their voices and their efforts for nothing. O how many, like cold and lifeless vapors, do not rise a foot off the ground, but should they meet with a beneficent Sun to warm up their efforts and elevate them, they would shine like so many stars. The rich harvest of the vines is thanks in good measure to the elms which they lean on for support.

To pass beyond the ordinary and excel in any profession of Letters is a labor of ultimate endurance and a challenge great enough to consume an entire life. Now what wonder is it, if we have no candidates willing to spend so much to get nothing, to sacrifice their lives to get no farther in so doing so than to stay alive?

Well-oiled vessels gain ten percent in speed and well-caulked ships sail faster. Ships which before moved dully, and as it were against their will, become so fleet that they rather seem to fly than to sail. Even in those who have talent, favor sparks Wit, and where a golden fleece is waiting at the finish, the oars, like the Argo's, move by themselves.

Finally, to be forced to dispute every day with poverty, to contrast every hour with her miseries, to scatter one's thoughts in the thousand different directions where needs demand, these are thorns where Letters find no nest. He who wants his bees to gather honey should not expose them to violent winds, for where the winds have

---

8 Ariosto, *Orlando furioso*, 35. 35.2/4:
    *Sono I Poeti e gli studiosi pochi*
    *E dove non han pasco e ricetto,*
        *Infin le fere abbandono I lochi.*
9 **Vitruvius, *De architectura*, 5.3.**

too much power, the bees can have none at all. In their trips from their hives to the flowers, and from one flower to another and back with their spoil, the winds will drive them off course and carry them astray. The heads of the Letterati, where other cares assail them, are incapable of doing decent work.

How, indeed, can the two coexist, to rack one's brain for a living and to use it for study? Therefore, well said he, whoever he was, and it holds true not for poets only, but for all Men of Letters.

> *Soft nests, sweet food, and temperate gales*
> *The swans desire; And none with pinching cares*
> *Come near Parnassus, and those who struggle on*
> *With nothing more than their fate and their want,*
> *Grow hoarse and lose both verse and voice.*[10]

Demosthenes speaking to the Athenians, said that it was an indecent sight to see the holy galley, Paralos, once used only for sacred purposes, to sail the priests to the sacrifices of Delphi, now profaned in the tawdry mission of carrying wood and livestock. At this the very winds are ruffled to carry it against their will and the seas sigh to see it so changed from what it was, and ought to be.[11] But is it any less unseemly that a soul of sublime understanding and elevated thoughts, sent into the world for its improvement, and more revered in Heaven than known on earth, should be forced into a life of begging for bread? Should one spend a noble mind fighting off nakedness, thirst, cold of winter, and hunger every day? His thoughts stray from the path of his speculations, bending to the call of importunate need, so that often the thread of his ideas is lost or impossible to finish, like that nimble-footed Atalanta, who by straying too far off course in order to snatch the golden apples of Hippomenes was left so far behind that she was twice beaten in the end.

> *The maiden is outstripped, the victor takes his prizes.*[12]

---

10  Guarini, *Il pastor fido*, act 5, scene 1:
> *Lieto nido, esca dolce, aura cortese*
> *Bramano I Cigni; e non si va in Parnaso*
> *Con le cure mordaci: e chi pur sempre*
> *Col suo destin garrisce e col disagio,*
> *Vien roco, e perde il canto e la favella.*

11  **Plutarch, *An seni gerenda res publica*** (*Should an elder be in government*).

12  **Ovid, *Met.*** 10.680: *Praeterita est virgo, duxit sua praemia victor.*

The satirical poet held in such scorn the palace of Numitor and under this name all the great households of his time, where beasts were housed and fed, but where men, and maybe more than men, got nothing:

> *He can spare the meat for a hungry lion,*
> *His house pet, and yet does not Nimirus begrudge*
> *The cost of sating the insides of a meager Poet?*[13]

Should the houses of the great be turned into temples where the heads of monkeys are adored, and buffoons are honored, while Men of Letters are outcasts? This is to apportion to the beasts all of the stars from the brightest down to the dimmest and to divide up the ample houses of Heaven among them, while burying the heroes of Elysium underground, aside Hell. A Scorpion, a Dog, a Hydra, a Goat, a Bull, they are placed over our heads with names of the zodiac, while an Achilles, an Orpheus, and all the chorus of demi-gods are consigned to below our feet. Are the beasts to be burnished by the rays of the Sun, while the great are sullied by the smoke of Pluto's kingdom? Seeing that the head, the seat of the understanding, was placed by nature above all the other parts of the body so that they as slaves should bear him as their king, how is it that the feet are on the top while the head drags in the dust? Must those of seemingly superhuman strength bear up, like the famous Milo, a great ox on their shoulders, while the poor philosopher Cleanthes to live like a man, is forced to work like a beast?

My design was to open this small work with the unique happiness of a Man of Letters, to show him to you, even when he wants for everything, as satisfied and blessed on his own and as what Seneca called him, a little Jove.[14] But what have I done thus far but exaggerate the cruelty of those who do not support and honor him, and his need for support and honor? In this I have shown more the culpability of those who neglect him, than any distress in him for being

---

13 **Juvenal**, *Satire* 7. 75/78: *Non deficit illi*
> *Unde emeret multa pacendum carne leonem*
> *Jam domitum. Constat leviori bellua sumptu*
> *Nimirum, et capiunt plus intestina poetae.*
14 Seneca, Letter 9.16

neglected.[15] For, if it is dug out of earth and stone, where it lay buried below ground in mines, gold that is discovered will show even more splendidly in the light of day. And the great stand to lose infinitely more by not digging it up and claiming it, than the gold itself if it lies hidden and unclaimed. Whatmore, the trespasses of the powerful in mistreating Men of Letters reveal the real merit that they have, since by not sustaining their greatness the mighty lose merit, and not by not honoring them they are made culpable.

Now let us see how a Man of Letters finds within himself the lively source of that famous and singular nectar of the gods containing in itself all other Tastes, so that he desires and enjoys nothing else. This is that Taste of Understanding abundant enough to be displayed in all parts of science and learning. (But to do so would be excessively lengthy and tedious). So, allow me, in a single field of the sciences, to display it for you as a specimen for them all. And while it may not rank among the best of the sciences, it stands out among the best known, for I am speaking about the vision and the cognizance of the Heavens. As seen by the eye, they emerge as the most spacious and the most beautiful among all of Nature's parts, as seen by the mind, they figure as by no means the least among the best.

---

15 In his 1684 revision Bartoli changed "cared for" *(curati)* to "appreciated" *(prezzati)*.

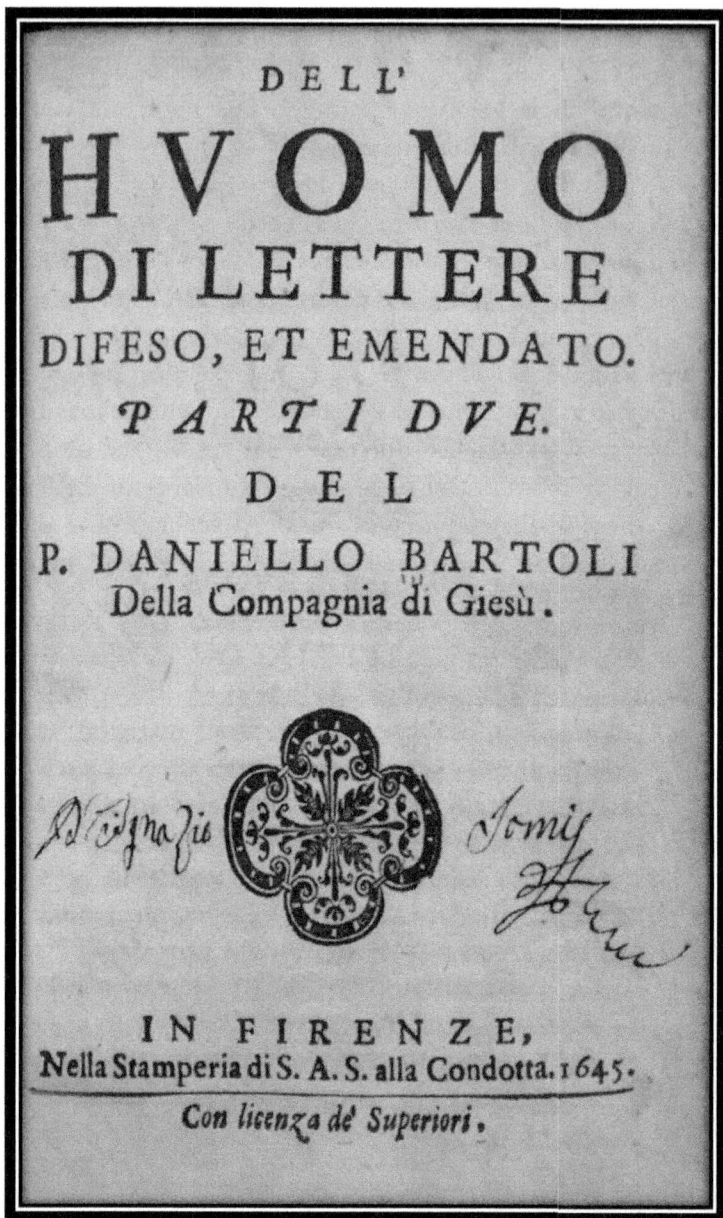

## 2  *The Taste of Understanding*: *Explained for all the Sciences, Through the Sole Cognizance of the Heavens*

It is the common teaching of the two most celebrated schools of philosophy, founded by Pythagoras and by Plato,[1] that the celestial spheres as they expand one above another in spaces of harmonic proportion compose in their revolutions the consort of a most perfect music. Macrobius gives the reason, drawn from the natural principles of sound, and states in conclusion; *"From this unimpeachable reasoning we can deduce that musical sounds proceed from the movement of the heavenly spheres, since the sounds must come from this motion and from the Divine Reason behind it causing these modulations"*[2]

And not for that this kind of music may not be judged by our ears, ought we not to believe it, or deny it, since its most delicate sound as it travels through our elements is completely drowned out and muted by their discordant noise, particularly where the noise grows the loudest. And well was it said elsewhere:

*Heaven is not mute, as is believed by some,*
*But we are deaf; for our ears are packed*
*With Earth's harsh croaking,*
*Amongs whose dissonants in vain we hope*
*T' aspire to th' heavenly harps' sweet harmony,*
*Played by the hand of the Delian Diety.*[3]

---

1 (Pseudo) **Plutarch, *De Musica***
2 **Macrobius, *De somni Scipionis*,** 2.1: *Ex his inexpugnabili ratione collectum est musicos sonos de sphaerarum coelestium conversione procedere, quia et sonum ex motu fieri necesse est, et ratio quae divinis inest, sit sono causa modulaminis.*
3 (Giovanni Battista) Bartoli, *Saggio di poesie morali* (Bologna, 1642):
    *Muto non è, come altri crede, il Cielo,*
    *Sordi siam noi, a cui gli orecchi serra*
    *Lo strepito insolente della terra*
    *Fra le cui dissonanze in van s'aspira,*
    *A l'armonia de la celeste lira*
    *Che si tocca per man del Dio di Delo.*
I have adapted the Salusbury translation of this excerpt from *Pastorale invito a cantare*, p..24. Italian Jesuits in Bartoli's day were forbidden to publish poetry. Nonetheless, this book, printed under his nephew's name, and these and several other unidentified verses, have been widely held to be his. Bartoli strenuously denied responsibility, if not authorship in his final corrected edition, *"E non fu*

Were it not, as Philo of Alexandria puts it, that God has saved us for a better time to Taste such sweet music, while his particular providence has in the meantime distempered and deafened our ears to it, we should otherwise remain delirious, ecstatic, and ravished out of ourselves by the harmony of those most regular bodies and would not only fail to cultivate the earth or attend to the duties of civil life, but finally forget our very existence, "*Heaven,* (says he*), by the perpetual concord of its movements gives forth such a sweet harmony that if it reached our ears it would excite such a mad love and desire for it that under its stimulus we should forget our need for sustenance, neither eating or drinking, as if we were already sufficiently purified for immortality.*"[4]

But to tell the truth, to feel in the heavens the Taste of such sweet harmony, and to have from there above such almost beatific delight, it is not necessary for us to desire that the music of those harmonic spheres (spheres, they call them those unwilling for them to be, as they nonetheless are, one single and liquid heaven)[5] should reach our ears. No less blessed can we feel as our imagination follows the flight of its thoughts. But I am not talking here, as do others, about poetry, the false inventor of illusions, leading us across the expanse of the Heavens, as it tells us: Here is Phaeton, more daring than prudent,

> *Daring to drive the eternal chariot,*
> *Youth reckless of his father's fears*
> *He unleashed the sky's furious fires*
> *Upon himself.*[6]

---

*mal detto da un mio compatriota, ingiuriosamente ristampato sotto mio nome.*"
*Opere, Le morali,* (1684), p.4.Bartoli seems to be involved in a 'jesuitical" equivocation.  In fact, this edition's titlepage (Milan, 1662) respectfully prints it under his nephew's name, but Domenica Brena's letter of dedication manifestly introduces it among the *'offspring of Bartoli's Wit.*"

4  **Philo of Alexandria,** *De insomniis,* (On Dreams): *Coelum perpetuo contentu suorum motuum reddit harmoniam suavissimam; quae si posset ad nostras aures pervenire in nobis excitaret insanos sui amores, et desideria, quibus stimulati rerum ad victum necessariarum oblivisceremur, non pasti cibo potuque, sed velut immortalitatis candidati.*

5 Note that Bartoli wants it both ways, employing the rhetoric of the traditional cosmological view of the crystalline spheres, while acknowledging, as an admirer of Galileo, that the sky is liquid aether.

6 **Seneca,** *Medea,* 599-602:

> *Ausus aeternos agitare currus,*
> *Immemor metae juvenis paternae*

Such poetry also tells of Vulcan, how he crashed from Heaven to earth in a single bound and how he paid for it merely with a foot out of joint. Here is where the Heavens ripped, for the gaping hole the Phlegrean Giants made there in their battery hurled against the stars, when the earth switched from thunderstruck to thunder striker. Here trod Hercules, here Prometheus, here Bellerophon, and whom you please. Now then, what I am speaking of here is that part of the noblest science that is the true interpreter of the mysteries and the register of the most occult ways of the Heavens. What opens the eyes to reveal how in their movements they are so immense and yet so delicate, in their influences so discordant and yet so unified in regulating nature; tracing the cycles they make, some so lazy and others so rapid, all to the same tempo, and almost moving together in the same dance, in obedience to the prime mover so strict, and in the liberty of their proper motions so free, so splendid, and so profound, so uniform, and so various, so majestic, and so lovely, rapid with such order, busy with such stillness, in the measurement of time, in the succession of days, in the changes of seasons, in such perfect concert. Eyes that can see so much, will make a ladder to climb up and see much more. Along the long chain of these heavenly beings (whose final link is fastened to the foot of the throne of Almighty Jove) one can rise even to the forms of the Archetypes, and to the Ideas of the First Mind, from whose invariable design are taken the weights, numbers and measures, the instruments, as it were, of the work of this great order of Nature and can recognize the lofty Wisdom, in such diversity of transmutations, of the One who keeps all steadfast to the course of an immutable Providence. He gave a secret order to the disorder of so many manifestations, chaining them together with indissoluble links to all his intents and purposes. Consequently, seemingly haphazard events of chance are really executions of a highly regulated Providence. One who can see objects of such lofty cognition, is he not in this alone more blessed than others in all their enjoyment of the senses? That great Platonic Philo can serve witness here where he said as proof, "*When the mind considers the course of the fixed and wandering stars, and the music they make together according to the most precise measures, one is drawn in by the love of such wisdom and led above all sensible elements to lose the desire for perceptible things. The mind is lead from sensory manifestations to the ideas behind their appearance*

---

*Quos polo sparsit furiosus ignes,*
*Ipse recepit.*

13

*and to perceptions of most exquisite beauty, by a sort of inebriation, wafting, as in a celestial Corybantic dance, to a love far above the manifest and intelligible, toward the very lord of all."*[7]

Some may see these rather as flourishes of art than real truths, and for not being experienced, so much the less to be believed. The best answer I can give them was given by Nicostratus, to a man of small mind, unsusceptible to the beauty of painting.

Zeuxis, that Sun of painters, whose work brought light to the art of painting, and cast his imitators into the shadows, drew on canvas the face of a Helen, of such noble workmanship, that the original was outdone by the copy, and the true Helen seemed to yield to her painted self, for if the real Helen drew a Paris from Troy to abduct her, the painted Helen drew the whole of Greece to admire her.[8] At his first look, Nicostratus, himself also a painter of no mean rank, as if he had seen not the head of Helen, but the head of Medusa, turned to stone. It seemed, by a mutual deceit, that Helen was alive in her picture, and Nicostratus was dead in his astonishment. Next to him stood an uncouth churl, a man with no eyes, standing by Nicostratus as he was stricken in amazement, like a statue looking at a painting. Turning to him and bringing him out of his trance, he asked, *"What is so striking in that Helen?"*[9] He asked too many questions in one. But as his eyes were no good to see Helen, neither were his ears suited to hear Nicostratus. The painter faced him with a look mixing compassion and scorn and said: "This is not a picture for bats. Pluck out those ignorant eyes you have, and I will lend you mine, and if now you are a mole with no eyes,

7 **Philo of Alexandria,** *In Cosmopaeia*: *Vagata (mens) circa stellarum tum fixarum, tum erraticarum cursus, et choreas juxta musicae praecepta absolutissimas, trahitur amore sapientiae se deducentis, atque ita emergens super omnem sensibilem essentiam, demum intelligibilis desiderio corripitur. Illic conspicata exemplaria, ideasque rerum, quas vidit, sensibilium, ad eximias illas pulchritudines, ebrietate quadam sobria capta, tanquam Corybantes lymphatur, alio plena amore longe meliore, quo ad summum fastigium adducta rerum intelligibilium, ad ipsum magnum regem tendere videtur.*
8 Bartoli added to the 1650 and 1684 Roman editions: *"How beautiful she was I will leave to your imagination, because I will not try to describe her, as no judge of beauty, and because I think that Helen should be drawn with no other brush than a smoking charcoal from the burning of Troy, only lighted by the fire that brought a city to ashes and destroyed a kingdom, and only shaded by the darkness of a perpetual infamy."*
9 **Aelian, 14**. 47: *Quid tantum in Helena illa stuperet.*

you'll wish you had all one hundred of the eyes of Argus. *You wouldn't ask me, if you had my eyes.*"[10]

Behold, the same thing happens when one remains stupefied gazing upon Nature's fair countenance, the sky. There God, as much as perceptible matter allowed, did design, copying them from his own, lineaments of such rare beauty where we find such delight, that it drives us out of our Wits, and makes our thoughts ecstatic, and our minds beatific. Everyone beholds the Heavens, but everyone comprehends them not, and between one who comprehends them, and one who doesn't, there is the same difference as between two people. One can see in an illuminated manuscript in Arabic, traced in gold, and outlined in azure, only the craftsmanship of the written characters, the other can read the words, and understand their meaning, so that what he sees with his eyes is the least of his pleasures.[11]

The Taste of Understanding is, indeed, like the sweetness of honey. To prove it the efforts of a long stream of words are less effective than the simple Taste of one drop. Nonetheless, I would like you to listen to the peerless moralist Seneca, when he talks about the great enjoyment to be found in contemplating the Heavens, up there where the mind conceives ideas higher than the world below, ideas higher than humanity. Listen:

*Imagine* (says he) *that you climbed to the highest sphere of the Heavens, so that you see at your feet Saturn, Jupiter and Mars turn in their several cycles, and under them each of the other planets revolving in their courses. There you behold their tremendous size, the unparalleled velocity of their cycles, the number without number of the stars, which here scarce seem sparks to you; there are worlds of light, no less than so many Suns. Then with eyes filled with the greatness of those spaces, and the mass of those vast bodies, look down on our sphere, and look for the earth. If you can see it, it will appear so small from the stars, that you must fix your steadiest eye, and pine for some Starry Messenger to help you see.*[12] Here below is

---

10 *ibidem: Non interrogares me, si meos oculos haberes.* The ecstasy or sense overload of Nicostratus illustrates the aesthetic character and discrimination of the *Taste* of Baroque Sapience., captured in the frontispiece of the Venetian editions, possibly by Salvator Rosa.

11 A striking and successful illustration of the relation of aesthetic perception to higher spheres of understanding.

12 A reference to the celebrated work and telescope of Galileo, *Sidereus Nuntius* (*Starry Messenger*) (1610).

*what you saw as the tiniest star, so that the straining eye is unsure if it can see, or just thinks it can see it; from there above that is how the earth is seen, so that catching sight of it you say: So that, there below, which I can hardly see, which I can scarce make out with my eye, is that the earth? Is it that dot split up into so many provinces, subdivided into so many kingdoms, for which we have invented manifold battle arts and arms for murdering, to capture and possess it? Sieges, assaults, conflagrations, batteries, pitched battles, ruins of whole nations done in no time that have so often made widowed nature weep, filling the air with the stench of rotting carcasses, damming rivers, and dyeing the corpse-laden sea red with great pools of human blood? Such are the incredible wonders of human madness? Our vastest desires are wasted on a dot. What, said I on a dot? on the least particle of a dot. What more would the ants do if they could talk? Wouldn't they too subdivide a handful of earth into many provinces? Wouldn't they set up their obstinate boundaries, not yielding an inch even to Jupiter himself, despite his thunder? Would they not plant a kingdom in a spot of ground, a great monarchy in a small field? A little rivulet of water would be for them a Nile, a ditch they would call an ocean, a stone as big as one's hand, they would style a great rock, one farm would be no less than an entire world. They would also raise bulwarks and bastions to fortify their states, they would levy armies in hopes of new conquests, and to dispute old disagreements and we would see in the space of two feet of ground, marching in order, with colors flying, enemy squadrons of black ants, advancing with alacrity, jostling, routing each other. Some would retire, the day being won, victorious; some would surrender conditionally or flee and hide, or die in battle to serve as booty for their enemies. Such a war between twenty thousand ants or more, waged to dispute a handful of earth, just the thought of it ought to make us laugh. What else do we do, cutting up a dot into so many kingdoms and destroying one another to enlarge them? Let the Ister be the natural border of Dacia, the Strimon of Thrace, the Rhine of Germany, the Parthians, let them be bound by the Euphrates, the Sarmatians by the Danube, let the Pyrenees divide France and Spain, the Alps Italy. "Such is the story in the small quarters of busy ants"[13]*

> You chalk out kingdoms, and assign them bounds,
> And measures, by the marks of blood and wounds;
> And yet herein you greatest folly show,
> In that by gripping much, you let all go.

---

13 **Seneca, *NQ*, preface,** 7: *Formicarum iste discursus est in angusto laborantium.* Bartoli has paraphrased and his rhetoric has amplified this excerpt from Seneca ending with a brief coda of the Latin that serves as a framework for the poetic variation on the same theme that follows.

*The whole world's every man's, and who so cares*
*To appropriate any part, divides and shares*
*What was his already. All men we one family be:*
*Ours is but one house, from sky to ground*
*And in this one house is our world home.*[14]

Come and see from here above your earth, look for your kingdoms, and see the patches that provide your noble titles. Find your tiny parcels in a dot, if a dot is even visible? And this is what makes you stride so haughtily? Come up among the stars not to see only, but to possess, if you will, a kingdom that can match your idea of kingship: Nor should you fight about boundaries, as all is your possession: nor ought you to fear exile, for as a common possession, no one can be expelled. Thus: *"It is a pleasure while wandering across the firmament of the stars to look down on the courtyards of the rich and laugh at the world and its gold."*[15]

What greater enjoyment is there, than to achieve so magnanimous a state of mind and so noble an understanding? Alexander was so taken with his great victories in the East, that when he received news from Greece of some martial deed, or some conquest, (at most of a castle, or of some petty city) he would say that it was like having word of Homer's battle of the frogs and mice.[16] O how small do the things that seemed so large down here appear when seen from the stars! And how we relish it as our thoughts grow large and our minds grow to scorn what others slavishly adore.

---

14 A second anonymous borrowing from the verses of the *Poesie morali*, p.15.
*Voi distinguete i regni, e a si gran lite*
*Segnate loro I termini, e le mete*
*E con cio stolti sete*
*Che per troppo voler impoverite*
*Tutto il mondo e d'ogn'uno e chi ne cerca*
*Per se sol una parte*
*Quel che tutto era suo divide, e sparte*
*Tutti gli huomini siamo una famiglia*
*Tutta dal sommo al fondo*
*E una sola casa, e nostra casa il Mondo.*
15 **Seneca, ibid.** (*NQ*, preface, 7): *Juvat inter sydera vagantem divitum pavimenta ridere, et totum cum auro suo terram.*
16 *Batrachomyomachia (The Battle of the Frogs and Mice)*, attributed to Homer.

What the good Seneca taught us to do; the great Anaxagoras had done long before. He only wanted to gaze on the Heavens saying he was born to watch them. So, he left his country, as a cemetery of the living, and so as not to let the earth interfere with his vision, he lived out in the fields, poor and unprotected. What? Did I say, poor and unprotected? He loved seeing above his head the beautiful canopy of Heaven's blue serenity, and himself crowned with a world of stars turning around him. The Sun would paint with gold his poor, ragged cloak, and Heaven would keep him informed of all its news. This was better for him than to be clad in purple, and as a crowned head to have the whole earth pay homage. But since, *"This consort of stars whose vast firmament is filled with beauty, does not appeal to the populace,"*[17] his countrymen of Clazomenae scorned him as foolish and expelled him as a wild man. To their vulgar scorn he contrasted Heaven's honors. He was unconcerned about his place among men on earth, but rejoiced to see the stars in Heaven, and mutually, to have them watch him with that loving eye Synesius speaks of: *"Those very stars seemed to look down kindly on me, as in their vast domain it was I alone intended for their contemplation."*[18]

What I have said to this point about knowing the Heavens, the focus of a small part of the natural sciences, has been to show how this understanding induces a certain beatitude of such exquisite Taste that it enchants the senses, and removes the desire for whatever is of a lesser order from the mind. And it should be understood as true for the many other noble and vast subjects, in which the Wits of letterati can enjoy enlightenment when they are set in front of the world (in the phrase of Pythagoras quoted by Synesius) as spectators in a theater of ever new and entirely noble wonders. *"Thus, Pythagoras of Samos claimed that a sage is nothing more than a spectator following the people and what they are doing. And hence he is brought into the world to witness their actions in something like sacred competition in the theatre of human affairs."*[19]

---

17 **Seneca, *NQ*, preface**: *Hic coetus astrorum, quibus immensi corporis, pulchritudo distinguitur, populum non convocat.*
18 **Synesius, Letter 101 to Pylaemon**: *Me stellae etiam ipsae benigne, identidem despectare videntur, quem in vastissima regione solum cum scientia sui inspectorem intuentur.*
19 **Synesius, *De providentia*, 2.8.1**: *Ita Pythagoras Samius, Sapientem nihil aliud esse ait, quàm eorum, quae sunt, fiuntque spectatorem. Proinde enim in*

Consquently, if the exercise of Letters, especially of those most demanding and most substantial, may be recalled from the Taste of speculating to the practice of living, I propose (as all the sages do agree) to call a Sage that Man of Letters whose mind has been refined by lengthy and upright use of intellect, and been purged of the dregs of sensuality and vice that make us brutes, so that whatever be the prosperous or adverse turns which befall him, he can weigh them on the scale of reason for what they are.

And it should not be difficult for me, as I lead you through some of the most fearsome misfortunes and sufferings, to show you that caliber of a man as superior to such tribulations as as the most distant stars are not eclipsed for being so far beyond the shadow of the earth.

---

*mundum, ac in sacrum quoddam certamen introductum esse, ut iis quae ibidem fiunt, spectator intersit.*

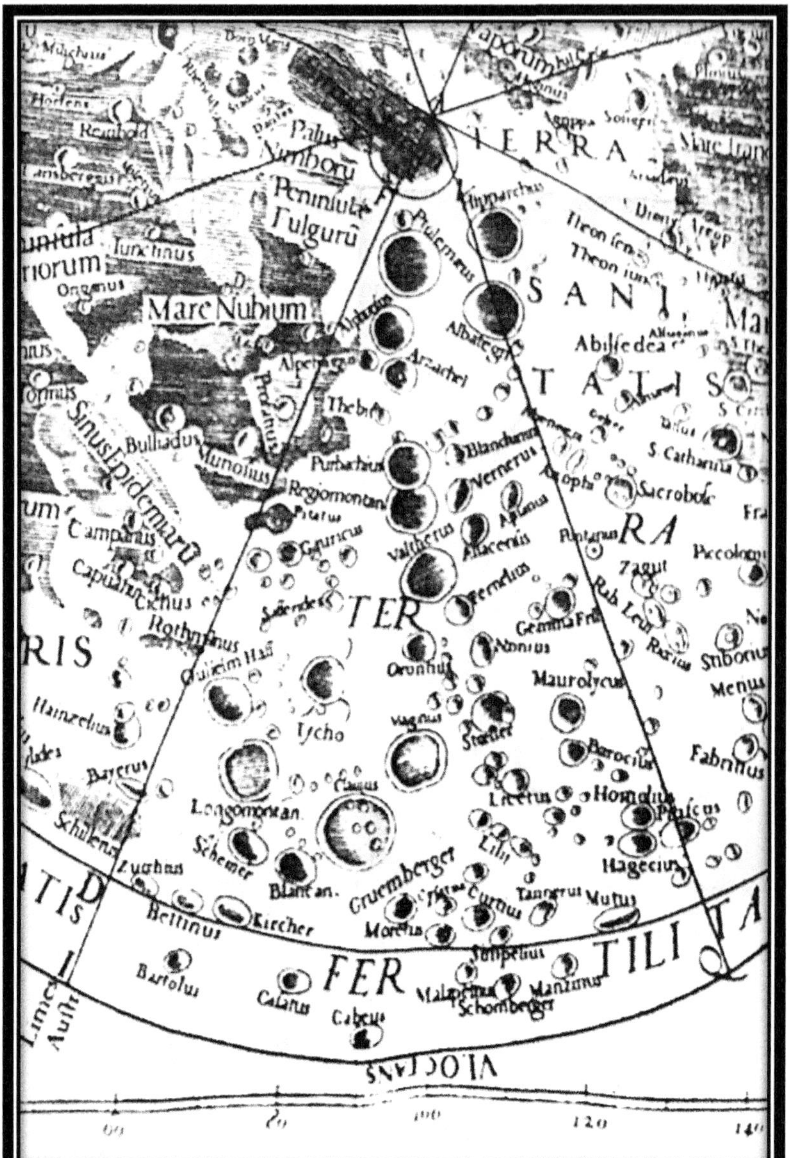
Mare Nubium
Sinus Epidemiarũ
Peninsula Fulgurũ
TERRA
SANI
TATIS
RA
TER
FER
TILI
Ptolemaeus
Hipparchus
Albategni
Arzachel
Alpetragius
Thebit
Purbachius
Regiomontan
Walterus
Tycho
Clavius
Maurolycus
Longomontan
Scheiner
Blancan.
Gruemberger
Kircher
Bettinus
Bartolus
Cabeus
Schomberger
Hageciu
Fabricius
Piccolomini
Abilfedea
Sacrobosc
S. Catharina
Campanus
Capuanus
Rothmannus
Bullialdus
Bayerus
Schilleru
Zuchius
Mutus
Theon sen.
Theon iun.
Lincus Austr

# 3  *Felicity of the Sages, even in Infelicity*

## 3.1  *The Sage in Poverty*

Poverty is one name, but not one single misery and, if you read encryptions, in this one word you will read a whole Iliad of evils. The poet with the title of **turpis egestas**, *(vile penury)*[1] placed it together with other monsters at the gate of Hell. And this was not unjust, for what it brings along to those dwellings where it is doorkeeper is sufficient for a whole hell of misery. Hunger inside eats the bowels alive. Nakedness outside exposes the flesh to ignominy. Shame forbids it from appearing in public. Necessity will not let it stay hidden. If embarrassment makes it silent, it undergoes a thousand hardships, if it begs for alms, despised, none notice. The evils it suffers are that much greater, the less they find compassion in others. But of the many griefs poverty has, there is none worse, specially to a man of sublime Wit, or noble extraction, than to be the subject of scorn and derision.

> *Nothing is worse about unhappy poverty*
> *Than that it makes men the butt of laughter.*[2]

This is the blackest shadow that follows it, this the heaviest chain it drags at its feet. And how many, not to show as trees without leaves, denuded to deformity, have dealt themselves the dagger, deeming death less insufferable than their agony?

Now this torturous and misshapen butcher (and if there were to be four Furies in hell, it would make the fourth), who would ever believe that when joined with Letters and Sapience (like a dissonant diatesseron, united to the diapente, makes the sweetest of all harmonies) it becomes lovely and pleasing beyond measure?[3]

Poverty with Sapience (says the Stoic philosopher) is a divine composition, which has everything and has nothing. Indeed, it can only

---

1 *Aeneid* 6.276.
2 *Juvenal, Satire* 3.152/3:
> *Nil habet infelix paupertas durius in se*
> *Quam quod ridiculos homines facit.*
3 **The 4th with the 5th makes the octave.** Pythagorean intervals, as treated in contemporary scientific writings cited below. Bartoli returns to the subject in his 1678 treatise, *Del suono e degli armonici tremori.*

give that without which one can have nothing because it alone is everything, namely Sapience. And is not this the condition of the gods? *"Now look at the world, you will see the gods naked, giving everything, having nothing."*[4]

What more can a man desire in the world than to be one who by philosophy, rather than by inheritance, has made the world his patrimony? The things that are ours as fortune and chance grant them to us them, are more others' than ours, more borrowed, than owned. They benefit us no more than a man's likeness turns a statue into a man. To know the world, says Manilius, this is to possess it, so that that to every Demetrius asking, *"With our country captured what is left for us?"*[5] with that same Stilpo of Megara we may respond, *"Nothing can take away from me what I possess."*[6]

To pilgrims on their journey, a little is not only enough, but more is an impediment. One whose thoughts are not confined within the walls of his home, as the center closed inside a circle, but rather has the wings of his mind always outstretched and headed where the desire for knowing new things calls him, he travels not only away from his home, but even away from himself, so that where he is not, is where he lives. Can it be dishonor or trouble to lack what, as a pilgrim, would be for him an impediment and a weight? From this Seneca fashioned the aphorism: *"If you want to purify your soul, you should either be a pauper, or live like a pauper."*[7]

But behold an eloquent Platonic who, for reproach or for scorn, was confronted with the public accusation, that poverty was dishonorable or reprehensible. If you (he answered his accuser) had as much of philosophy as you have riches, you would understand that I, being poor, am the rich one, and you, being rich, are the poor one. *"For he has most who desires least, he has what he wants who wants very little and*

---

4 **Seneca, *De tranquillitate animi*, 8.**5: *Respice enim mundum: Nudos videbis Deos omnia dantes, nihil habentes.*

5 Seneca, *Letter* 9.18/19: *Quid capta Patria superfuerit nobis?*

6 *Ibid., Nullum vidi qui res meas auferret.* See Laertius, *Stilpo*, 2.11

7 **Seneca, *Letter*** 17.5: *Si vis vacare animo, aut pauper sis oportet, aut pauperi similis.*

*considers riches in wealth and goods not above what a man has in his own soul.*"[8]
In the sea of this life against the tempests and the currents that keep
us from port, not the man who is overloaded, but the one who swims
nude will make it. This simple coat that covers me, or this plain staff
I lean on, do they make me contemptible? Tell me what more had
Hercules, son of Jove, conqueror of the world, and a demigod? "*Even
Hercules, light of the world, destroyer of beasts, conqueror of peoples, a god, before
he was conveyed to heaven for his bravery and as he roamed the earth, had no more
than a skin for a mantle, no more than a staff for a companion.*"[9] Even the
foremost gods themselves, what do they have in their domain for their
wealth? Large veins of metal to extract silver and gold? Oceans to fish
pearls, shells to press for purple dyes? Kingdoms, vassal and subject
peoples for exacting tribute? Or rather having nothing but themselves,
but blissful in themselves alone, and seeming poor because they have
nothing, yet rich in abundance, because they need nothing? "*Therefore,
among us whose needs are the least, he will most be like God.*"[10]

Let, therefore, Socrates the pauper, but Socrates the Man of
Letters, go through all the markets and ports of the world and inspect
piece by piece the immense store of goods boasted of by riches and
honors. His bliss is in what he knows, and he cares not for what he has
not. So, let him declare, and all his peers repeat it with him, "*How many
are the things that I don't need!*"[11]

Alexander cried warm tears when he heard the philosopher
Anaxagoras (Anarxarchus) reject the idea that Nature, either from
avarice would not, or from sterility could not, produce more than one
World. As she had no rein to her power, nor limit to her will, he
contended that in the spaces of the immense universe, it has
reproduced the numbers of the infinite, and extended all its being to

---

8 **Apuleius,** *Apologia,* 20: *Namque is plurimum habet qui minimum desiderat:
habet enim quantum vult qui vult minimum, et idcirco divitiae non melius in
fundo, et in foenere, quàm in ipso hominis aestimantur animo.*
9 **Apuleius,** *Apologia,* 2: *Ipse Hercules illustrator orbis, purgator ferarum,
gentium domitor is inquam Deus cum terras peragraret, paulò prius quam in
coelum ob virtutes adscitus est, neque una pelle uestitior fuit, neque uno baculo
comitatior.*
10 **Apuleius,** *Apologia,* 21: *Igitur ex nobis cui quam minimis opus sit, is erit
Deo similior.*
11 **Laertius,** *Socrates,* 2.25: *Quam multo ipse non egeo!*

all its potential, responding to the Ideas of innumerable Worlds, by creating each one. Of only one was Alexander only in partial possession out of the many there could be, and therefore he roared with sorrow, *"the way wild beasts rip to pieces more than they want out of hunger."*[12] Yet he, the master of Greece, Persia, of the Indies, *"Out of many kingdoms he berought together one great kingdom,"*[13] but he thinks himself the poorer by what he does not have, and what he does not have is the extent of what he desires. *"What matters the number of kingdoms he has seized or how many he has given away, or what the tribute of his nations amounts to? Whatever he does not have, is as much as he desires."*[14] So, Alexander is poor, and in the riches of half the world he has nothing, because half the world is nothing in comparison to the infinite worlds he desires.

Meanwhile, Crates, a Man of Letters, who has nothing but himself and the tattered philosopher's mantle he covers himself with, more to hide his nakedness, than to show he is a philosopher, lives on earth like a Jove in Heaven, richer for everything he does not have, than Alexander, with all that he possesses: *"Alexander weeps for the infinite worlds he heard about from Anaxagoras (sic), and the learned Crates goes on his way in his mantle living as at a feast with jokes and laughter."*[15]

I wish I knew how to describe accurately for you that famous Diogenes, when he drew Alexander to see him (not so much as a visitor, but rather as an admirer). He was sought out by the master of the world and still paid him no attention. *"His eminence seemed to set him above the man who had all the world at his feet."*[16]

---

12 **Seneca, *Letter* 94.**62: *Immanium ferarum modo, quae plus quam exegit fames, mordent.*

13 **Seneca, *Letter* 94**. 63: *in unum regnum multa regna coniecit.*

14 **Seneca, *De beneficiis*,** 7.2: *Quid enim interest quot eripuerit regna, quot dederit? Quantum terrarum tributo premat? Tantum illi deest quantum cupit.*

15 **Plutarch, *De tranquillitate animi*,** 4: *Flet Alexander propter infinitos mundos ab Anaxagoras (Anaxarchas) auditos, cum Crates, pera, et palliolo instructus vitam tamquam festivitatem quandam per jocum, et risum ageret.* Bartoli has misread Plutarch's text and confused Anaxagoras with the Anaxarchus who accompanied Alexander to India. See Laertius, *Anaxarchus*, 9.61.

16 **Seneca, *De beneficiis*, 5.4**: *Supra eum eminere visus est, infra quem omnia jacebant.* Rosa's 1662 etching (above) of this scene quotes Juvenal, *Satire* XIV, 311/4.

I shall take from Claudian a symbolic image, which can portray
him more to the life, than if Apelles himself had painted him,

*This is a stone that is called a magnet,*
*Dark and lowly, it does not adorn the hair of an empress,*
*Nor the white neck of the virgin, nor shine in the buckle of a sword.*
*But if you see the wonders worked by this black stone*
*Then it outshines the value of any from the East.*[17]

---

*Sensit Alexander testa cum vidit in illa*
*Magnum habitatorem, quanto felicior hic, qui*
*Nil cuperet, quam qui totem sibi posceret urbem.*
17 **Claudian,** *Magnes*: *Lapis est cognomina Magnes:*
*Discolor, obscurus, vilis. Non ille repexam*

His prickly beard, his unruly mane, his dangling forelocks, his ragged clothes, his rough and ill-bred manner, his extreme poverty, did they not make him seem like a naked, black, heavy, unshapely piece of stone? Moreover, a barrel was his house, and for him it was all the world, because from all the world he wanted only that. He turned it around at his pleasure, scoffing at the celestial spheres and the wheel of fortune, because neither those with their cycles, nor this with its downturns, could stand against the revolutions of his barrel, nor could the heavens give anything good to him who covets nothing, or fortune take aught from him, who as naked can be stripped of nothing. But, in a man so disheveled and so poorly lodged, such virtue and such a forceful (let me say) magnetism,[18] where do they come from that he, obscure and beggarly, could draw to himself the most illustrious and most opulent monarch of the world? Thanks go to philosophy that Diogenes, as a sun covered by clouds, or a Venus clothed like a satyr, shone forth so, that he could allure such a king and transport him to admire and revere a ragged beggar. What, Diogenes a beggar? Let his riches be put on the scale to counterbalance those of the immensely rich Alexander. Diogenes of all that the Macedonian offered him, accepted nothing, because he needed nothing. Alexander misses even what he does have, because he misses what he wants, desiring to be transformed into, and to be Diogenes. Therefore, Diogenes, *"Far more powerful and wealthier by far was he, than Alexander who possessed everything. For what the one would not take was more, than what the other had to give."*[19]

---

*Caesariem regum, non candida vergine ornat*
*Colla, nec insigni splendet per cingula morsu.*
*Sed nova si nigri videas miracula saxi,*
*Tunc superat pulchros cultus et quidquid Eois*
*Indus litoribus rubra scrutatur arena.*

18 William Gilbert's *De magnete* (1600) and the force of magnetism it propounded influenced the cosmic philosophy of Jesuit scientists, such as Niccolò Zucchi, Bartoli's teacher, as a possible alternative to Galileo's revolutionary Copernicanism.

19 **Seneca, *De benificiis***, 5.4: *Multo potentior multo lucupletior fuit, omnia tunc possidente Alexandro. Plus enim erat quod hic nolet accipere quam quod hic posset dare.*

Therefore, Letters and contented poverty,[20] for him where they are united— compose that happy temper of the Golden Age, when free from all fear of loss everyone lived pleased with what was his— that is, content with himself, and rich in needing nothing, which means without desiring riches. Thus, Palemon and Crates— two friends, two philosophers, two beggars— were hailed by Arcesilaus as honored relics of the Golden Age.[21] And between others' riches and their own poverty, they lived like that friend of Seneca: *"Their contempt for all things was not such, that they would not permit others to have them."*[22]

The rich are not so blinded with the splendor of their gold that they cannot see, at least in part, the value of these assets. In a host of rich and ignorant men, a poor Man of Letters stands out as a rag among silks, homespun cloth against purple robes, the thinness of his face is worn by study and made pallid by books as he stands among round and ruddy faces. They see themselves as sheep covered with golden wool and regard the letterato as the ancients saw a great god, graven in a base stone— or molded in clay— but in no way less honorable than if it were cast in gold and inlaid with pearls.

That adventurous ship, the first of them all to pass through the long Straights of Magellan with him at the helm, circumnavigated the whole earth, and so was named Victory. Returning to Europe and drawn into port, it was hailed by all as the second Argo of the world. Those sides which had been proof against the batteries of storms; of oceans never seen before, those faithful sails braving strange winds; that rudder, that mast, those sail-yards; yes, all its parts were judged worthy of the noblest stars in Heaven, since she had overcome the elements and pursued the conquest not of a fleece, but of a world of gold. Nor did her being partially in pieces— her mast shaking, her yards disjointed, her sides disarmed, her sails tattered, and her poop deck collapsing— render her any less praiseworthy and beautiful. The other ships in the port, all decked out, beheld her with a certain envy and her damages wreaked by the tempests and the long voyage, like

---

20 The title of Bartoli's next book, *La povertà contenta* (1650), mentioned by Salvator Rosa in his *Letters* to G.B. Ricciardi.
21 Laertius, *Crates (of Athens)*, 4.22
22 **Seneca, Letter 62**.3: *Non tanquam contempsissent omnia, sed tanquam aliis habenda, permisissent.*

the scars of a captain warrior, they deemed more honorable, than the beauty of their own fineries. To her they struck their sails, furled their yards, lowered their colors, they were rich with cargo, rich with gold. The Victory— empty, shattered, disfigured— they adored as their mistress. Behold, the condition of a poor letterato among a number of rich and ignorant men; they feel, although often unawares, envious for the inner riches they wholly lack, which they perceive so abundantly in that pauper. *"There is nothing more wonderful and entirely pleasurable than to observe mature men and elders, respected by the world and enjoying an abundance riches of all sorts, confessing that they do not possess what is the highest good."*[23] Now if the rich be the trees in a great grove of branches thick and spreading everywhere with beautiful fronds, does that make the poor Man of Letters a leafless trunk, and half naked— but so what?

*As the mighty oak standing in a fruitful field*
*Bears the tributes of ancient peoples and the gifts of the chieftains,*
*No longer standing fast by strong roots*
*Is fixed by its own weight,*
*With its nude branches in the air*
*And only the trunk with shade to give*
*Though in the high wind it may totter*
*Surrounded by so many solid and robust trees*
*It alone is venerated.*[24]

---

23 **Tacitus,** ***Dialogus de oratoribus***, 1.6: *Ullanè autem ingentium opum, tam magnae potentiae voluptas, quam spectare homines veteres, et senes et totius orbis gratia subnixos, in summa omnium rerum abundantia confitentes, id quod optimum sit, se non habere?* This treatise on oratory is now identified not as the work of Tacitus, but of his contemporary, Quintilian.

24 **Lucan**, *Pharsalia* 1.131/9:

*Qualis frugifero quercus sublimis in agro*
*Eximias veteres populi, sacrata is gestans*
*Dona ducum, nec jam validis radicibus haerens*
*Pondere fixo suo est, nudósque per aera ramos*
*Effundens, trunco, non frondibus efficit umbram.*
*Sed quamvis primo nutet casura sub Euro*
*Tot circum sylvae firmo se robore tollant*
*Sola tamen colitur.*

## 3.2    *The Sage in Exile*

Those ancient Sages, masters of Sapience, who when they were alive, had Greece, and when they were dead, had the whole world as their audience, left us as an infallible maxim: For the mind to learn philosophy, and not to wander in error, the foot must go wandering through many different lands. We may reach Sapience in no other way than by going to many sages, in many lands, pleading for it as beggars. Truth, (said they), a native of Heaven, is a sojourner — a passing pilgrim on Earth— and can only be found along the pilgrim's journey itself. He who seeks it, acts like rivers that grow larger the longer they flow. At their sources they were but tiny steams, and as they flow along, they grow as large as the sea. The vapors of the earth could they ever become stars, if they did not quit the land as mud and raise up to the Sun and so find happiness as pilgrims in Heaven, rather than as settlers on earth?[1] Men are not like the planets— most potent when they are in their own houses. Indeed, it often turns out that our stepmother is our land of birth and our real mother a foreign land. Certain plants in their native soil feed on poisonous humors but transplanted to a foreign clime, they lose their toxins and become wholesome food. His country ought to serve the sage as the horizon of his stars— for birth, not for burial. There, he first sees the light, as the dawn of his Sapience; progressively, he ascends to other lands until he reaches the high noon that knowledge attains on earth.

This was the sage teaching followed by those wise men and put in practice by them, as they had their nature in common with the Heavens as in their movement they find their tranquility. On their long travels they hastened to new Academies of Letters where some new increase of Sapience they might discover. Their life was, according to Synesius, a perpetual hunting expedition, now to Greece, now to Egypt, now to Persia, now to the Indies, where the lure of the richest spoils drew them. In this way Pythagoras, Socrates, Plato, Democritus, Diogenes, Anaxagoras and hundreds more did roam through foreign and exotic lands and gleaned what best they had to offer, the way that certain well-favored springs, as they wander as pilgrims through the

---

[1] From Pliny. See such vapors rising in Poussin's *Blind Orion searching for the Rising Sun*, 1658, at the Metropolitan Museum, NY.

bowels of the earth, do pass through precious veins— some of gold or silver, some of emeralds or sapphires. These they imbibe, transporting the very essence of their most wholesome qualities.

Now here is how the Taste for Letters can make leaving home behind (for the man with such a yearning) not only tolerable but extraordinarily congenial, so that when it happens, exile has no other punishment than its name. For the man with no gifts but what the ignorant crowd calls the gifts of fortune, leaving home, no doubt, feels like it does for a featherless chick chased from his nest. His exit is his fall, and his fall his ruin. But the man with strong feathers and ready wings will trade the straw nest where he was buried for the ample spaces and the open air of the great sky and make it as much his own as the freedom of flight which carries him aloft.

"Who took you from your country?" (said a shepherd to Tityras) "Who set you wandering as a pilgrim, to live as a stranger in foreign parts?"

*And what was it that made you visit Rome?*[2] Tityras replied, *"Weariness of servitude, thrust me from my native nest; Love of liberty brought me to live in foreign land."*

*Freedom, which lately looked down on my helplessness*
*As the shavings falling from my beard whitened.*[3]

Petrarch sagely takes this up, *"He, in his shepherd's words, says that he was glad to leave home to find his freedom, and it makes you, a philosopher, cry?"*[4]

Let the Moors of Spain weep,[5] as they are driven back to their Africa, a land fit for such monsters. They go not as men changing countries, but as men crashing down from Heaven. They turn their weeping eyes back at every step to see Granada and swear that straight above that kingdom lies Paradise. Such language is used by Sybarites,

---

2 Virgil, *Eclogue* 1.27:

    *Et quae tanta fuit Roman tibi causa videndi?*

3 Virgil, *Eclogue* 1.28/9:

    *Libertas; quae sera, tamen respexit inertem,*
    *Candidior post quam tondenti barba cadebat.*

4 **Petrarch** (1304-1374), *Rerum familiarum*, 2. **Letter 4**: *Ille in sermone pastorio ut libertatem inveniret, patriam se reliquisse gloriatur, tu philosophus defles?*

5 Giovanni **Botero** (1544-1617), *Relazioni universali*, 1, on Granada.

who love their country as a stable because they lead the lives of animals, or of fools, like that Athenian simpleton who said the Moon of Athens was fuller than the one in Corinth. It wasn't that the Athens Moon was fuller, but that his head was emptier: "*The same thing* (I say with Plutarch) *happens to us when we leave our land; we are puzzled to see the sea, the air, the sky, as if they were missing something they had for us at home.*"[6]

With the country of Stilpo in ruins, in the universal weeping he alone can smile; despite the loss of everything, he is serene. He departs alone and naked, carrying with him all that is his, because he carries just himself, the Sage and Letterato. Antisthenes commented: "*A sage, when all is lost, nonetheless is sufficient unto himself.*"[7] The people of Clazomenae, as we said above, may banish the great Anaxagoras as unworthy of the name of citizen and exile him from the city. He does not grieve, as if he were not quitting his country, but a prison stuck in a remote corner, too small for his great soul. He points to Heaven as his country, and to the stars as his fellow citizens. Wherever he goes he has Heaven for the same roof, his house is not gone— he is only changing rooms: "*Who cares if he is somewhere else? Other valleys, lakes, rivers and hills are his view. The Heavens always stand above him; his mind can convey its thoughts around the world; with the roof of Heaven always above, he is simply changing sleeping quarters.*"[8] The Athenians mock Antisthenes, because he has no house in the world, but all the world is his and he has the last laugh: "*For I am like the cockles in their shells. They always have a home.*"[9] He can live in the open, as the demigods live in the Elysian fields, where

None have a secure home.[10]

Diogenes may be thrown out of Sinope, he will be as grateful to those who proscribe him as Theseus was to Hercules, his deliverer,

6 **Plutarch,** *On Exile,* 6: *Et hoc idem accidit nobis, cum extra patriam constituti mare, aërem, coelum dubii consideramus, quasi aliquid eis desit eorum, quibus, in patria fruebamur.*
7 **Laertius**, *Antisthenes*, 6.10: *Sapiens autem, etiam si omnia desint; solus sufficit sibi.*
8 **Petrarch, ibid.**: *Quid enim refert quam diversa parte consistat? Valles quidem, et lacus, et flumina, et colles alios videt. Coelum unum est. Illuc aninum exigit, eo cogitationes suas ex omni mundi parte transmittit; nec aliud quam sub tecti unius amplexu ex alio in alium thalamum transivisse cogitat.*
9 *Quia quasi cochleae sine domibus numquam sunt.*
10 *Aeneid* 6. 673: *Nulli certa domus.*

31

when he fetched him by force from that unhappy stone, on which his punishment was carved,

*There he sits and will for all eternity.*[11]

Hercules saved him from that loathsome idleness which alone stood him for a great Hell and returned him to his liberty. Scoffers may jeer at Diogenes in exile, his rejoinder: "My fellow citizens have condemned me to leave Sinope, I have condemned them to stay." The sage knew they were the real exiles, banished from the rest of the world, confined within the walls of one city, more than he— banned from only one city, with the whole world for his country. Being far from Sinope for him was like being a man thrown overboard in a sudden sea storm and driven by the waves to a rocky precipice.[12] From those cliffs he watches as others are shipwrecked and he calls his misfortune fortunate. He does not long for the ocean that cast him ashore; but abhors it. He does not envy those in danger there; but pities them.

Would you like a picture or just a rough sketch by the hand of the worthy Seneca who draws to the life the state, the employments, the ordinary pastimes of the greater part of men in their cities?

Behold— a world of people who are always busy, doing nothing. They are less idle while they are sleeping than while they are working, "*If you see them leaving home and ask, Where to? What are you up to? They answer, "Sorry, friend, have to go." Should I see some people, I'll get busy. With no plan they wander around searching for something to do. What they had intended to do, they don't because they got distracted.*"[13] Did you ever see a long line of ants, one after another busily climbing up a stump until they get to the top, as if they were touching the very Heavens and greeting the stars? Then they go down on the other side and back to the ground: "*Many follow a pattern of life that not without cause may be described as a busy inertia. They return home totally exhausted and swear they don't remember why they left home or where they were. Then, meandering the next day, they follow the*

---

11 *Aeneid* 6. 617: *Sedet, aeternumque sedebit.*

[12] This is a prophetic simile, as Bartoli would find himself there off Capri, little more than a year later.

13 Seneca, **De tranquillitate animi**, 12: *Horum si aliquem exeuntem domo interrogaveris, Quò tu? Quid cogitas? Respondebit tibi; Non me Herculè, scio. Si aliquos videbo aliquid agam. Sine proposito vagantur quaerentes negotia, nec quae destinaverunt agunt, sed in quae incurrerunt.*

*very same course.*"[14] Can it be a matter of grief or sorrow for someone with the eyes of Sapience in his head, a good judge of the truth, to be cut off from such a life? Would he not rather say to those who stay behind what Stratonicus, (lodging in Zerif) said to his host. He asked what crimes they punished with banishment and was told that swindlers were punished with exile, "So why," said he, "don't all of you become swindlers to get out of here?"

When leaving one's country, one leaves behind all one's possessions. This, as Plutarch said, is no worse a loss than the old skin a snake leaves outside his pit as he creeps inside. Without it he is younger and quicker. And it costs a Man of Letters less than anyone else, for he will never want for a home and a living. Everywhere he goes, he will be received like ships from the Indies, full of gold and pearls, welcomed by the ports where they drop anchor.

Scipio, that Hercules of Rome, tamed not one monster, but all of Africa, the mother of monsters. He conquered Asdrubal, killed Annon, captured Syphax, destroyed Carthage, subjugated Libya— peerless, he earned more triumphs than anyone ever. When he became the Sun of Rome's empire, he brought tears to the weak eyes of envy and, as the distinction of his merits grew, he came to be regarded in a negative light. His inferiors began to think he was getting too big, as he had as the foundation of his glory the ruins of Carthage. This was a grandeur that overshadowed the merits of others. The brighter he shone, the more they felt overshadowed. And because no laurels can survive the thunderbolts of evil tongues, nor can preeminence escape them, after his glorious triumph, adding Africa to the glory of his name, as Scipio Africanus— he found in Rome monsters worse than he had seen in Africa: accusers, slanderers who, under the protection of Portius Cato, summoned him to court hoping to have him condemned. Guilty of what? Only of what is an insult to envy. But the great man did not want to make his enemies laugh or cry. He removed himself from eyes that examined his every move. And in voluntary

---

14 ***Ibid.****: His plerumque similem vitam agunt, quorum non immerito quis inquietum inertiam dixerit. Hi deinde domum tum supervacua redeuntes lassitudine, jurant, nescisse se ipsos quare exierint, ubi fuerint: postero die erraturi per eadem illa vestigia.*

exile, he left Rome which was worse than Carthage, in that, from the Carthage he destroyed, he got a triumph; from the Rome he preserved, he got exile. He retired to Linternus, a small port in a great storm, and changing profession, from a warrior he became a farmer. And with that same hand that had planted the palms of such glorious victories in the dry sands of Africa, he took over a small farm. Afterwards, in a strange *quid pro quo*, he changed his sword for a hoe, his battering rams for plows, horses for oxen, trenches for fences, ditches for furrows, the formation of squadrons for the arrangement of trees, the routing of armies for the uprooting of thorns; in the end, battles for toils, and victories for harvests. But the privet around his farm was not thick enough for the troubles of Rome not to penetrate. Nor did his rustic simplicity so disguise him that public cares did not upset him. In the voluntary banishment that he unwillingly accepted from his ungrateful country he departed, rather than be expelled. From then on, he held enkindled in his heart such a flaming passion against Rome that it was not extinguished, and even when he expired, he kept this fire alive beneath the ashes of his bones, buried far from his heartless fatherland.

This is the advantage of a great mind over a great heart. A man of great knowledge and of such valiant and ready Wit as Scipio, after Rome was abandoned, could say, as Socrates, when he was turned out of Athens: "*For me the whole earth is the same mother, the whole of Heaven is my roof, the whole world is my country.*"[15] He could leave the City of Romulus, to enter (as Musonius said)[16] the City of Jove, not surrounded by walls, but enclosed by the vast convex of the Heavens, where all languages are spoken, as it contains all nations of every climate. It is a noble city whose senators are the gods of Heaven as its people are senators of the earth. He may have exited Rome like a tiny stream between narrow banks runs its lowly course. Come to the sea (where the masses see it die) from a stream, it becomes the great sea and extends as far the sea stretches; so to say, it bridges the confines of one world and another. But this will take the virile virtue of a great Spirit that deems it unworthy to love servitude to one small corner,

---

15 *Mihi omnis terra eadem mater, omne coelum idem tectum, totus mundus est patria.* See Cicero, *Disputationes tusculanae*, 5.108.
16 In **Stobaeus**, *Florilegium*, 29.78: *De exilio.*

rather than the liberty of feelings and thoughts that sets it on top of the world.

He who is separated from his country, let him imitate the Moon. The farther it is from the Sun, the more it is filled with light. Given the growth and acquisition of new knowledge that accompanies daily familiarity with men of greater stature than he, he must imitate the example and the words of Alcibiades. An outcast from his country, he was welcomed by a foreign king and greeted with the offer of three important cities: "*We would have perished, had we not perished.*"[17]

How great is the obligation of Sapience to banishments, voluntary and enforced! In this way Pallas Athena has gained more and different advantages than when she sailed in the ship of the Argonauts on the quest for the Golden Fleece.

Before the art of navigation, the world was half unknown; mostly uncultivated, all barbarous.

> *Uninquisitive a man only knows his own shores*
> *And grows old behind the plough of the family farm,*
> *Rich in simplicity, and he owns only what he was born with.*
> *He has no concept of the world's riches.*[18]

Who then possessed the world, or knew its dimensions— or what it contains? The sea was idle, the winds unprofitable; the stars of Heaven were neither studied nor used.

> *No one yet knew the constellations*
> *And the stars that decorate the Heavens*
> *It was not then done.*[19]

Now, all the world is made but one realm, whereas before, every realm seemed a world. Each country goes not without the other's produce, hoards not its own. In exchange for what it lacks, it can exchange what it has in supply. This makes a single body of the whole world. One part

---

17 *Perieramus, nisi periissemus.* Not Alciabiades and Tissaphernes. See Plutarch, *Themistocles*, 29.

18 **Seneca,** *Medea,* 331/4:

> *Sua quisque piger littora norat,*
> *Patrióque Senex factus in arvo*
> *Parvo dives, nisi quas tulerat*
> *Natale solum, non norat opes.*

19 *Ibid.*, 335/37: *Nudum quisquam sidera norat,*

> *Stellisque, quibus pingitur aether,*
> *Non erat usus.*

can easily come to the aid of another in need. Now the whole of Heaven is but one roof and all men know each other as one and the same family.[20] We may now chant with greater truth, what the verses of Manilius spoke:

> *Nature was still hidden, we explored it all*
> *A whole world we took into possession*
> *We were gazing at the realm of our Maker.*[21]

What would the Indian Gymnosophists, the Greeks, the Chaldeans have had, if they were happy with what they were born with and had not set out from their country as Ulysses in his fortunate wanderings in search of that Sapience from others, which they lacked? Look how much better a seeing eye is than a blind one, says Philo of Alexandria.[22] So much more is that man worth whose thirst for knowledge has led him journeying as a pilgrim and voluntary exile through many lands, than the one who lived like the trunk of a tree; it rooted where it first sprouted, spent its life in the same place and there it finally rotted.

## 3.3   *The Sage in Prison*

The souls of the philosophers (said an ancient sage)[1] have their bodies for houses, the souls of the ignorant have them for prisons. This is because the first are withdrawn into the body in time of sleep and repose, and leave freely at their pleasure to wherever their fancies carry them; the others, shut up in the narrow walls of their bodies, are tied with as many chains as they have limbs; they see no other light than what comes through the tiny openings of two pupils. They are confined, for they have no thoughts other than what their bodies dictate. So, if the ignorant go to prison, they are prisoners twice. The sages, no. Their finest part can suffer confinement no more than the

---

20 This discourse on early modern mercantilism reflects the global philosophy expressed in Bartoli's poetry as the coda to the Senecan *excursus* in chapter 2.
21 **Manilius, *Astronomica*, 4. 875/7:**

> *Jam nusquam Natura latet: pervidimus omnem*
> *Et capto potimur mundo: nostrumque parentem*
> *Pars sua conspicimus.*

22 Philo of Alexandria, *De Abraham*, 4.25.

1 **Epictetus**

wind can be imprisoned in a net, or the light trapped in a crystal. The Tullianum of Rome, the Cave of Syracuse, the Lethe of Persia, the Ceramo of Cyprus and as many of yesterday and today as are famous or infamous prisons of the world— none are so deep that they can bury, or so dark that they can blind; so narrow that they can bind, so fortified within double walls that they confine a truly philosophical mind. This is owing to Sapience. Plato calls it the wings of the soul. It carries the mind in flight, not only outside prison, but if it wills, outside the world. The Stoic says, "*So now his thoughts of the whole of Heaven travel to all past and future time. Our frail body, guardian and binder of the soul, this too is thrown over. Insults and sicknesses work on it. But the soul is sacred and eternal, and no hand ruffles it.*"[2]

Therefore, a prison to a wise man is no prison, but a house, since he is at liberty to go out when he wants. "*But the soul accompanies every man, and where it wants to go, it can travel.*"[3]

Unimportant to the soul are the whereabouts of the body, while its thoughts are outside the body. Thus, Hermotimus, whose soul left his body at will, went traveling to diverse places, even into the remotest climes, to see what the world was doing. He felt so little— he didn't even know he was in pain— so that while his body was being burnt alive in one place, his soul, not knowing it, was rejoicing in another.[4]

Socrates had a small remedy against the unending disturbances of the always bothersome Xanthippe. He would go to the upstairs part of the house while she made the bottom floor insufferable with her shrieks. What better way to escape the darkness, the close quarters, the boredom of solitude in prison than for the mind to climb to the stars, to bask in their light, to follow their cycles, to measure their magnitudes, and so to travel in the company of the Intelligences so

---

2 **Seneca, *Consolatio ad Helviam*, 18**: *Nam cogitatio ejus circa omne coelum, et in omne praeteritum, futurumque tempus emittitur. Corpusculum hoc custodia, ac vinculum animi, huc, atque illuc jactatur. In hoc supplicia, in hoc latrocinia, in hoc morbi exercentur. Animis quidem ipse sacer, et aeternus est, et cui non possit iniici manus.*
3 **Tertullian, *Ad martyres*, 2.**10: *Totum autem hominem animus, circumfert et quo velit transfert.*
4 **Pliny**, 7.52.

masterfully making them move ? *"The body feels no pain, when the soul is in Heaven."*[5]

A pleasant folly was recounted by Horace of a Greek fool. For many hours of the day he imagined himself in a packed theater watching characters go on stage, listening to excellent tragic plays recited by the very finest actors! He was the happiest of men in all Argos:

> *He thought he was in a theatre watching a play,*
> *a happy spectator applauding in an empty theatre.*[6]

His friends, trying to be sympathetic, were unknowingly cruel. For by the power of hellebore when they resettled the brains in his head, they took the joy from his heart. He would not have exchanged his folly for all the wisdom of the world and, being cured, he rued his new wisdom and envied his old folly. His friends had deprived him of an innocent source of joy and had brought him back to old drudgeries. When they turned him from an imaginary spectator to the role of an actor of tragedy, to them he unleashed his dolorous complaint:

> *You have killed me, my friends,*
> *You would not grant me, said he, this special pleasure*
> *And have wrenched my senses from a most enjoyable illusion.*[7]

Hence, a foolish fancy of the mind may make someone happy, by driving him out of himself and fixing his attention on an object of pleasure. So why can't Sapience accomplish in a head full of noble and sublime knowledge, what folly can accomplish in a head empty of sense? Sapience can offer your mind spectacles so pleasant you forget where you are. From a prison you may travel to the bowels of the earth, or to the watery abyss, now on the ocean, now from the air, now tossing in the wind, now around the Sun and among the stars, by and by, to the farthest reaches of the cosmos — even to the immensity of outer space. These are the speculations that transport our minds and bless us in their contemplation. They are the true dreams of waking

---

5 **Tertullian, ibid.**: *Nihil crus sentit in nervo, cum animus in coelo est.*
6 **Horace, 2, Epistle 2, To Florus:**
> *Qui se credebat miros audire tragoedos;*
> *In vacuo laetus sessor, plausorque theatro.*
7 **Horace, ibid**: *Me occidistis amici,*
> *Non servastis, ait, cui sic extorta voluptas.*
> *Et demptus per vim mentis gratissus error.*

eyes, giving in equal measure repose and delight. As said that excellent Platonic, Maximus of Tyre: *"Are you familiar with the spectacle of the philosopher like the one I am talking about? In sleep, in a vivid reality, as it flies around, yet is attached to body, the soul travels in the great world. One is borne from the earth to the sky and travels across the universe by sea and flies over it on the air. It goes around the earth with the sun, circles around the moon and joins the stars in their chorus; nothing short of being unison with Jupiter, governor and commander of the universe. What a blessed operation! O beautiful vision! O truest of dreams!"*[8]

Someone who is capable of such thoughts when he is put in prison can say with Tertullian, *"Remove the name of prison, and call it a retreat"*[9] He changes place, but not fortune. He alters the condition of his body, but not the employment of his mind. And as the poet says of the demigods: they do the very same things below in the Elysian fields which they would do living here on earth.

> *Those cares of the chariot, and of arms,*
> *And the job of feeding the neighing horses*
> *Are still done the same as on earth.*[10]

Thus, the sage in prison has the same noble purpose of mind, his one and only mandate, to climb to higher degrees of better understanding as he did when he was free: *"doing the same as on earth ."*[11] He will go to prison, not for obscurity and infamy, but to bring it light and glory. He follows behind the great Socrates: *"Untouched by the ignominy of the place, it seemed no prison where Socrates was."*[12]

---

8 **Maximus of Tyre**, *Dissertations*, 28: *Scis enim philosophi spectaculum cui maximè simile dico? In somnio nimirum manifesto, et circumquaque volitanti, cujus, integro corpore manente, animus tamen in universam terram excurrit. Ex terra effertur in coelum, universum mare pertransit, universum pervolat aërem. Terram ambit cum Sole, cum Luna circumfertur, caeteroque astrorum jungitur choro, minimumque abest, quin unà cum Jove universa gubernet, et ordinet. O operationem beatam! O spectacula pulchra! O insomnia verissima!*
9 **Tertullian,** *Ad martyres,* 2.8: *Auferamus carceris nomen, secessum vocemus.*
10 *Aeneid* 6.653/6: *Quae gratia currum*
> *Armorisque fuit vivis, quae cura nitentes,*
> *Pascere equos, eadem sequitur tellure repostos.*
11 **Ibid.:** *eadem sequitur tellure repostum.* The refrain echoes Virgil
12 **Seneca,** *De consolatione ad Helviam*, 13.4: *Ignominiam ipsi loco detracturus, neque etiam poterat carcerem videri, in quo Socrates erat.*

But this is not the only gift of Letters for the sage in prison, one far greater is when (which very often occurs) the prison becomes a lyceum, and with feet fettered in shackles, the hand is free to take up a pen. Living in a cell, known only to himself, like the silkworm in its cocoon, "*Already changed and winged.*"[13] the writer flies everywhere in his books and becomes, in the school of a prison, a public tutor to the world. The Sun, leaving our hemisphere and going underground, gives to our world a world of stars, so that his loss is our gain, and his absence is his honor. Pearl oysters that lie at the bottom of the sea, chained to a rock, without light— indeed without eyes— produce pearls. When they are freed from the deep and taken from darkness into the Sun's light and encased in gold, they ornament royal crowns and are held in veneration by the world. Thus, Anaxagoras between the four walls of a narrow prison found the squaring of the circle.[14] Thus, Naevius the poet, switched from the bottom of a tower to the heights of Mount Parnassus where he wrote most of his poems.[15] And, because no one would imprison Euripides, he shut himself up in a dark cave and there wrote those tragedies which have had the world for theatre and applause ever since. The prisons which confined these famous men forbad them to be seen. But their writings revealed more of them to the world than their faces would have. Of the effigies of Brutus and Cassius which were not shown at their public funeral, Tacitus said, "*They shone resplendently by the very fact that they were not exposed to view.*"[16] Like them, being hidden in the shadows of a prison drew to these men more resplendent rays of glory than if they had been living in public.

How aptly may be said of them what Tertullian says of the light of day after it lowered into the western ocean, as if buried below ground: "*Back with its glorious light, its generous beauty, with the same and entire sun renewing everything in the whole world, it consigns the night to its place of death, sending the darkness back to its place of burial.*"[17] These Sages went to prison

---

13 After Horace, 2. 20 to Maecenas, v. 9/10: *Jam mutatus in alitem,*
14 **Plutarch, *De exilio*,** 27. Better to understand that he worked on it.
15 **Gellius, 3.2; 15.20.**
16 *Tacitus, Annals,* 76: *Eo ipso praefulgebant, quod non visebantur.*
17 **Tertullian, *De resurrectione*,** 12: *Rursus cum suo cultu, cum dote, cum sole, eadem et integra, et tota universo orbi reviviscit; interficiens mortem suam noctem; rescindens sepulturam suam tenebras.*

as seeds fall in the fields, buried, but not dead. Still in the ground, they shoot up energetically through the earth and their rich grains demonstrate that while they seemed dead they were working to sustain many lives. Locked in towers, their thoughts turn with indefatigable speculations to serve the public good. As town clocks walled in towers, they point out the hours with a moving finger and bestow the activities of the public with regularity. They might be hidden in caverns of living stones, but like the fabled Echo of the poets, when they lost all their other vital parts, they still had a loud voice which, pronounced and reverberated by the stones of their prison, was heard throughout the world. Of all of them may be said what the author of the *Metamorphoses* said of Echo.

> *Hiding and invisible to the light.*
> *She is heard by all. Her sound is where she is alive.*[18]

Solitude, and silence are the indivisible companions of study. To find them some have buried themselves in the most private hiding places of their houses— some in the woods, and in caves. But such men as these already had them as their companions in prison where. they were much less alone in such company while their minds focused on their thoughts. From down below their Wits were as farsighted in attaining enlightenment in all forms of knowledge, as from the bottom of that famous well, the eyes (of Thales) could even see the stars at noon.[19]

## 3.4   *The Sage in Sickness*

Poetry had a Deucalion who could make men out of stones. Philosophy had a Zeno who could make stones out of men. Deucalion, the restorer of the world, was left on top of the naked peaks of Mount Parnassus, the only refuge left in a world buried in a deluge and become all sea. He threw over his shoulders the stones that were the bones of the great Mother, and according to the oracle,

> *Stones (who can believe this, unless as the witness of antiquity?)*
> *Began to lose their stiffness and hardness*

---

18 **Ovid, *Met.*,** 3.400/1:
> *Latet, nullaque in luce videtur,*
> *Omnibus auditor. Sonus est qui vivit in illo.*
[19] Plato, *Theaetetus*, 174a; Aesop's Fable.

# Felicity of the Sages

*Gradually softening and taking shape.*[1]

On the other hand, there was Zeno. He injected a vein of stone into the men who were his students and made them unfeeling and hard by rooting out every emotion from their hearts. The Stoa, the porch where he taught, was more of a sculptor's studio where they made statues than an academy of Sapience where they made philosophers. His first and last lesson was teaching how to set the mind inside a royal fortress against the surprises of love; the attacks of hatred, the sieges of hope, the batteries of desperation, the scaling ladders of daring,— in short, so that neither the arms nor the arts of any emotion could force the heart to surrender or cede its position, by concessions or treaties. In the tempest of a sick body, of distraught humors, of life endangered, he would have the spirit stand: *"Immobile as a cliff battered by the sea."*[2] Battered, but unmoved by the waves, it shatters them at its feet and dashes them into foam. All the pain we suffer, however tight the wrack may twist each member, must not let us show a distressed paleness in our faces or the weakening of courage in our breasts. We must not allow a moan to escape from our mouths, nor a single tear from our eyes. Indeed, as the torments increase, our faces should show increased happiness. Similarly, the Heavens appear most serenely limpid when the north winds are blowing hard and cold.

But why speak of Zeno and the Stoics? Take Epicurus himself, that animal whose soul was only salt to keep him from rotting alive from his pleasures. He taught that the man who has not learned how to turn thorns into flowers to get honey from bitter absinth, to exchange his sorrows for jubilation and his miseries for enjoyment, can never be happy. Enjoyment is the source of beatitude (said he); a man cannot be blessed, if he does not always feel blessed and must learn how to find pleasure in his torments as well as in his enjoyments. *"What* (said Epicurus quoted by Seneca) *if the Sage is burning alive inside the bull of Phalaris; he will cry out: Sweet it is, nothing bothers me."*[3]

---

1 **Ovid,** *Met.*, 10. 32/5:
> *Saxa (quis hoc credat, nisi sit pro teste vetustas?)*
> *Ponere duritiem caepere suumque rigorem*
> *Mollirique mora, mollitaque ducere formam.*

2 *Aeneid* 7.586/7: *Velut pelagi rupes immota.*

3 **Seneca, Letter 66.**18: *Quare Sapiens in Phalaridis tauro peruratur, exclamabit: Dulce est, ad me nihil pertinet.*

But the Stoics were asking for too much when they couldn't find it in themselves to make sages of others without taking away their humanity. Other schools more prudently taught that the affections should not be pulled out by their roots as poisonous but, as wild and thorny plants, they should be improved by grafting. Many voices, without a skillful artist to tune them, make a most unpleasant noise, but if reason can impart tempo and measure, they make music of the sweetest harmony. But those rigid schools, by imposing their strict injunction to eradicate its passions from the heart, have this much to offer: that true philosophy can grant us sufficient control of our emotions so that even if it does not inure the senses to pain, nor imbue our spirit with such stupor as not to feel it, at least it guards the spirit from abandonments of despair or outbursts of frustration. Thus, despite the raging storm of our body's suffering, we never lose heart or peace of mind.

Here is a sage in sickness. Don't see him lying on a bed, but embarked on a ship, not in the fever and pain of his virulent sickness, but in whirlpools and breakers of a long and unrelenting tempest. The sails flap, the planks groan, the mast trembles— everything shivers from poop to prow; the ship is in danger. But this is not the signal of sinking; it is the flow of nature. The experience of the pilot and promptness of the sailors will steer it, I'll not say, unruffled, through so many tumults, but safely through so many dangers. Sapience sits as helmsman to focus the mind and govern the emotions. In one tempest of sufferings, as virulent as they can be, where another ship would sink, a sage in infirmity will sail through, if not with the serenity of calm waters, at least with the assurance of reaching port.

You shall see in a body battered, a mind so firm; in a body in complete havoc, a mind so composed, that you might think you are seeing two persons in one man— one a philosopher, the other an invalid. This latter is like the side of Mount Olympus thick with clouds, soaked by rain and struck by thunder; the former, like its lofty peak, always enjoys the heaven's serenity, always sees Sun or stars. On one side, it is a cloud melting into rain; on the other, it is a rainbow, cheerful in melancholy and smiling through the tears.

Now if you want to know how this happens, ask me the question. A mind at peace, does it not benefit the body's health? They are so bound together that one is in sympathy with the other and, as happens with strings tuned together, when you play one, the other, untouched, will sound. The emotions of the mind are the winds, the humors of the body the sea, while the winds roar, the sea grows rough and tempestuous. On the other hand, Seneca says, "*What enhances the mind, also benefits the body.*"[4] So that if philosophy did nothing else but teach us to see death as it really is— which it has encouraged through so many noble and high-minded aphorisms— how many virulent paroxysms of fear, sometimes deadlier than the fevers themselves, can such wisdom relieve from our hearts? How many men, wholly safe and half sound, at the least touch of illness, die just out of fear of death, and take their own wretched lives for nothing? Think of that Diophantus who hanged himself by a thread taken from a spider's web.[5]

Aeneas coming to Hell's gates, had a terrible time facing centaurs, harpies, chimeras, gorgons, hydras. So, when he saw them his blood rushed to his heart in fear, as his hand rushed to his sword in defense.

> *And he did not understand that the pale lives were without bodies*
> *She told him they flew around the cave as imagined shapes*
> *He might strike, but in vain, the sword would cut through shadows.*[6]

The sage sick man does just the same. The fears of death which in sundry frightful shapes make towards him from the gates of Hell, he knows they are "*bodiless phantoms*"[7] and remembers what that Roman sage wrote, "*It is not from men alone, but from things themselves that we must take the mask and restore their real faces. Take off this pomp you hide behind, to terrify simpletons. You are the same dead man my servant and my handmaid held in scorn, etc.*"[8] Fools who want medicines for maladies, have no remedy against fear. It freezes them more than their fevers burn. They will not look at anything or be looked at by anything that

---

4 **Seneca,** *Letter* **78**.3: *Quidquid animum evexit, etiam corpore prodest.*
5 *Epigraphia graeca*, Greek anthology, 11.111.
6 *Aeneid* **6**.292/4:
> *Et ni docta omnes tenues sine corpore vitas*
> *Admoneat volitare cava sub imagine forma*
> *Irruat, et frustra ferro diverberet umbras.*
7 *Aenied* 6.292: *Tenues sine corpore vitae.*
8 **Seneca,** *Letter* **24**.13/14: *Non hominibus tantum, sed et rebus personae demenda est, et reddenda facies sua. Tolle istam pompam sub qua lates, et stultos territas. Mors es quam nuper servus meus, quam ancilla contempsit, etc.*

reminds them of death. They are like that simpleton who, so as not to be seen by the fleas that were biting him, turned the light out:

*So that these fleas, he says, can't find me.*[9]

Fears have all too good an eye— they are expert at seeing better in the dark than in the light.

Granted that mental attitude has such impact on what the body feels, what great advantage is there for the sage in infirmity that he can keep a brave spirit and a tranquil mind, so that fear is powerless to cause him anguish or discouragement? The very intensity of the sickness is soothed by his tranquility of spirit and mitigated in its fury: *"You can make your illness light if you think it so. Everything depends on one's opinion; ambition, luxury, greed. We suffer what we think we suffer. One is only as miserable as one thinks."*[10]

But keeping sickness in check is trivial, if it is not assuaged. It is assuaged— believe me, blessed— when the mind is occupied elsewhere, which is an easy prescription for a man of study. Then the mind is relieved of feeling the present pain, like a heron, in a hail storm or in the rain, who flies above the clouds to enjoy the blue sky.

Syracuse stands captured by Marcellus and is full of the shouts of the victors and the shrieks of the vanquished. While the soldiers are breaking in and the populace is running through the streets, only Archimedes has his mind so centered on the lines of certain mathematical figures which he is engaged in describing, that he doesn't see, know or hear a thing of what is going on outside. He is so lost in his thoughts that when a hasty soldier finishes him off, he knows he is dead before he knows he is dying— more aggravated that he has not finished his demonstration than that his life has finished. On the other hand, there is Solon gasping his last. While he lay dying, he overheard some philosophers arguing some point or other by his bedside. So he forgot he was dying and calling back his departing soul into his head, as one who wakes up or rises from the dead, he opened his eyes and ears— and did not finish with living until they finished with their dispute. Seneca, didn't he once (as he himself relates) escape the fevers

---

9 **Epigraphia graeca**, Greek Anthology, 11.432: *Non me, inquit, cernent amplius hi pulices.*
10 **Seneca**, **Letter** 78.13/14: *Levem morbum dum putas facies. Omnia ad opinionem suspensa sunt. Non ambitio tantùm ad illam respicit, aut luxuria, aut avaritia. Ad opinionem dolemus. Tam miser est quisque quàm credit.*

that were after him by scampering, as they were coming on, to hide himself in the most secret speculations of philosophy? The angelic St. Thomas Aquinas, did he not ignore the smart of a bad burn by channeling his whole soul most sagely into a profound lucubration, a state of reflection he was familiar with in his studies?

Your body is confined to a bed, but don't let your mind be tied down; you can absent yourself from your sufferings by dwelling with your mind in a separate place. "*What is it that the untutored lack in dealing with sickness of the body? They have no training in finding inner peace. They have lived mostly in their bodies. But the man who is great and prudent wrests his soul from his body; he is principally occupied with his better, godlike side, dealing with the side of suffering and illness only as he must.*"[11] What he means, (and Seneca is speaking here of the sage in infirmity), is that he is like a compass, with one part immobile and stationary on one foot, and the other moving around it, describing larger or smaller circles, as it circles at a lesser or greater distance from the center.

But, behold, in the example of one man the precepts of all. Posidonius, a sage in infirmity, authenticates what I have been saying: that Letters and Sapience carry the sickbed above a flood of sufferings, just as crocodiles carry their nests above the flooding of the Nile.

This man was a philosopher, infirm for many years and laden with more maladies than limbs. In every part of his body he had great pains. Had his ills been distributed among many men, they would have filled a whole hospital of sick people, whereas being all collected together in his body, they didn't even amount to one sick man. Thanks to his fortitude of mind standing in for his weakness of body, the sufferings of his ailing limbs did no more pierce his heart than arrows can strike the guts of an elephant, because they fall off his thick hide.

*So many spears cannot inflict a mortal wound*
*His entrails lie safe inside.*[12]

---

11 **Seneca,** *Letter* **78**.10: *Illud est quod imperitos in vexatione corporis male habet. Non assueverunt animo esse contenti. Multum illis cum corpore fuit. Ideò vir magnus, ac prudens animum deducit à corpore, et multum cum meliore, ac divina parte versatur: cum hac querula, ac fragili quantum necesse est.*
12 **Lucan,** *Pharsalia,* **6**. 213; 211:
*Tot jaculis unam non explent vulnera mortem.*
*Viscera tuta latent penitus.*

*Felicity of the Sages*

A grand proof of Roman valor was given by Mutius Scaevola to King Porsenna. More suffering from his mistake than from his burning hand, he watched intrepidly as it was burning in the fire, as he had watched it scornfully make that mortal, misguided thrust. His foe, the king, was so greatly astonished that he was constrained not only to commend his would-be killer for his anger at not succeeding, but also to protect him against himself by removing the fire from under that illustrious hand, only fit for luster and more to be celebrated for its error than has it struck the right man. This was just a single act, a single hand, for a short time, of a man criminally guilty of death, of a man bitterly furious against himself.[13] Posidonius so many years in his sickbed, an Anaxarchus in a grinding mortar,[14] tormented in one part after another, consumed by his pains and surviving his ongoing death only to take longer dying— he regarded himself and his sufferings with not only a dry eye but with a cheerful one. He took his very illnesses as subjects for his philosophy, changing his chamber into a school and his bed into a lecturer's chair. In a word, he did as the Moon, which though it falls into eclipse and loses its light— does not lose the path of its cyclical movement but stays on course nonetheless— as if she were yet as filled with light as she was before.

Men flocked from all parts to Rhodes, to hear and see a man, who from his own wounds produced balm for others. He had more admirers as he lay on his bed than that famous Colossus of brass, erected at the gate of the port— the pride of Rhodes and wonder of the world. Pompey the Great, passing through Greece was drawn by the fame of Posidonius and wanted to see him. He arrived just at the time when the sage was more than ever being hammered by his pains. He came, he saw, and he was conquered. Pompey seemed the patient in compassion with the torments of Posidonius. Posidonius seemed the healthy one in extensive discussion with Pompey and arguing the

---

13 Livy, *Ab Urbe Condita*, 2.12/13.
14 This is the same philosopher Bartoli misread as Anaxagoras in Plutarch who tormented Alexander with the idea of infinite unconquered worlds, (p.24) whose skull was crushed by Nicocreon, tyrant of Cyprus, (Laertius, *Anaxarchus*, 9.58). Bartoli reveals a certain historical confusion ignoring the time gap between pre-Socratic Anaxagoras and Aristotle's pupil which is repeated in the Subject Index of his 1684 *Opere.*

truth of his topic: *"Nothing is good, unless it be honest,"*[15] with such cheerfulness of face and constancy of mind that, as he was being torn apart by his pains, instead of screaming out, he chastised them as someone else might a beast, saying: *"Pain, you can do nothing. However much you torment me, I will never admit you are an evil."*[16]

Thus Sapience, which is the summit of the noblest Letters, better than the waters of the Styx for Achilles, can render the spirit invulnerable to the wounds of the body and keep the mind as far alienated from all sense of its sufferings, as it can keep its thoughts focused on happier matters.

Let the Sage be poor— put him in prison. Banish him to exile— afflict him with infirmity. Here, in two words, is the medicine for each of these maladies. *"Do I fall into poverty? I am in good company. Am I exiled? I will take where I am sent as my birthplace. Am I put in chains? So, what? Has not nature saddled me with the heavy weight of my body? Shall I die? That would mean that you can no longer afflict me with sickness, you can no longer chain me up, no longer will I have to die."*[17]

Thus, I have demonstrated how a Man of Letters can find happiness alone with what Letters provide.[18] But in order to highlight with greater clarity the small light I have shed on such an illustrious theme, I shall show what stands in its shadow. So, if I have shown you how Sapience can find wellness, even in misery, now I will show how Ignorance can be miserable, even in wellness.

---

15 **Cicero, *Tusculanae disputationes*** 2.61: *Nihil bonum est, nisi quod honestum sit.*

16 *Ibidem*, 2.62: *Nihil agis dolor, quamvis sis molestus nunquam te esse confitebor malum.* Cicero also frequented this Stoic philosopher's lectures in Rhodes in 77 BC and corresponded with him.

17 Seneca, *Letter* 24.17: *Pauper fiam? inter plures ero. Exul fiam? Ibi me natum putabo quò mittar. Alligabor? Quid enim? Nunc solutus sum? ad hoc me natura grave corporis mei pondus abstrinxit. Moriar? Haec dicis: Desinam aegrotare posse, desinam alligari posse, desinam mori posse.*

18 A masterful coda to the four vignettes of *The Felicity of the Sages* distilled in Seneca's words to be reflected in the the five-sided mirror of *The Infelicity of the Ignorant* that it introduces.

LA GVIDE

DES BEAVX

ESPRITS.

*COMPOSE'E EN ITALIEN*
*par le R. Pere Daniel Bartoli*
*de la Compagnie de IESVS.*

Et traduit en François par vn Pere
de la mesme Compagnie.

CINQVIESME EDITION.

Imprimé au Pont-à-Mousson.

Et se vendent à PARIS, Chez CHARLES CABRY
à la Place de Sorbonne , proche l'Escole.

M. DC. LXIX.

**Vertheidigung**
der Kunstliebenden und
Gelehrten
anständigere Sitten.
Aus dem Italianischen ge-
dolmetschet
von
Einem Mitglied der Hochlöblichen
Fruchtbringenden Gesellschafft
den
Kunstliebenden.

RESPICE FINEM.

Nürnberg/
Gedruckt und verlegt bey Michael Endter/
Im Jahr 1654.

# 4 *Infelicity of the Ignorant, Even in Felicity*

## 4.1 *Ignorance and Sanctity*

Sanctity is a pearl of such great price and inestimable worth that even not set in gold— not sparkling amid the lights of the intellect, not illuminated by the sciences— it is not in the least diminished in its value, nor less precious to that great Merchant who gives everything he has for just one.

The scales of God do not weigh the beauty of our understanding, but the goodness of our will. What speaks to the heart of God is not acute insight but burning emotion. The wretched Lucifer knows this. He had the fire and splendor of Wit; but wanting the ardor of love, ambitious to be the Sun of paradise, he became the prince of infernal darkness. He crashed down with the other stars he tore from Heaven and showed by how much deeds far outstrip facts, while the ignorant of Earth struggle up to the place where the learned angels of Heaven fell down.

God never asked for a man's head, yet he wants the hearts of all. As he dictated the creation of the world to the pen of the great chronicler Moses, he did not give instructions about the great expanse of Heaven, the number of the stars, the influence of their aspects, cusps and trines. He did not examine whether they have their light from the Sun, or contain the source of it in themselves, in what ways the planets move, the reason for the spots on the Moon, or the causes of eclipses; nor if the Heavens are solid, if the sun is calid, how the rainbow is painted, how the winds run through the air, who moves the sea with ebb and flow, who rumbles to make the earth quake. St. Ambrose says, *"Such things don't concern us, since they provide no benefit."* [1]

He said only what he needed to lay in the mind the foundations of faith. He said what was necessary to know for the fullfilment of his law. The rest he omitted, as the *"Vanities of a perishable knowledge."* [2]

And the Wisdom of the Father— his living Word, the great exemplar of all Ideas— came to the school of a stable, upon the chair

---

1 **Ambrose,** *Hexameron,* **6.**2.8: *Quae nihil ad nos, quasi nihil profutura praeteriit.*
2 *Ibid.: Marcescentis sapientiae vanitates.*

of a manger, in a forum of oxes and asses, to teach in the silence of midnight, with the sound of his crying, the occult verities of human philosophy. Did He live in the academies a professor of Letters, a partaker in disputations, a scribe of science? Rather, regarding Letters, the tiny amount He had to add was less than the smallest letter, (as St. Augustine put it so well) *Iota unum* (*one iota*), even less than the smallest of all letters, *Unus apex,* (*one tittle*)?[3]

He came, it is true, to convince the philosophy of the academies of their ignorance and to make the wisdom of the world appear foolish. Hence, he did not employ the high style, nor the subtleties of ingenious discourse. With the simple word of his mouth, *Fecit lutum de sputo* (*He made mud with spit*).[4] He used parables and a manner of speech not only simple, but common and with this He restored the vision to our dim-sighted eyes.

And for Apostles, the legislators of the world, the oracles of true answers, whom did he chose? Whom did he call? The rude and ignorant, instructed with no other than the talk of "hoist the sails, weigh anchor, make to shore" that they learned in the school of fishermen. Yet, says Theodoret, with the solecisms of these unlettered men he confounded the syllogisms of the philosophers.

Thus, God honored Sanctity without Letters— the simpler, the better; the less enfeebled by hypotheses; the fuller and meatier in its affections.[5]

He knows much, indeed, everything, who only knows God. If he does not— even if he knows everything else— he still knows nothing. Origen observes that Caiaphas, a bad politician and a worse priest, told the truth to the Jewish satraps, the sworn enemies of Christ, "*You know nothing, Truly they knew nothing, not knowing Jesus, the truth.*"[6]

Lord, may I deserve the words of praise that Pope St. Gregory uses to honor that good monk Stephen: "*He was rustic in his speech, but*

---

3 *Augustine, On the Sermon on the Mount*, 8.20.
4 *John* 9.6/7.
5 **See Bernard of Clairvaux, *Sermon 36, On the Canticles.***
6 *John* 11.49: *Vos nescitis quidquam;* **Origen**, *Commentary on John: Vere enim nihil noverant, qui Jesum veritatem ignorabant.*

*learned in his life.*"[7] May the Lord teach me and reveal Himself to me, that is all I want to know and I will leave the Samaritan woman with the well of human wisdom that springs from the earth and with it the urn to bury the desire of ever again wanting it.[8]

Until now I have spoken with language of others, not with my own. What I have said is not entirely true, but it is what some preach as true. Some, I say, "*who, with the pretext of ignorance*"[9] (says Nazianzen), claim to be followers of the fishermen and condemn the learning of others. Either they want it not or cannot learn it for themselves.

An ecclesiastic could read no other books, understand no other philosophy, than that of his revenues. He defended himself behind the shield of the apostle, who called Letters a poisonous plague: "*for the letter kills.*"[10] This was his interpretation of the text of St. Paul. It moved Thomas More to mock or to chastise him, by writing this epigram to him, but in him how many does he call out?

> *Great father, at all times you cry* **the letter kills**,
> *This* **the letter kills** *is all you have to say.*
> *But you got it right, there's no letter can kill you,*
> *As for Letters, you don't know a single one.*[11]

That Sanctity without Letters is very precious and excellent, none will deny. That it is better to be a Saint than a Man of Letters, who would doubt it? But is it not better to be both holy and wise than just holy? Who could reasonably contest this?

To be, as Christ said of the great Baptist: "*A lantern burning and shining;*"[12] a lantern where light and fire, flame and light are united,

---

7 **Gregory the Great**, *Homily on the Gospels*, 25.8: *Erat hujus lingua rustica, sed docta vita.*
8 *John* 4.25.
9 **Gregory Nazianzen, *Orationes***, 27: *qui ad inscitiae praetextum.*
10 **Paul, 2 *Corinthians*** 3.6: *littera enim occidit.*
11 **Thomas More**, *Epigrammata*, Froben, Basel, (1530):
> *Magna Pater, clamas. Occidit littera: In ore*
> *Hoc unum, Occidit littera, semper habes*
> *Cavisti benè tu, ne te ulla occidere possit*
> *Littera. Non ulla est littera nota tibi.*
12 *John* 5.35: *Lucerna ardens, et lucens.*

which is that very **Perfectum** of St. Bernard,[13] in which both parts run
together: **Lucere et ardere**. (*to give light and to burn*). To have as the
holy animals of Ezekiel, **Manus sub pennis** (*the hand under the wings,*)
namely, the works of hand, and the flight of mind. (*Ezechiel*, 1.8). To
carry in the mouth, as the spouse in the Song of Songs, the
honeycombs from heaven and earth, with the honey of eternal life for
oneself and with the wax tapers of the sciences to illuminate others.
To unite, as in the Ark, the law and the manna, as in paradise, the Tree
of Life with the Tree of Wisdom, in short, love and understanding. Is
this not the earthly vestige of the beatitude of heaven? Is it not to be
the throne of that great Monarch and God who sits upon the
Cherubim and rides upon the wings of the wind?[14]

One of the most signal honors God can bestow is the gift of
knowledge in the branches of learning. By giving to Abraham one
more Letter for his name, he did him a most extraordinary favor.
(*Genesis* 17.5) Chrysostom says, *"Just as kings give their prefects' golden tablets
as commissions and signs of their dignity, so God, to give due honor to that just
man, added a Letter to his name."*[15]

What shall we say of those to whom God adds, not only a
Letter to their name, but the great cognitions of learning to their minds,
making them more like Him, the more their understanding is perfect?
Before this the Spouse asked for nothing. She begins the Song of Songs
with the request of a kiss, by which she meant that her husband should
be her teacher and with his love also give her knowledge— love, with
the meeting of their lips— knowledge, from the full kiss. St. Bernard
interprets, *"She asks for a kiss, that is, she prays the Holy Spirit to receive the
Taste of knowledge and the seasoning of grace. And it is well that the knowledge
which is given with the kiss is received with love, since a kiss is a sign of love."*[16]

---

13 **Bernard of Clairvaux, Commentary on Psalm 23**.
14 Although Bartoli's sermons were lost in the shipwreck off Capri. this
section gives a good idea of the tenor of his sacred oratory, effectively
orchestrated rhetoric and moral persuasion, *intendere ed amare*, a
hallmark of his eloquence.
15 **John Chrysostom, Homily 2, On Isaiah**: *Ut quemadmodum reges
praefectis suis tabellas aureas tradunt, signum videlicet principatus sic
Deus justo illi, in honoris argumentum, unam litteram dederit.*
16 **Bernard of Clairvaux, Sermon 8**: *Petit osculum, id est, Spiritum
Sanctum invocat, per quem accipiat simul et scientiae gustum, et gratiae*

Those that are thus privileged, are the **Filii Lucis** (*sons of light*) who are called, as Bede construes it, by the illustrious name of Day, in that place where the prophet says: "*One day tells another, from this day we receive the most limpid and most lucid intelligence to contemplate divinity.*"[17] And as, according to the saying of St. Ambrose, "*This very day is the Son, whose Father reveals the day of His divinity in its mystery,*"[18] so, to these sons of light the same **Dies filius** (*Day-Son*), principal font of all knowledge does impart his splendors, enriching them with wisdom. These, says Origen, are the golden candlesticks by whose light the Ark is made visible and the sanctuary illuminated. These are the lilies, in the truths they understand, candid and white, and in the charity with which they love; vermillion and red, these are the hierarchs of the kingdom of God that add the **Docere** (*teaching*) to the **Facere** (*doing*), the shining stars, **in perpetuas eternitates**, (*Daniel*, 12.18), the precious stones, the foundations of the golden Jerusalem which is the title of honor the great Augustine bestowed on the very eloquent St. Cyprian. And both of these men did merit it, and along with them (Dionysius) the Areopagite, Athanasius, Basil, Nazianzen, Chrysostom, Jerome, Ambrose, Gregory and many others who were great marvels no less for the profundity of their understanding than for the sanctity of their lives.

Gregory (Nazianzen) the Theologian calls a man endowed with Sanctity and devoid of Letters, a man deprived of one eye,[19] because even to know God and hence to love Him, the learned sciences, for one equipped to use them as guides, bestow great enlghtenment.

And here see under the image of a solecism noticed by St. Ambrose, a secret mystery cited by David: "*My eyes have grown weary waiting upon thy word, saying, when shall I be consoled?*"[20] How will you make

---

*condimentum. Et bene scientiae quae in osculo datur, cum amore recipitur; quia amoris indicium osculum est.*
17 **Bede, On Psalm 18**:(Psalm 19.2): *Dies Diei eructat verbum, per diem enim accipimus limpidissimum, et lucidissimum ingenium ad divina contemplanda habentes.*
18 **Ambrose, Stromata**: *Ipse est Dies filius, cui pater Dies divinitatis suae eructat arcanum.*
19 **Gregory Nazianzen, the Theologian, Oration 20.**
20 **Ambrose, On Psalm 118** (119.82): *Defecerunt oculi mei in eloquium tuum, dicentes, Quando consolaberis me?*

this agree with the laws of grammar, **oculi dicentes** (*eyes..saying*) in the plural, with the first person singular, **Consolaberis me** (*shall I be consoled*)? Perspective teaches that the centric lines of both eyes, called the axes, join to towards a single point so that both the eyes serve as one, for they do not see the object doubly, but singly, as if from one eye. Moreover, sight is stronger with two eyes, more distinct and better able to judge distances. If to know and see God the eyes of faith and knowledge must go together, (the concept, perhaps, of the royal saint (*David*), can anyone doubt that this way of seeing is better and stronger? Therefore, the Sciences are not detrimental to Sanctity; rather they assist it as companions, or at least they attend it as handmaids.[21]

Regarding the example of Christ, to see how little he favors the sanctity of the ignorant over the sanctity of the Sages, it is enough to point out that when He took up the great bundle of our miseries and so generously opened His arms to them, alone among them He only kept out Ignorance, and would not allow her darkness any part in the light of the world.[22] In poverty needy, in weakness unsteady, in solitude abandoned, in scorn despised, in nakedness confounded, in tribulation aggrieved, on the cross blood-soaked and acquainted with grief— as the prophet (Isaiah) said, full of pain from head to toe: among such manifold maladies, He had no place for ignorance. Under the rugged skin of the savage Esau, He spoke with the voice of Jacob for, as the Wisdom of the Father, ignorant he was not, and ignorant, as the teacher of the world, He showed Himself not to be. For if He talked in a way no more elevated than he did, it was because the eyes of bats cannot bear the sun— even a lantern is too much. But if He was silent then, he has spoken ever since over these last sixteen golden centuries which the Church has seen. He has spoken, I mean, through the tongues and the pens of so many of the world's illustrious teachers, who from Him, as springs from the sea, have taken all the clarity and all the profundity from that store of great learning which, to the profit of posterity, they have so copiously illustrated in their works. St.

---

[21] An interesting essay in scriptural exegesis by optical science in the erudite *ars rhetorica* characteristic of Bartoli.

22 Here the sacred orator invents an original (?) trope on ignorance as beneath the dignity of suffering for his peroration.

Augustine says, "*Praise the Lord, young men; let your old age be youthful, your youth be aged, so that your Sapience is not proud, nor your humility without Sapience: Praise the Lord from this day forward, now and forever down through the ages.*"[23]

## 4.2 *Ignorance and Rank*

Foolish beyond measure are those sculptors who do not know how to sculpt a giant of terrible aspect, unless he has the pose of fury with arms flung open and legs awkwardly astride, as if he were measuring the world in one step. The same, says Plutarch, is true of those princes who believe they are most majestic when they look most fearsome. And so, they assume an austere manner and with artificial severity, crease their brow and harden their gaze, so that you are almost reminded of what the poet said of Pluto:

*The greater part of a cruel reign*
*Is the king himself, whose person engenders fear*
*Among the fearful.*[1]

How apt would it be if we were to whisper in their ears what a very prudent emperor told the Senate of Rome when he understood the plan they had to remove him because, beset by gout, he could not come to direct public affairs in person. He had himself carried into the Senate and showed with a long oration that his mind was as good as his legs were bad, and confounded them with his parting rejoinder, "*Didn't you know that the head commands, not the feet.*"[2]

A reputation of great wisdom makes the powerful respected, not a threatening grimace. One is not more majestic for being more intimidating. He who knows more, can do more. He who rules all eye and all sceptre, (the image and the character used by the Egyptians to

---

[23] **Augustine, *In Psalm* 112**: *Laudate igitur pueri Dominum, sit senectus vestra puerilis et pueritia senilis ut nec Sapientia vestra sit cum suburbia, nec humiiltas sine sapientia ut laudetis Dominum ex hoc nunc et usque in saeculum.*

[1] **Seneca, *Hercules furens*, 725/7:**
*Magna pars Regni trucis*
*Est ipse Dominus, cujus aspectum timet*
*Quid quid timetur.*
[2] *Nescitis caput imperare, nonpedes?*

symbolize the idea of a king), he, above others, is most princely, and
godlike.

Nor can one ever be sufficiently knowledgeable, as an arbiter
of public and private interests, if his Wit, and hence, his judgement, are
not informed by those elements of learning which dictate what he
must— and what he may— do as a prince, as a judge, and as a father.
Otherwise, a prince's dignity is diminished by the measure of his lack
of knowledge, so that it behooves him to see through eyes of others
or to put the eyes of others inside his head for him to see.

Some may be loath to submit their highest faculty— their
understanding— and make themselves beholden for this to inferiors.
They may want to resolve by themselves what ought to be measured
on surer scales and with greater weights than their limited knowledge.
Xerxes would say, *"The ignorance of the ruler is sure to run the ship of state
aground."*[3] He who lacks knowledge will either commit errors harmful
to himself and others, or so as to avoid such errors, he will have to
share his decision-making and be left a prince by half and handicapped.
Whereas only those will retain their integrity, who, in proportion to the
state they govern, can maintain in equal measure the equilibrium
between knowledge and power.

The Emperor John had rather die than lose a hand wounded
by a poisoned arrow, reasoning that single-handed he could be no
more than half an emperor or handle the reins of sovereignty, for
which two hands are little enough. Without knowledge one is missing
half the stature of a full prince. Does he not seem, in his ignorance, to
be but half a prince?

What in the devil's name entered the head of a certain man,[4]
for him to write and teach in his history that the most necessary
attribute of a prince is ignorance? A single line was the entire
encyclopedia he had Louis XI give as his sole precept to Charles VIII,
his son: *"If you can't dissemble, you can't rule."*[5] This man held it to an
infallible maxim that one man cannot be both learned and prudent,

3 *Tum vero, ignorantia principis, regni navim agit in syrtes.*
4 Philippe de Commynes wrote the penetrating and skeptical history the reign of
Louis XI.
5 *Qui nescit dissimilare, nescit regnare.* Here Bartoli approaches the
controversial political philosophy of Machiavelli, but he equivocates by
dismissing the greatly discussed role of dissimulation as ignorance.

having to reject the speculations of science for the practice of government. Doing so places the sceptre in the hands of a king, with the sword at his side and the ears of King Midas on his head, *"His ears slowly circling as do those of an ass"*— *"ears geared for even greater lies."*[6]

In this way Agrippina brought up Nero— her son, her husband and her parricide— removing him from his more serious studies, lest transformed into a philosopher, he should cease to be the beast that he was. The emperor Licinius schooled himself in this fashion. He condemned Letters as guilty of high treason in the first degree, though they never bothered him; for never entering his head, they never met him, because he turned into an animal as soon as he became a man.

Let them stand up against this squalid show of deviance, perhaps, or of folly, from among a hundred others, an Augustus, a Germanicus, a Titus, a Hadrian, a Marcus Aurelius, an Alexander, a Constantine, a Theodosius, all crowned with double laurels, as sages and as emperors. They have Augustus at the front of their august body. According to Suetonius and Dion Cassius, every day, even at the height of warfare, in his tent in camp, he would set apart some time for study, so that no day would pass in the which he failed to exercise his human faculty, and nonetheless, for forty years he governed the whole world so well and so wisely. Then came the total ignoramus Domitian, busy several hours a day swatting flies, boasting for everyone he killed that he was Apollo battling a Python.

Behold Alexander Severus, reverenced as Jupiter on Earth, not so much for the thunder in his hand as emperor, as for the Pallas Athena in his head as a philosopher. Then look at the hare-brained Caligula, showing up in public dressed as Bacchus, crowned with ivy, a tiger skin for a mantle. He looked more like a beast than a god and supplied answers as absurd as his outfit in the mutterings of a drunkard.

What made Thracian Cosingas throw up ladders towards Heaven on the very top of a mountain, as if he had a front row there and got straight from the mouth of Juno the directives he issued in the

---

6 **Ovid**, *Met.*, 11.34: *Aures lentè gradientis aselli;* **Tertullian**, *De pallio* 2: *Aures aptas grandioribus fabulis.*

interests of the public good?[7] Wasn't it that the laws and edicts of the powerful are so much more willingly received when they appear to come from a mind of superior knowledge and nobler vision? Therefore, in my judgement, it was not so much out of the call to explain the motions of their revolutions— or, at least, to track the spheres that move effortlessly in the Heavens— that the most famous schools of the philosophers ascribed Motor Intelligences to their workings, but rather so that the world should feel better satisfied about its governance by believing that the revolution of the stars was due to dynamic intelligences directing the principles and tempering the influences upon which, as they believed, the well-being or misfortunes of both public and private affairs are dependent.[8]

The boy Alexander could hear the voice of Aristotle, his tutor. He spoke in his father Philip's stead, with his teacher's tongue in a solemn reception for the ambassadors of the Persian king and answered the questions they had to test him with, winning for himself the name and title of great king, while he was only a little prince. They declared, *"This boy is a great king, but ours is enormously wealthy."*[9] So he sparked in the Persians a great desire to have him for their king, because they had come to know him as a sage. Doubtless, if you forgive this magnanimous monarch for some few of his sins of youthful passion and for his excessive pride and warlike temper, if his behavior otherwise is equitably measured, rather than according to the malicious view of Seneca, in this instance more Cynic than Stoic, one may take the verdict of the sage Plutarch: *"One may proclaim him in the context of his particular deeds, a philosopher."*[10]

The prince and his court are like a statue in its niche, one taking decorous and mutual ornament from the other. Now what does a prince of Letters have for his niche? What kind of court? Nero, a musician surrounded by a chorus, like an Apollo among the

---

7 **Polyaenus,** *Statagems of War*, 7 (Macedonian, 2nd century A.D.)
8 Here a plausibly modern and somewhat shocking demystification of the outworn harmonics of Ptolemaic cosmology and, by extension, of the hieratic mythology of sanctioned power, articulately nontraditional.
9 **Plutarch,** *On the fortune or the virtue of Alexander*, 2.11: *Iste puer Magnus est Rex, noster autem Dives.*
10 **Plutarch,** *On the fortune or the virtue of Alexander*, 1.10: *Libet ad singulis ejus actiones exclamare, philosophice.*

muses. Elius Verus, the emperor of the wind, in the garb of Aeolus among his courtiers, dressed one as Auster, the north wind, another as Zephyr from the south, another as Boreas from the cold. A wise prince among sage courtiers shows as the sun among the sirens. They enchant the planets with their song, while he is the sun that Cleanthes called their plectrum, because his playing regulates and accords the harmonies of their lyres.

Manilius said that if the Heavens were like a court in musical concert, *"The stars are like the court's great nobles, etc."*[11] And the emperor Julian saw the sun as a king around whom the planets turn in homage.[12] So who would object to calling the court a Heaven and a prince with the light of knowledge and the heat of power, a sun in the middle of so many stars, namely, the learned men about him who take light from his wise discourses and send it back to him, exchanging illuminations. This has greater truth and merit than the fictive and manmade heaven of Cosroes, king of Persia,[13] painted in the vaulted arches of a spacious chamber, as in an open sky of celestial blue, strewn with stars of gold and displayed in certain moving spheres, one set inside another in orderly fashion. It represented the whole vast space of the universe and in the middle the barbarous king sat there prettily, looking more like a spider in the center of its web than a monarch in the middle of the world.

Seneca has no better concept to express the blessed state of his Jupiter than by placing him amid the gods of his court, as a sun in a circle of the most limpid diamond mirrors. By the mutual transmission of rays from him to them, and from them to him, the light of the individual knowledge of each is shared by all, and this common knowledge is absorbed individually by each. But if Jove should from on high cast his eyes down here below to the learned court of a prince of Letters, he might exclaim in amazement or delight as he did when he saw the whole world displayed in the small globe of the great Archimedes:

> *In the small glass was everything to be seen*
> *He laughed and gave the gods these words:*

---

11 **Manilius, *Astronomica*** 5.740: *Sunt stellae procerum similes, etc.*
12 **Julian (the Apostate), *Orationes*,** 4.
13 **Cedrenus,** *Synopsis of History,* (Byzantine, 11th century).

*"Has the power of mortal progress reached such a point?*
*that our creation can be displayed in such a delicate globe."*[14]

Dionysius of Syracuse aspired to philosophy, so he could tyrannize his subjects' souls with his words as successfully, as he so unjustly tyrannized their bodies with his sword. Therefore, he invited Plato and had him brought to Syracuse from Athens. It would have taken no less a master to smooth that rough stone where it proved impossible to carve an intelligent Mercury. For while Plato could make philosophers of men, he could not make men of beasts. He came with his mouth filled with Attic honey, but that sponge steeped in human blood could not sip a single drop. Nevertheless, while Dionysius heard him lecture the whole court was turned into a different scene, as those enchanted castles which at the beck of a magic wand change from one thing into another. The royal palace, the slaughterhouse of Syracuse and more the cave of Cacus than a princely palace was suddenly changed into a lyceum grove— no, Sapience's temple— where the men, and even the stone walls, were philosophizing, with all the stonework written over with geometrical demonstrations or calculations of philosophical numbers. Dionysius had managed to bury the name of a public butcher under that of a philosopher. Those who up to that time he had horrified as a Fury from Hell, began to respect him as a demigod among princes. This is what Letters can accomplish in a prince; this is what, as a patron of Letters, a prince can achieve in his court![15]

---

14 **Claudian,** *Letter* 16, *De sphaeram Archimedis*, 68.18:
*In parvo cum cerneret omnia vitro*
*Risit, et ad superos talia dicta dedit*
*Huccine mortalis progressa potentia curae?*
*Jam meus in fragili luditur orbe labor.*

[15] This enthusiastic dithyramb on court patronage reflects the younger Bartoli's ideal of the Este court and its Renaissance traditions, more than its current state and, notwithstanding his own commission, *ex officio* to the Jesuit curia as historiographer, he gradually turned toward more collegial institutions, like the French Academy (1635) and the Royal Society (1660).

## 4.3    *Ignorance and the Profession of Arms*

It may be hard for me to show how Letters in a soldier don't amount to a string of pearls around his neck or make him more like a bride than a warrior. Some are of the opinion that Letters weaken courage and take from the heart the energies then used by the head, spent writing with the pen, rather than fighting with the sword.

> *Sometimes a serious application to the gentle arts*
> *Softens a man and he loses his ferocity.*[1]

The most ingenious animals, they say, are the most fearful while the strongest and best fighters are the fiercest and roughest. Philosophy, law, and poetry serve as no greater ornaments for a soldier, than swordplay for a poet, musketry for a jurist, or jousting for a philosopher. Hercules grasped this and set the example for others like him when he broke his lyre on the head of his master Linus and quit his school. The plectrum was not suited to hands wielding a club, nor the sweet sound of music to ears attuned to the bellowing of the bulls, the roaring of the lions, the hissing of the hydras and the shouts of the tyrants that he was born to destroy.

Certainly, I do not pretend to argue that a man of war ought to be a Plato, an Archimedes or a Homer, but that the polish of some laudable study should refine his Wit, the way splendor enhances his armor and painting adorns his shield, should not, I think, raise any reason for contention.

An eagle with eyes so trained on the sun and talons so strong for prey, a Hercules who knows how to tame monsters with his hands and carry the Heavens on his head, an Apollo at whose side hang both harp and quiver, a Pallas with a pen in one hand and a spear in the other, in short, a warrior with some smattering of Letters— what is wrong with that? May rust on a soldier's Wit mean luster and beauty when on his sword and armor it means dishonor? Are they such sworn enemies the pike and the pen, the strength and the sense to combat as a warrior and to discourse as a writer?

---

1 Ovid, *De Ponto* 2. 9.47:

> *Scilicet ingenuas didicisse fidelier artes*
> *Emollit mores, nec sinit esse feros.*

63

It is argued among critics which is the greater happiness, **Facere scribenda,** *(to be doing and writing)* or **Scribere facienda** *(to be writing and doing).* Whichever you choose, there is no question that together: *"Happiest are those who embrace both."*[2] That with the sword in your hand you do deeds worthy of immortal memory and hold in the same hand a pen to commit them to eternity, faithfully recording what that hand has courageously achieved, historian of itself, is a double glory, like the sun that needs no outside light to prove how great it is. Is this not the acme of glory accessible to human achievement?

And this truth has its shadow. For the accounts of historians are quite often liable to be incomplete, if they appear too late, or subject to suspicion, if they appear too early. So many in our day offer the histories of the battles of others, focusing on the victories of their commercial success. I mean certain men keep themselves from starving from hunger by selling the immortality of fame to whoever pays the most. They are the greedy ravens who will sing the **Victor Caesar,** not to who wins, but to who feeds them, vilest glowworms who from their bellies illuminate the deeds of others and seek food for themselves. Like the parasite of the warrior Pygopolynices in Plautus,[3] they concoct their histories to the aromas of the table and offer praises proportionate to their hunger. How much better is it for a man to be his own historian and use his pen according to the requirements of honorable fidelity, not allowing the addition of anything false and, for the love of glory, not allowing the omission of anything true?

Julius Caesar is less indebted to his sword than to his pen. The one slew his enemies, while the other keeps him alive today in the world and leaves imperishable his double glory as historian and conqueror. The brave Roger, king of Sicily, either to confess his debt to his sword, or to express his gratitude to it for opening his way to more than one kingdom, had this ingenious inlay inscribed on it:

**Apulus, et Calaber, Siculus, mihi servit, et Apher.**
*(For Puglia and Calabria, Sicily and Africa it has served me.)*[4]

---

2 *Felicissimi quibus contingit utrumque.*
3 **Artotrogus in Plautus,** *Miles gloriosus.*
4 Pandolfo **Colenuccio** (1444-1504), *Historia Neapolitana.*

Now Caesar might have placed an inscription on his stylus, rather than on his sword, listing the victories of so many battles, the glories of so many triumphs, for while his sword by fighting gave him victory on the battlefields, his stylus by writing gave him the nations of the whole world for a theatre and the applause of all succeeding ages for a triumph.

We can laugh at the vanity of that Greek sculptor[5] who came before Alexander dressed as Hercules to say: *"Sire, the virtue of your heart and the valor of your sword have transformed the world into a temple in your honor. Only missing is a statue of you which should be larger than any made for others. Your giant virtue, which challenges the Gods, ought not be compared to mortals. My ambition is to consecrate my work to your name, not so much to make you immortal in sculpture, as to clothe sculpture in the mantle of your honor. So, I propose to carve you from the highest mountain of the world and make you equal to Heaven, since you are already greater than Earth. See in distant Thessaly, Athos, the king of mountains who bends his stately peaks and begs to be transformed into you. I shall carve it so that you have one foot set in the sea and the other set on land, and these two great elements shall serve as your base. I shall have one of your hands pour a river falling from a great urn and in the other you shall hold a city. Nor should it be too much for your hands to hold a city and a river, not for you, who has the whole world in your grasp."*

Alexander with one and the same smile accepted and refused the profuse offer of the sculptor. He had, as much as any, a passionate desire for greatness, and to make his memory eternal for posterity, but he wanted to be known by the world as a mighty warrior and not as a huge colossus. So, in refusing the chisels of Stasicrates, he pined for the pen of Homer and envied the fortune of the great Achilles who had valor from himself and praises from Homer, fame from himself and glory from Homer. But, really, wouldn't it have been better for one so rich in countless deeds of heroism, who had no need of aggrandizing tales, to have a historian, rather than a poet? And if so, why should I be envious of others for the honor of making me happy by making me eternal if I can procure it for myself, by making my hand as skillful with the pen as it was with sword?

I shall skip over the necessary role, in the profession of arms, of eloquence to reanimate, to reprehend, and to restrain the soldiers

---

5 **Plutarch: Stasicrates; Vitruvius: Dinocrates**

and over the need for great familiarity with ancient and modern history and with those parts of geometry which pertain to war machines and fortification. Needful also, at times, is astronomy, so as not to lose, as has happened unluckily more than once, a day's march and an army through the havoc caused by a sudden eclipse of the sun. This makes ignorance the only excuse, after the example of Romulus, who reckoning by a year of only ten months, was told,

*Once indeed, you were better versed in swords than in stars, Romulus.*[6]

Of all this, as not the business of any but war leaders, I have nothing to say. Let me just mention in conclusion:

Not always is one in the field and in armed combat, as in peacetime or when the necessity of rest and recovery may recall one to civil life. This calls for some cultivation of Letters, ans is required in social conversation with persons of quality and of parts, so that one's voice does not mimic the drums gone speechless in peacetime that sounded with such clamor in wartime. Or obedient to the ancient custom of those good Roman warriors, when war is over, must one go back to farming the land, as if a military man were a wild beast, so that once he has seized his prey from the settled areas, he must return to the forest and to go back to life in the woods?

Paulus Aemilius, after he vanquished King Perseus and subdued Macedonia, stayed to celebrate victory with the lords of that kingdom in a series of banquets. He used so ingenious a method in martialing the courses that the table seemed a pitched field where the ranks of dishes confronted the guests, began the skirmish and gave the first assault, gradually retreating with the empty and disarmed and giving way to fresh recruits marching up to relieve them. There were delicacies still holding their prime positions on the table and there were some seeming to give orders as to who should retreat first and who later. Some came up under covert and in stealth as insidious; others attacked in the open. In conclusion, the contents were no less delightful than the manner of marshalling the courses and all the invited guests showered their applause on Paulus Aemilius, who

---

6 **Ovid,** *Fasti,* 1.27: *Scilicet arma magis quàm sydera Romule noras,*

replied: "*It is the commission of a real man to brandish his sword with the greatest terribility as well as to provide his entertainment with the greatest conviviality.*"[7]

But if the knowledge of a soldier only goes so far that the transition from times of war to times of peace means it is only the change from the unpleasantness of the camp to the pleasures of the city, to turn, like Ajax, from a a great warrior yesterday, into a flower today,[8] this is a very paltry kind of insight and, as such, might better be done without. More honorable and delightful is the entertainment afforded to Wit by Letters. Are they not the best means to sweeten natural ferocity and to humanize that untamed and savage quality that characterizes the bloody profession of arms?

Of arms, Cassiodorus stipulates: **In bello necessaria, in pace decora** (*Necessities in war, ornaments in peace.*)[9] Of Letters, it may with as much justice be held, with the times changed, and said, **In pace necessariae, in bello decorae**. (*Necessary in peace, adornments in war.*) Achilles had two lessons every day; one in the desert where he grappled with lions, the other in the cell of Chiron where he plied the lyre harmoniously and learned the secrets of natural philosophy. He was training to live both in times of war and of peace; in war terrible to his foes, in peace amiable to his fellows. This also was the glory of that Roman Achilles, Scipio Africanus, the Great. In war, he was like lightning, all fire with magnanimous passion; in peace all light with sparkling Wit. It was as wonderful to see him fight as it was to hear him discourse, as Velleius said: "*He always practiced the arts of war or peace, always regular in arms and in study, challenging his body with dangers and his mind with the study of the sciences.*"[10]

Very rare are such as he and it is almost a miracle to find ears accustomed to the sound of trumpets and the beating of drums that are yet not too deaf for the voice of Sapience to be distinctly

---

7 **Plutarch, *Symposium*, 1**: *Ejusdem viri esse et armatam aciem quàm maximè terribilem, et convivium quam jucundissimum instruere.* See Plutarch, *Aemilius Paulus*, 28.5

8 The Homeric hero, Ajax, after his disgrace and suicide, was transformed into a flower related to Hyacinth. See Ovid, *Met.*, 13.397/8.

9 **Cassiodorus *Variae* 7.18**: *Formula de armifactoribus.*

10 **Vellieus Paterculus, *Historia* 1**: *Semper enim, aut belli, aut pacis serviit artibus semper inter arma, ac studia versatus, aut corpus periculis, aut animum disciplinis, exercuit.*

understood. Rare are the martial sons of Hercules who, after their labors, consecrate to Mercury the offering of olive wood they take from Pallas. But those few, more exceptionally distinguished for being more unique than rare, bring together two incomparable, indeed, divine qualities united in their person, **terrorem pariter, et decorem**, *(strength and distinction in equal measure)*. This is the formula Cassiodorus used to describe a squadron of armed galleys; on parade unequaled in beauty, in combat unequaled in terror.

## 4.4    *Ignorance and Riches*

Those who use Letters for profit, and use their god, Mercury, as the goldsmiths use quicksilver, to separate others from their gold— and keep it for themselves— would be hard put to understand the problem that ignorance represents for a rich man. For if his hands are full, why should he empty his head, or rack his brain? He has already found the quintessence of good fortune which they say is money. If it is made of gold, it makes no difference if that means the Ram of Phrixus,[11] or that bestial philosopher, the Golden Ass.[12]

In today's world money is what buys love and honor and you can have no better Letters of recommendation than Letters of credit. No ink writes better than that used by bankers.

> *Once Wit was more precious than gold,*
> *But now the great hoards have it for nothing.*[13]

What's the good of having so much philosophy and so much knowledge in one's head, if they only serve to crack it open so the brains fall out? Take the ancient philosophers and you'll choose the hands of Midas to make gold over their heads to ape their follies. They tear out their eyes to see better in the dark, and in order to be eagles, they turn into moles. They throw their riches into the sea, becoming beggars to avoid poverty.[14] They live in places rocked by continual earthquakes, thinking that living is better when they are always in

---

11 Ovid, *Met.* 7.7/8. Added in later editions.
12 Apulieus, *The Golden Ass.*
13 **Ovid**, *Amores*, 3.8.2/3:
>          *Ingenium quondam fuerat pretiosius auro,*
>          *At nunc barbaria est grandis habere Nihil.*
14 Crates.

danger of dying and that they dwell in greater safety when any minute their home may become their tomb. They live in barrels— more like a dog in his doghouse, than a man in his dwelling.[15] One throws himself into Mount Aetna, the other into the sea; this one because he cannot grasp the reasons for its fluctuations, the other because he cannot trace the origin of its fires.[16] Pythagoras transforms himself into a hundred beasts; Socrates, standing for a whole day in thought, on one leg, looks like a crane; Anaxagoras, fixedly staring at the sun, like an eagle; Xenocrates is a marble without feelings; Zeno, a stick without emotions; Diogenes, a dog, Epicurus, an animal; Democritus, a madman, always laughing; Heraclitus, forlorn of hope, always crying. **"O curas hominum!"** (O, *the cares of men!*).[17] Wouldn't it be better not to have a head than to have one full of such follies? And this is what it means to be a philosopher? This makes a letterato? Pearls, round and rotund (both properties of rich idiots) are the world's most precious, most treasured things. Make me of gold and, though I may be a calf, I shall be worshipped as a god, an apotheosis begun of old by the Israelites in the desert and still observed today, without end.

This is the philosophy of many rich men and they sing it in a chorus of contempt for the learned, especially if they seem poor, starving and in rags, if not naked.

Now, on the other hand, I wish I had a pen with enough talent for me to draw for you a lively image of the deformed features of the ignorant and rich. I know you would recoil with the same feeling of horror that Orcagna, an excellent painter in his day, triggered in many friends when he unveiled a horribly ugly head of Medusa. For this he had searched out for his painting and pieced together in one the worst monstrosities he could find among the hundred disgusting and monstrous creatures he had collected to this end.[18]

The Spartans held in abomination idleness and luxury, the enemies of their severe republic. So, they called all the people to a

---

15. Diogenes
16 Aristotle and Empedocles.
17 Persius, *Satire* 1.1.
18 For some reason Bartoli attributes this well-known story associated with the famous sculpture of Benvenuto Cellini (1500-1571) to his predecessor, the painter Orcagna (1308-1368). Cellini's *Perseus and Medusa* stands in the so-called Loggia of Orcagna in the Piazza della Signoria, Florence.

general assembly and brought them to look down from above on Nauclides. He was so fat that from head to foot he seemed all belly.[19] That was all there was to do with him. His corpulence convicted him of being an idler and he was banished for being useless. He was punished as a slight to everyone, as he was no good to anyone but himself. Now conjure up a rich ignoramus and you shall see in him, not a man, but a living touchstone in the shape of a man, to make out gold and silver. By touch alone he can recognize and identify them, but for all other purposes he stays a stone. You are looking at a sponge. For what he can suck up, he is all eyes, but otherwise he feels nothing, as he is not even an animal.

Dress him in the most delicate fabrics; in the whitest linens, in the finest silks; clothe him in the finest wools dyed in two shades of purple— if he runs into Demonax, he will get to hear what the blunt philosopher already said to someone like him:[20] *"Sir, this wool was worn by a sheep before you, that is why it fits you perfectly, and is so well-suited and complimentary, for it feels it hasn't lost owners, just switched them. The color of its dye doesn't change that it's wool, though it is finer. Likewise, the shape of a man that you take on doesn't change that you are a sheep, though you have a finer coat and look more distinguished."* Put him in a house decorated with all the trappings, all the noblest decorations, and what have you? Whoever passes by and knows the background of the property's owner will say, as the acquaintances of a certain pensioner Vatia, retired to his country villa, would say as they were passing: *"**Vatia hic situs est.**"* (Here lies Vatia buried.)[21] Hear Seneca give the reason, *"**Vivit is, qui se utitur.**"* (One stays alive, only he's of some use.)[22] It is not the man whose head serves his stomach, gearing the thoughts he has in one to keep the other full: The stomach should serve the head and supply it with the vitality that fuels human activity, otherwise, he goes on, *"Those who withdraw and waste away live in their homes as if they were already in their graves. You can carve*

---

19 **Aelian**, 14.7.
20 **Lucian**, *Demonax*, 41.
21 **Seneca**, *Letter* **55**.4
22 **Seneca**, *Letter* **60**.4.

*their names in the marble over their threshold, they have predeceased their own death."*[23]

Themistocles, that sagacious Athenian, knew quite well how to read the character of someone rich and ignorant. He was looking for a husband for his daughter. She had no dowry, for he was a poor man, and someone came to him with an offer of marriage. True, he was rich, but he lacked the currency of even two Letters of learning. While someone else would have run after this golden bait and thanked his good fortune with the hecatombs of Pythagoras, he backed away with that golden dictum worth more than all the wealth of that ignoramus: *"I prefer a man with no money, to money with no man."*[24]

And here, before I close this chapter, I cannot fail to felicitate certain happy families where it is not wealth inherited from ancestors, but Letters and culture that pass down as a sacred trust over the generations, father to son.[25] As in the offspring of eagles: *"Misbred is the eaglet whose eyes shy from the light."*[26] The eaglet that cannot endure the sight of the sun lies under suspicion of different blood. One is suspected as spurious if from birth he does not show the same vivacity of Wit and love of Letters. Family trees like these are truly happy for always having some golden branch, not only because *"With one severed, another golden bough is never wanting,"*[27] but because in every age, they have those bearing fruit, those in flower and those budding, matching the different ages of life to the different stages of a life in Letters— which are: to learn, to possess, and to teach.

Of great beauty was the tradition of the Spartans who separated into three choirs after the three ages of man, old age, virility and youth, and they would sing together in certain public processions, The elders, **"Nos fuimus fortes"** (*Strong were we*); those in their

---

23 *Ibidem: qui latitant, et torpent, sic in domo sunt tanquam in conditivo. Horum licet in limine ipso, nomen marmori inscribas, mortem suam antecesserunt.*
24 Plutarch, *Themistocles*, 18.4: *Quaero virum qui indigeat pecunia, non pecuniam, quae indigeat viro.*
25 The courts of Renaissance Italy produced many families with a tradition of Letters, like Bartoli's. His grandfather served the Este dukes of Ferrara in Tasso's day, as did his father, and a nephew also became Daniello Bartoli, S.J.
26 **Claudian**, *On the Consulate of Honorius,* 3, preface: *Degener est qui lumina torsit.*
27 *Aeneid* 6.143.

manhood, "***Et nos modo sumus***" *(And we are strong in turn,)* to which the young replied, "***Et nos erimus aliquando***" *(And so shall we be, whenever).* [28] Is there any music equal to this, when it happens that in one house the grandfather, the son and the grandchild; the first, with a distinguished career in Letters, recounting the curriculum of his honors who says that glorious ***Fui***; then, the second, wearing his badges of honor and basking in his success, can say ***Sum***; and the last giving hopes and beginning to fulfill his promise, will say ***Ero***; and one day he will say ***Sum*** himself— and finally ***Fui***? This is to chain together a precious descent of children, like jewels, with golden links. This is to make a succession of descendants for posterity, like a rich vein of diamonds; each one by itself is an inheritance which together make a great treasure chest of riches.

## 4.5    *Ignorance Confounded, Condemned to Silence, when it is Finer to Speak*

To the Taste of Understanding which, as I said above,[29] is savored by Men of Letters in their exercise of Wit and in the acquisition of truth, I will finally contrast the Distastefulness of Ignorance, condemned to be silent in the company of educated men. The man who knows little must either keep quiet or speak. And he feels ashamed either way, for silence accuses him of his ignorance and speaking will convict him of it. A case in point is Alexander, who understood little about painting and was visiting the school of Apelles.[30] In his comments, he mistook caricatures for sketches, blots for shadows, and errors for artistry and he became the butt of the apprentices smirking among themselves. In gatherings of the learned those miserably ignorant are condemned to stand like mute consonants between vowels, with no sound of their own. Among the strings of the lyre they are untuned and sound only as dissonant. Like the tyrant Dionysius, their ears are not on their heads, but on their feet. They hear only what

---

28 **Plutarch,** *On the ancient customs of the Spartans*, 15.
29 Chapter 2.
30 **Plutarch,** *Megabiz*, *How to tell a flatterer from a friend*, 15. Bartoli cites Apelles and Megabyzus, in Plutarch. For Alexander, see Pliny, 35.85 quoted in Salvator Rosa 's 1662 etching, *Alexander the Great in the studio of Apelles.*

is base and vile and their heads are missing a mind fit for subjects of noble intelligence.

Naturally, as with jars, the more they are empty, the more sound they make. A man furnished with the smallest brain will produce the greatest stream of words. These types are more eager to pass themselves off as learned than they are afraid to show their ignorance. They talk freely of things which they know nothing about and earn from their listeners the same reward allotted to the ambitions of Neanthes.[31] Convinced that he, too, was a son of Urania, furtively he filched the lyre of Orpheus from the temple of Apollo and walked into an open field, in the dark and still of the night, to have nature's complete attention. Then, with his plectrum, he started to strum that luckless instrument. There was not a single chord, at the touch of such a rude hand, but did respond with a mournful *Oimè*, bemoaning in its own language being more tortured than played. If ever it was true that the lyre of Orpheus had the power to uproot trees and make stones fly, it should have been while it was being so harshly mishandled by Neanthes. But, in this case, what the lyre failed to do was done by wild beasts. Awakened by his jarring noises, a pack of hardy mastiffs, judging the player more by his sound than by his looks, **Asinum ad Lyram** *(an ass to the lyre)*,[32] tore him to pieces. And so, if he was no Orpheus in the beauty of his music, he lucklessly imitated him in the misfortune of his death.

Less stridently, yes, but withal more publicly and by more mouths that disconcerted instrument of solecisms, Ignorance, is torn to pieces as people recount in derision the absurdity of its statements, the blithe assurance of its definitions, the ardor of its justifications.

Have you ever heard two such types, even more completely obtuse than that perfect circle of Giotto, discussing a question between them, or (as it happens) resolving a problem? It brings to mind the words and the laughter of Demonax when he overheard two of them arguing aloud. One had nothing to say on the topic, the other had nothing to answer on it. To one he says, *"That's a goat you're milking"* and to the other, *'That's a sieve you're holding under it."*[33]

Certainly, you are moved, (is it more to compassion or to laughter?) when at times you may hear such types as these reciting or reading what they have written on subjects of even notable interest. Their extremely long discourses, not once even in a single line out of many bring focus or make a point on the theme at hand, so that the topic being discussed might well deal with them as Diogenes did with an inept archer.[34] Seeing in a hundred shots that the man never so

31 Lucian, *Adversus indoctum* (*The ignorant book collector*), 12.
32 Greek proverb, ὄνας λύρας (onas luras). Fable in Aesop, Phaedrus, Lucian, *Dialogue of the Courtesans*, 14, Boethius.
[33] **Lucian, *Demonax*,** 28.
34 **Laertius, *Diogenes*,** 6.68.

much as once hit the mark, he ran and stood at the target, confident that the fellow would hit everywhere but in the direction of his aim.

You might be well be reluctant to concede as the merit of extraordinary Wit the ability to speak at length for hours, and while speaking of everything else under the sun, never once touch even slightly on the subject at hand. The emperor Gallienus, during a grand hunting party, decided to award the victory to the man who, after ten spears flung at close range at a large bull, managed never to hit him even once. On sending him the crown he explained to those surprised at his decision: "*This man is an expert greater than all of you. For, to throw ten spears from close up, against so great a target and not to hit it, that is a thing which no one else could do.*" And these are the merits, these the rewards of the sons of Ignorance, when they play to the crowd and beg for applause.

But if, by misfortune, they hear the jeers they deserve, instead of applause, the most unrepentant among them will be ready with a list of bitter rejoinders, such as, *envy is the mortal enemy of virtue*, or *from the shining lights of glory arise the black shadows of malice*, also *slander is a companion to justly awarded desserts, like the admonishing slave in the chariots of triumphant conquerors*.

From the less brazen are heard these ordinary excuses, supplied on the slightest occasions, *That the difficulty of the matter, and the towering sublimity of the subject, fit only for the Wit of an Atlas, was beyond their capacities*. Sometimes, the perfect excuse for them might be the one used by the famous Faustulus. When he was thrown from the saddle by the ant he was riding to the merriment of bystanders, he reminded them that a similar fall befell Phaëton. This is the text:

> *Faustulus was riding an ant as if he were a large elephant,*
> *He fell off and hit the ground on his back.*
> *Directly the ant gave him a kick that was almost deadly.*
> *He was distraught and fighting to stay alive.*
> *But this is what he had to say: "Why do you laugh, tools of envy?*
> *So, what if I fell? Didn't Phaeton fall the same way?"* [35]

---

35 **Probinus quoted by Ausonius**:
> *Faustulus insidens formicae, ut magno elephanto,*
> *Decidit, et terrae terga supina dedit.*
> *Moxque idem ad mortem est mulctatus calcibus eius.*
> *Perditus, ut posset vix reperare animam.*
> *Vix tamen est fatus. Quid rides improbe livor?*

Along with the taunts earned as the fruit of their ignorance by those who don't know what they are talking about and become the subject of laughter, we should not forget the snickers merited by certain unspeaking and unspeakable individuals outfitted in the garb of letterati, but truly without any outfitting of good Letters. In addressing them by their titles one should not say doctor, but **vox praetereaque nihil** *(talk and nothing more)*.

The skin of the Nemean lion was worthily worn on the shoulders of the great Hercules. It was never more worthless than when it was worn by a woman: *"The lion had to be brushed down so as not to hurt a delicate shoulder, his fur was supplemented by false hair. He would have roared aloud from vexation if he could. Certainly, the Nemean sighed pitifully (if his native spirit had a say) when he saw his lion's share lost."*[36] No otherwise do the gowns and the titles, the insignia and features proper to Men of Letters, react when they are worn by people without Letters or civility. They see themselves condemned to be perpetual liars, in that they tell those who see them: *"This is a lion, who is really an ass; Here goes a doctor, who is like certain books* (as Lucian told such another) *that are painted skillfully and gilded gloriously on the outside cover and inside absent of any letters, pages of blank paper."*

How many such are seen to make their way so proud and stately resembling that perfect sphere of the geometricians that touches the ground only at one point? Seeing what they look like, they forget what they are, and like Alexander's steed Bucephalus in his trappings, they will allow none to touch or look at them, but the ruler of the world.

Such a one was that little man, upon whom Lucian so masterfully whets his Wit.[37] This man, as many also nowadays, measured his knowledge by the Letters that he had, not in his head, but in other men's writings. As if the Wits of philosophers enclosed in their books were, as the Wits of Ariosto's Orlando, in a vial,[38] and just

---

*Quod cecidi? Cecidit non aliter Phaëton.*

36 **Tertullian, *De Pallio***: *Credo et jubas pectinem passas, ne cervicem enervem inureret stiria leonina; Hiatus crinibus infartos, genuinos inter antias adumbratos. Tota oris, contumelia mugiret si posset. Nemea certè (si quis loci genius) ingemebat: tunc enim se circumspexit leonem perdidisse.*

37 **Lucian, *Adversus indoctum*** (*The ignorant book collector*).

[38] *Il senno d'Orlando, Orlando Furioso,* XXIII.

by sniffing their brains could inhale them all, so that their heads would become the library of as many authors, as they had books on their shelves. "*In the houses of the idle and pretentious you will find all the orations and all the histories and inscriptions from floor to ceiling.*"[39]

But collecting books in this manner, to wipe the dust off them every day without using them to remove the rust from the brain, this is in the judgment of Sidonius. "*Loving the parchment more than the Letters.*"[40]

This is to make the house more admirable than its master, as happened with Archelaus.[41] People flocked from all parts to see his palace, which had been painted by Zeuxis, while (as Socrates said) no man would move a step to see the owner. "*What sight is there sweeter to a free and unspoiled spirit born for honest pleasures than to see a numerous concourse of brilliant men in his home and know that it is not for money or for some matter of law, not for his official function or administration, but for himself alone.*"[42]

---

39 **Seneca, *De tranquillitate animi*, 9**: *Sic apud desidiosissimos videbis quidquid orationum, historiarumque est, et tecto tenus extructa loculamenta.*
40 **Sidonius Apollinaris**, Letters, 5.2.: *Membranas potiùs amare quàm literas.*
41 **Aelian,** 14.17
[42] **Quintillian** (Tacitus*), **De oratoribus Dialogus,** 6.2: *At quid dulcius libero, et ingenuo animo, et ad voluptates honestas nato, quàm videre plenam semper, et frequentem domum concursu splendidissimo hominum, idque scire non pecuniae, non orbitati, neque officii alicujus administrationi, sed sibi ipsi dari.*

THE
LEARNED·MAN
Defended
and
Reform'd:

# THE
# Learned Man

### Defended and Reform'd.

*A Discourse of singular Politeness*, *and Elocution;* seasonably asserting the Right of the *Muses*; in opposition to the many Enemies which in this Age *Learning* meets with, and more especially those two *IGNO-RANCE* and *VICE*.

### In two Parts.

*Written in Italian by the happy Ten of* P. Daniel

# BARTOLVS, S. J.

Englished by *Thomas Salusbury.*

*Scientia est de numero bonorum honorabilium.* Aristot. l. 1. De Anima.

*Scio neminem posse bene vivere sine Sapientia studio.* Seneca Epist. ad Luci.

*Pulchrum est in omni Artium genere excere.* Sabellic. lib. 10. de cultu & fructu Philos.

VVith two Tables one General, the other Alphabetical.

*LONDON,*
Printed by *R.* and *W. Leybourn,* and are to be sold by *Thomas Dring* at the *George* in Fleetstreet neer St. *Dunstans* Church, 1660.

# PART TWO

*The Defects of Men of Letters cannot reasonably be held as prejudicial to Letters themselves. Nor should we believe that what stems from the vice of misuse is a natural condition. The horizon will mar the sun with the impurities in the atmosphere. The earth's reflections, (if it were true, as some erroneously believe) appear on the moon as so many spots. The vapors in the air make the stars appear unstable, and in continual motion. So does this mean that the sun is besmerched? That the moon is muddied? That the stars are inconstant?*

*Nothing in the world is so innocent, that it is not made guilty through the flaws of those who abuse and diminish it. Arms spawn exacters of cruelty; scepters are the mainstays of ambition; beauty is made the agent of lust; riches, ministers of luxury; honors, upholders of pride; nobility, a license for ostentation. But why examine one by one the most excellent things if even sanctity can be used by hypocrisy and religion made the pawn of interest? Therefore, the misuse by some of Letters no more renders them guilty than flowers are shorn of their innocence and beauty because spiders feed there and draw venom from them.*

*Letters are the light of the intellect. Light, whose property is always to issue directly from the center of the sun in straight lines, has its rectilinearity together with its existence and only travels in straight lines. Now, if Letters, which come from the glorious Father of lights whose gift to us they are, were to shine the rays of their unswerving revelations along the right road of truth and reason, would they not be happier by far? And would not the world be far happier with them?*

*But, since the desire for such righteousness counts for very little, while claiming to have it would be too much, I thought it would be reasonable on my part to single out in some chapters and headings where Letters have been abused most, whereby they not only inflict public harm, but also serve to mislead beginners lacking instruction in how to use them. And it is from both these predicaments that I have drawn what I have written here in order to encourage those who, with the recognition of their errors, may want some stimulus to emend them.*

# 5        *PLAGIARISM*

## 5.1    *Thieves Who in Various Ways Appropriate the Work of Studies not their own*

The ancient art of thievery, the natural daughter of necessity, then the adopted child of convenience, is as involved with Letters as it is with money. Clement of Alexandria[1] traces its origins to such ancient times that the works of the most ingenious Wits no sooner surfaced than they were stolen. The painted Helens of great artists were no sooner seen than they found a Menelaus and a Paris and their legions to carry them off. Some think (I will apply in jest that ancient saying of the comic)[2] that only a **Homo trium litterarum** *(a man of three letters)* makes him a **Fur** *(thief)* and it is only the vice of men of few Letters to steal the labors of the learned, which they use to elevate and enrich themselves. Nonetheless, the noblest Wits and most learned pens have honored this art and helped themselves to what others have done, so it holds no less true for them than for great lions and small ants, that

*It is good to feast on prey and live on rapine.*[3]

The writings of the great Aristotle are famed to be a beautiful mosaic, created according to his design but with material, for the most part, borrowed from others. So that, while Speusippus spent a fortune to buy Aristotle's books,[4] if Democritus, and others whose works of Wit Alexander collected together for his teacher were to take back what was his, this seeming Phoenix in others' plumes dressed down to himself would come out...a crow.

On the score of Philolaus, Plato heard himself vilified as a thief by a slanderer.[5] Not that he had copied a good deal of his *Timaeus* from him, but rather served it up in a sauce stewed in the writings of that second Pythagoras. Here is how Timon puts it:

*You spent a great deal of money on this small work*

---

1 Clement of Alexandria, *Stromata*, 2,1. The idea that the achievements of Homer and Plato were stolen from Moses, "*the theft of the Greeks*".
2 Plautus, *Aulularia*, 2. 4.46/7.
3 *Aeneid* 7. 749: *Convectare juvat praedas, et vivere rapto.*
4 Three talents, Laertius, *Speusippus*, 4.1; Quoting Favorinus, *Memorabilia*.
5 Gellius, 3.17: Timon of Phius.

*And you gained your learning with what you purchased to write it.* [6]

And.certainly, we could use, if there were one, an Archimedes for books to tell the difference between the original and the borrowed, as he could by separating the mixture of two metals.[7] Were there but an Aristophanes, a judge who could understand the language of the dead when they speak from the mouths of the living.[8] Were there but a Cratinus to put books to torture and write the indictment of their stolen parts, as he did with the poems of Menander, of whose thieveries he composed six books,[9] then you would see how true it is that Mercury, the god of Letters, is also the god of thieves.

But in my estimation, the whole crew of those who in their books publish the labors of others under their own names may be separated into three orders, one worse than the other. The first are those who, gathering one thing from one and another from another and changing their titles and inverting their order, compose books as they make garlands, where many small pieces make a big piece, many flowers make a wreath. They have the discretion to steal a little from everyone, so that few notice and none will complain of the theft. They might say they are not stealing, but only clipping chips off the coin.

The names of these authors are sumptuously written in capital letters on the title page of the work. One is amazed to see them the fathers of such prodigious offspring, when it is clear they have neither the power to produce them nor the seed to engender them.

*He sees it bears new branches and fruit from others.*[10]
He may have holdings, but he knows that he has neither the revenue nor the capital sufficient for so great a purchase.

These types have a law never to mention the authors whose writings they have hunted down. They are right to suspect their thefts will be identified as poaching. They pay no mind to what the elder Pliny said: "*Sordid and wretched are the minds of those who would rather be caught stealing, than make restitution, though it would be far better for them in the long*

---

6 **Gellius, 3.17.**: *Exiguum redimus grandi aere libellum.*
  *Scribere per quem orsus perdoctus ab inde fuisti.*
7 **Vitruvius**, *De architectura*, **preface, 7.**
8 **Aristophanes, *The Wasps.***
9 Lelio Gregorio **Giraldi, *Historia poetarum*,** De poetas (Ferrara, 1545).
10 Virgil, *Georgics* 2.82:
  *Miraturque novas frondes, et non sua poma.*

*run.'*[11] Nor do they observe the ancient custom, reported by M. Varro, of adorning the wells with sweet smelling garlands of flowers once a year in thanksgiving for the clear and wholesome waters that they supply.[12]

It often happens (and this is the ultimate refinement of the art of thieving) that the culprits will chastise as ignorant and condemn as unlettered those very persons from whom they have taken their best material, so that by impugning their source's learning, people won't detect their thievery. Torrential waters act just so when they break their banks in the swell. They uproot, steal and bear off everything that stands in their way, but from what they carry off, they swallow the solid parts and only show the stumps, the chaff— the flotsam. This is how the Harpies work.[13] They sate their hunger at a banquet but are not satisfied with just grabbing what they can carry and befoul what they leave behind. This is to treat good writers as that scoundrel Dionysius treated friends. According to Diogenes,[14] he used them like the jars of fine spirits. He would drain them when they were full and when they were empty smash them to pieces. This is acting just like the infamous monsters in the straights of Messina below the lighthouse, Scylla and Charybdis. The first smashes the ships, and scatters their goods, the second takes hold of them in its whirlpools and swallows them up. These two don't seize what's not theirs to throw it back, they swallow it: *"They don't spew out what they shipwreck, they devour it,"* said Tertullian.[15]

They should hear as addressed to them alone what the great moralist Plutarch has to say in a different context: *"We must not begrudge the glory of those who have helped to bring us on high, not act like the little bird of Aesop, Regulus, who deserted the Eagle when he tired and could fly no more."*[16]

Worse than these are the second kind. They get their hands on— I know not how— the unfinished writings of excellent masters of Letters, these pious collectors, as an osprey will sweep down on

---

11 **Pliny, *In praefatione operis*,** 23: *Obnoxii animi et infelicis ingenii esse deprehendi in furto malle, quàm mutuo (mutuum) reddere; cum praesertim sors fiat ex usura.*

12 Varro, *Rerum rusticarum*, 3.22: *Fontinalia*: October 13.

13 *Aeneid* 3, 209.

14 **Laertius, *Diogenes*,** 6.50.

15 **Tertullian, *de Pallio*, 2**.3: *nec expuunt naufragia, sed devorant.*

16 **Plutarch, *Precepts on government*,** 12, 806: *Non debemus suffurari gloriam eorum, qui nos in altum extulerunt, necesse ut Regulis Aesopi, qui deseruit Aquilam cùm ea lassa ulteriùs non potuit volare.*

unfledged eaglets fallen from their nests and take them up as abandoned and exposed infants to take in them as its own. The burden of their ignorance outdoes in them the infamy of their stealing. They have no mind to listen to what Synesius says: "*It is more sacrilegious to steal the deliberations of the dead, than their clothing, what they call scavenging.*"[17] O, the host of those, if they could only rise from below ground, or but raise their heads from their tombs, to see their works appropriated by persons with no right of succession, *ab intestato*, who would chime in with that forlorn shepherd of Mantua,

*Now, time to graft the pears, Meliboeus, to bind up the vines.*[18]

It was a most respectful rule of the excellent and discerning painters of Greece, followed in all ages, to honor the memory of the worthy masters in that art, by not applying their paint brushes to works which the artists, overtaken by death, had left either without the final touches or unfinished. This was to attest that those remains, even unformed and incomplete were more excellent than if other hands had finished them most scrupulously. Of this the Natural Historian says: "*What is even more remarkable is that the last paintings of these notable artists, though left unfinished, such as the Dawn by Aristides, the Sons of Tyndarus by Nichomaches, the Medea of Timomachus, the Venus of Apelles, were held in admiration more greatly than if they had been completed.*"[19]

Now in the world of Letters, for many there is no such well-considered and respectful law because they are exceedingly greedy for the aura of a man of Wit, and will put their hands on the unfinished works, not theirs, not to complete them for the author but, against every good mark of justice, to claim the property of others as their own belongings.

✕He who finds a treasure on his land can have it all to himself, as emperor Hadrian set down,[20] but if it is found on someone else's land, he must split it and give half to the owner of the property. This

---

17 **Synesius, *Letter* 143**, To Herculium; *Magis impium esse mortuorum lucubrationes, quam vestes furari, quod sepulchra perfodere dicitur.*
18 Tityrus reacts to his expropriation in Virgil, *Eclogue* 1.74:
   *Insere nunc Melibaee pyros, pone ordine vites.*
19 **Pliny**, 35.21: *Illud per quam rarum, ac memoria dignum, etiam suprema opera artificium, imperfectasque tabulas, sicut Irin Aristidis, Tyndaridas Nichomachi, Medeam Timomachi, et Venerem Apellis in majori admiratione esse quam perfecta.*
20 **Aelius Spartianus, *Hadrian*, 18.** (*Historia Augusta*).

law, which applies to money matters, should with even more justice be observed concerning the products of the Wit.

Then there are the third sort— and they are intolerable— namely, those who to another's work add nothing but their names. They are insignificant men whose little features figure nowhere in a book except on the facade. As the nag of the fables who had nothing of the lion but its skin, they claim all the rest for themselves. As if the ownership of a book were the same as dedicating a new temple to a god, where all it takes is carving the god's name above the facade. Caligula, that beast dressed as an emperor, cut the head off the statue of Jupiter Olympus and, so he would be adored as Jupiter, he had his own head placed there. What do you call that? The Persians considered it the worst sin to be a debtor— and next, to be a liar.[21] Those who steal in this way are each of the two., they are indebted to others for what they do have, holding it by false claims of ownership in no other way but by shameless lies.

Someone of this stripe was castigated for such a theft. They expected that, unable to hide the fact with lies, he would at least hide his face for shame. Brazen as he was sly, he set to defending himself behind the shield of that sympathetic psychology so bandied about by would-be philosophers and came up with this passionate retort: No one could prove him to be the robber of the writings of another unless they could prove that their minds were different. For two Wits who are uniform and consonant in genius will have, by virtue of sympathetic union, both the same movements of mind, and the same order of thoughts. Now we can leave it to Kepler, Mersenne, and Galileo[22] to investigate the mysterious reason why two strings tuned to the same octave, the diapason, and the fifth, a diatessaron, so accord the one with the other in sound that if one is touched, the other not touched trembles and moves. Here though, is a problem harder to solve, (if in uniform Wits there may be, as in musical chords, those regular vibrations, which encountering harmonic numbers of perfect consonance, occasion like motions). How is it possible that two brains

---

21 **Plutarch, *de vitando aere alieno*,** (*Against borrowing money*).
22 **Kepler, *De harmonica proportione* 3** (1595) / **Mersenne, *Questions on Genesis*** (1623) / **Galileo, *De novae philosophiae*** (*Two New Sciences*, 1638); Also, Johannes Kepler, *Harmonices mundi* (1619) Marin Mersenne, *Traité de l'Harmonie universelle* (1636), Vincenzo Galileo, *Della musica antica e della moderna* (1581).

by way of consenting sympathy are tuned to select one and the same argument, to explain it with the same form of expression, never differing a word, nor even an accent mark? In the end, with such exact resemblance of stature, voice, and features that they outdid the Menecmi twins of Plautus, even though:

> *The twin boys were so alike, that neither their nurse*
> *Whom they called mamma could tell them apart*
> *Nor even their own mother who had given them birth.*[23]s

The skill many have in stealing writings not theirs has spawned the preoccupation to safeguard them jealously along with the quarrels that arise when they are stealthily stolen.

Even Nature herself has taught the animals a double lesson about things most precious and most sweet: that their Wits must ever more artfully protect them against thieves and that thieves will be ever more avid to ferret them out. Thus, pearl oysters— mothers of pearl— when the morning's light finds them, will close, and if someone takes one in hand while it is still open, though it is otherwise blind, "*When it sees a hand, it closes, and protects its wealth, knowing what they are looking for. And if a hand intrudes, it will cut it with its tip, a completely justified punishment.*"[24]

The bees, with a very bitter overlay protect their hives, "*Against the avidity of other insects, aware that what they are making may spark cupidity.*"[25] And since,

> *Nothing is more dangerous than a thief with nothing*[26]

against these thieves, it is never enough for Mercury to keep watch with the hundred eyes of Argus. Consequently, we have the world of quarrels which engage so many authors, so many books.

In all this patience is most difficult and distress most reasonable. Even dead statues of brass, if in the night they are knocked over by thieves intending to smash them to pieces, while they have no

---

23 **Plautus, *Menecmi*, prologue:**
> *Ita forma simili pueri, vel nutrix sua.*
> *Non internosse posset, quae mammam dabat*
> *Neque mater adeò ipsa, quae illos pepererat.*

24 **Pliny, 9.35**: *Cum manum videt comprimit sese, operitque opes, gnara propter illas se peti; manumque, si praeveniat, acie sua adscindit, nulla justiore poena.*

25 **Pliny, 12.6**: *contra aliarum bestiolarum aviditates: Id se facturas consciae, quod concupisci possit.*

26 **Martial, *Epigrams*, 63.12**: *Nil est deterius latrone nudo.*

way to feel pain, they do have a voice to complain: "*They are not entirely mute, when they are struck by thieves, they warn the guards with their ringing.*"[27]

But, behold, in two short reminders, the remedy against the vicious hunger after others' labors. The first is to persuade yourselves that the world will not investigate so ineptly that, given time, from public knowledge, from the fame or rather the infamy of the evidence, from witnesses, the theft is not discovered and who the culprits are. You must never, however stealthly you are, think that you won't be found out. You turn upside down the order of things, because you put others' property to your own use. Even if, as a clever Cacus you can turn around the footprints of your prey as you bring it home dragging it by the tail, a Hercules will come without fail, and by those very prints will track down the theft and the felony and punish its author.[28] You, on your own, will let slip from your mouth, or pen, certain words, as clues that are alerts about the crime. In this too you are like the raven. He never robs neatly enough that with blood on his beak or the prey in his mouth he doesn't crow. And before he knows it, the stones are flying to chase him away:

> *If the raven could eat without making noise,*
> *He would have more booty and less trouble and aggravation.*[29]

Even when you keep silent, your papers speak against you and your books will prosecute the case. With this assurance Martial, whose epigrams helped many to pass for Wits and poets having passed them off as their own, wasted no words on accusing thieves or in self-defense:

> *There is no call for me to defend myself or my books*
> *My defense is your pages that tell you are a thief.*[30]

The second reminder is for you to be convinced that it is much less grievous not to show as learned, than to show as ignorant without something that's yours—and criminal by stealing from others. If your head is poor in the hair that indicates thoughts and the riches of the mind, don't uproot the hairs of the dead and make an ill-shaped wig.

---

27 **Cassiodorus, *Variae*, 7,** formula 13: *Nec in toto mutae sunt, quando a furibus percussae, custodes videntur tinitibus admonere.*
28 *Aeneid*, 8. 209/10.
29 **Horace**, *Letter* 7. 50/51: *Nam tacitus pascit si posset corvus, haberet*
        *Plus dapis, et rixae((multo) minus, invidiaeque.*
30 **Martial, *Epigrams*, 1.34:**
        *Indice non opus est nostris, nec vindice libris*
        *Stat contra, dicitque tibi tua pagina, Fur es.*

*Nothing looks worse on a bald head than a hairpiece.*[31]

Better to be poor with one's own, than rich with what belongs to another. To say, "this is mine, though not a lot," is far sweeter than saying "this is a lot, but it is not mine." The loveliest verses that Manilius could read in his poems, were this pair,

*I speak on my own. Nothing here is owing to magic or theft,*
      *This work comes from me.*[32]

Write so that on all your compositions you may attach that distich that the poet Ariosto wrote over the portal of his house.

*Small, but suited to me, not entailed and not unkempt,*
*Home, all paid for with my own money, sweet home.*[33]

## 5.2  *We Should Not take From Others, But Create new Things of our Own*

The desire to become immortal for posterity through one's books should launch the Wit to invent on its own, rather than sharpen its talons to prey upon others' work. Many are convicted of plagiary and have their names proscribed and their fame confiscated while. they might well have secured immortality for both the one and the other. And oh! How much more might Letters flourish, and in how many other and better ways might we spend our time, our studies, and our Wits? Instead of this vile and useless task, **Quadrata rotundis** (*squaring the circle*), of making a silhouette of what others have fleshed out in the body of their works, all the workings of our thoughts should be focused on enriching the arts and the sciences with new discoveries, things unknown to our forebears for the profit of generations to come. One single page like this would be enough to win for us the honor for which the weightiest tomes often strive in vain.

Seeking out new things is by itself— even if we don't find them—not without its praises, because  it is useful: "*Much is brought to*

---

31 **Martial,** Epigrams, 83.11: *Calvo turpius est nihil comato.*
32 **Manilius, *Astronomica* 2.**57:
            *Nostra loquar, nulli vatum debebimus orsa*
                  *Nec furtum, sed opus veniet.*
33 In Bartoli's native Ferrara, Via Ariosto, 26:
         *Parva, sed apta mihi, sed nulli obnoxia, sed non sordida,*
            *Parva (parta), Meo sed tamen aere, domus.*

*the process of invention by the mere hope of making a discovery.*"[1] And the man who is inspired by noble thoughts would rather make his own hard way toward Heaven than follow behind someone else on earth so that with the Poet he may say:

*Mine were the first steps into the unknown*
*My path was untrodden by other footprints.*[2]

It may well befall someone who aims for Heaven to fall more often than somone who stays on the ground, yet that *"failure while daring great deeds,"*[3] brings great glory and the glory of the flight outstrips by far the failure of the fall. Even today the generous passion of the young Icarus, who aimed for the stars, gets greater kudos for his flight than blame for his fall:

*The ploughman at his plough looked up in amazement*
*At what is in the sky,*
*He thought it must be a god.*[4]

Let me say that it is hard to climb without falling or tripping, since often our knowledge is more what we believe, than what we know, more in not seeing our errors, than in not making them. I feel the same about the life of Letters as Seneca's friend in another context: *"If it is my lot to fall, let me fall from Heaven."*[5] I would have our Wits treat our thoughts, as eagles treat their chicks. Before they are full-fledged and their wings have begun flying, they throw them out of the nest to hunt, as if to say, "You are now full-fledged eagles, why do you idle in the nest? You have talons, and beaks, are you not ashamed to be fed like so many baby swallows. Go and find food on your own. That is why you have a strong grip; that is why you are eagles."

Every thought not focused on finding new knowledge in Letters, in the opinion of Hippocrates missed the mark that all men of Letters with a straight aim must set as their target. He wouldn't have us piece together the leftovers of dead writers, **quasi bona**

---

1 **Seneca, *QN*, 6.5**: *Plurimum enim ad inveniendum contulit, qui speravit posse reperire.*
2 **Horace, *Epistle* 19**.21/2:
    *Libera per vacuum posui vestigia princeps*
    *Non aliena meo pressi pede.*
3 Ovid, *Met.,*2.328: *Magnis tamen excidit ausis.*
4 **Ovid, *Met.*, 8**.218: —*Stivaeque innixus arator*
        *Vidit et obstupuit; quippe aethera carpere possit*
            *Credidit esse Deum.*
5 **Vagellus in Seneca, *QN*, 6.2**: *Si cadendum est mihi, coelo cecidisse velim.*

***naufragantium*** (*as the booty of shipwrecks*)[6] but wanted us to launch our ships forth to gather up new goods to endow the world with greater riches and ourselves with greater glory. *"My goal is make new discoveries, to come up with what is still unknown. This will set what has previously been hidden to good use. Such is the vocation and the responsibility of science.*[7]

Indeed, by looking for things previously unfound, how many have found things previously unlooked for! Just the drive to convert some baser metal into gold has triggered new thoughts and focused the Wit. Specifically, now there are the wonders of nature that the art of chemistry can test and explore.[8] And what mines of new discoveries to build a truer natural philosophy have been revealed in their marvels for those yet to come. They will know how to test and explore these sciences and discover how, along the path of experiment, to penetrate to the primary structures of their function in natural. It happens (said a fine man) the same way it did in Aesop for the sons looking for gold. As their father lay dying, he told them he had buried gold in his field. All of them started digging so that the field, from the barren land it had been, became fertile, not bringing forth gold, but rather a plentiful harvest of crops, as good as gold.

Truth has not gone sterile, no matter how much she taught our ancient fathers. *"Even regarding those held to be the sagest of mortals, they may have known a great deal indeed, but not everything."*[9] With their studies, they have not fished out all the pearls; with their speculations, they have not discovered all traces of the truth. Valiant they were, it is true, but no match for Hercules. Noone has found or marked the boundaries of nature that should prevent someone from venturing beyond where the pillars have been set. The Moralist says, *"The truth is open to all and is not fully known, there is much that remains to be discovered in the future."*[10] And, as the Spartans said, neither rivers nor mountains assigned boundaries to their kingdom, it reached as far as one could throw a spear. In like manner the arts and sciences expand as far as the sharpness of our Wits

---

6 Legalism.

7 **Hippocrates,** *Art of medicine*, **preface**: *Mihi verò invenire aliquid eorum, quae nondum inventa sunt, quod ipsum notum quam occultum esse praestat, scientiae votum, et opus esse videtur.*

8 Bartoli's father was a chemist and apothecary.

9 *Columela, de re rustica, in fine*: *Etiam quicunque sunt habiti mortalium sapientissimi, multa scisse dicuntur non omnia.*

10 **Seneca,** *Letter* **33**.11: *Patet omnia veritas, non est occupata. Multum ex illa etiam futuris relictum.*

can make them stretch. It is not the ocean where Pope Alexander the Sixth drew a line from pole to pole through one of the Cape Verde Islands and set the boundaries of their navigations, for the Castilians; from there west; for the Portuguese, from there east. **Patet omnibus veritas.** (*The truth is open to all*).

Some of the ancients wanted to draw this line of demarcation between Greek and Latin poetry. But Horace wanted to cross it, weaving together in his crown the laurels of Athens with those of Rome, as he offered the lyric poetry of the Greeks upon the Latin lyre. He was scolded by his seniors and his compositions were rejected as the children of a bastard muse and spurned as two forms together in a single monster. This impelled the poet to take up his pen in defense of his plectrum and in the context of his defense he made public the culpable envy and the malice of his opponents. He said that their hatred of his compositions was not so much from love of the antique beauty of the ancients as out of their envy of his modern elegance; that their words against his mastery testified to their own shortcomings; that they were ashamed to learn from him, a young man, what they as seniors were incapable of inventing; that in his rivals this was the origin of all their malice.

> *They will say that nothing is right, unless they approve,*
> *For the elders deem it unseemly to be at a disadvantage*
> *Before smooth-faced youngsters with something to teach them.*[11]

And, doubtless, we may say with the man in Minutius: "*Why should we complain, if the truth has ripened in our own day?*"[12] Was the treasury of invention so definitive among the ancients that it can never be renewed? And yet, what Arnobius wrote of religion holds concerning the truths discovered every day by our increase of knowledge, "*It is not that what we believe is new, but that we have lately come to learn what we should believe.*"[13]

Who then will prescribe bounds and limits to the free flight of ingenious Wits or confine them within the narrow space of what is

---

11 **Horace, *Book 2, Epistle 1*.** 83-85:
> *Vel quia nil rectum, nisi quod placuit sibi, ducunt;*
> *Vel quia turpe putant parere minoribus, et quae*
> *Imberbes didicere senes perdenda fateri.*

12 **Minutius, *Octavius*,** 38.7: *Quid invidemus, si veritas (divinitatis) nostri temporis aetate maturuit?*

13 **Arnobius, *Adversus nationes* (*Against the Heathen*),** 2.72: *Non quod sequimur novum est, sed nos serò didicimus quod nos sequi oportet.*

already known? As if nothing were left to create? If such a law as this had been known of old, today we would know nothing: "*Never would a thing be invented, if we were satisfied with what already has been discovered. Besides, just following behind someone else, comes up with nothing, invents nothing, doesn't even experiment.*"[14] And of men like this, in my opinion, we may say, as Dante very finely said of the fearful sheep that follow their leader:

> *As silly sheep, when two or three more bold*
> *And venturous than others leave the fold,*
> *The rest, afraid, dejecting eyes and head,*
> *Without inquiry, follow those that led:*
> *And if one stay, the rest in heaps, bestride*
> *Him, not knowing why, and simply there abide.*[15]

Let us add what Lactantius has to say to Dante's words. "*Why are there some who seek knowledge by looking for the truth as established; who want to achieve Sapience without having any questions, following the lead of their forebears, like sheep?*" [16] Most appropriate is the answer that the Echo of Erasmus gave to that miserable Ciceronian, who cried, **Decem annos consumpsi in legendo Cicer-one** (*Ten years I spent studying Cicer –one*) and heard in reply **One** *(Ass)* which was as much as to say that wanting to become an ape of Cicero, he made himself into an ass, by poring over his Tully.[17]

But the courage to undertake and the good fortune to succeed in the discovery of new and useful things, I must admit, is not for everyone; ordinarily, one who sets out on this enterprise feels fearful and frightened and may let others persuade him to hold him back.

---

14 **Seneca, *Letter* 33.**10: *Numquam enim invenietur, si contenti fuerimus inventis. Propterea qui alium sequitur, nihil sequitur, nihil invenit, immo nec quaerit.*
15 Salusbury's Englishing of **Dante, *Purgatorio* 3**, 79/84:
> *Come le pecorelle escon dal chiuso*
> *Ad una, due, e le altre stanno*
> *Timidette atterrando l'occhio e 'l muso*
> *E cio che fa la prima e le altre fanno*
> *Adossandosi a lei s'ella s'arresta*
> *Simplici e quete, e lo perche non sanno.*
16 **Lactantius, *De origine errorum* 2. 8**: *Quare cum sapere, id est, veritatem quaerere, omnibus sit innatum, Sapientiam sibi adimunt, qui sine ullo judicio inventa majorum probant, et ab aliis, pecudum more, ducuntur.*
17 **Erasmus**, *Ciceronianus* (1528).

The fixed stars do not move by themselves, they are held by the Heavens and borne along by the universe, and they are not blamed as unruly or condemned as errant. Inversely, the planets are most voluble in moving on their own. As they variously temper their simple and very regular movements they give the appearance of climbing and descending, of going fast and slow, which makes the simple folk call them irregular in their movements, confused in their cycles, not in orbit but in error, tracing not circles, but labyrinths.

Alexander had a heart so great and so large that he could conceive within it the desire for a world of worlds, but coming to the Eastern Ocean he confessed himself not too great for this one small world and was worried that his fortune on land might prove different on the sea. He struck sail to wishes tempting him to search across the ocean for new places to conquer. Chastened by his fear he demonstrated his prudence and covered his retreat with the counsels of others, making a show of compliance to the arguments of his counselors dissuading him, "Great Monarch,[18] little more than Greece sufficed to make Hercules a demigod. Will not the whole Earth suffice to make you a Hercules? Do not lose this world while you are in quest of another. If there were more land on the other side of the ocean, your enemies would have fled there. To hide from your arms— and from you— they have gone to bury themselves in hell. Be content that the confines of your kingdom have stretched to the very boundaries of nature. This shore will preserve the imprint of your vanquishing footstep for all time. In marking the reaches of human generosity, you will be the Hercules of the East, as Hercules was the Alexander of the West." With that Alexander, "*came full stop and suffered defeat by the great orb of the world.*"[19]

That generous Columbus, set against the ocean as in a flood of water, discovered new lands and new worlds. Had he done no more than this! Despite the repulses of two republics and one king, he followed the advice of the winds blowing from the West and whispering in his ear, "see yonder ample lands, whose scents we waft so powerfully." He weighed anchor and set sail with a frigate and two caravels and launched into the bosom of the vast ocean. Never could his course be changed or reversed, neither by a sea uncharted and held

---

18 **Seneca the Elder,** *Suasoria* 1.
19 **Lucan,** *Pharsalia* 3. 234: *Constitit, et magno se vinci passus (fassus) ab orbe est.*

to be innavigable, nor by the length of a voyage with no end in sight. He was deterred neither by meeting with monsters, nor by the plotting of his men, nor by the want of food in a situation with no hope of outside assistance, nor by the frequent tempests that tossed him into unknown climes, nor by the long and excessive calms that took him upon the confines of the torrid zone where the Heavens for their excessive heat seem like hell. Otherwise, Europe would now be without not just aromatic spices and precious mines, but without the knowledge of that half a world, America. Nor would Columbus have won for himself from the kings of Castile the privilege of attaching to to the quartered arms of his house the motto heralding his discovery of the New World,

**For Castile and for Leon, Columbus found a New World.**[20]

Not only this honor, but those immortal merits whereby all ages acknowledge their debt to him, and through him, to Genoa and to all of Italy for the property of an entire world? No different is the man who in the world of learning undertakes to be first on the path to discover new lands (no less than in navigating uncharted oceans). Twixt the troubles and trials of his long journey of unremitting study, amid frequent internal outbursts of desperation, he must conquer himself a thousand times, with his eye, like those glorious heroes, conquerors of the Golden Fleece, more on the glory of the goal, than on the worry of the way.

> *You alone, Glory, enflame minds and spirit,*
> *(Jason) sees you, in verdant youth, immune to old age*
> *Standing on the shore of Phasis and calling the young men.*[21]

And so Homer, the first poet of heroes and the first hero of poets, is doubly great, as there was no one before for him to imitate and no one after to imitate him. First, he was greater than all those who came before; second, he was greater than those who came after him. This is the great panegyric that Velleius Paterculus coined in few words, instead of all the tributes attempted by so many more, "*Neither before him was there anyone for him to imitate, nor after him was there anyone who*

---

20 ***Por Castilla, y por Leon, Nuevo Mondo hallò Colon***. Oviedo, *Historia de las Indias*, 2. 7 (1535).
21 **Valerius Flaccus,** *Argonautica* 1.76-8:

> *Tu sola animos, mentemque peruris*
> *Gloriae, te viridem videt immunemque senectae*
> *Phasidos in ripa stantem juvenesqve vocantem.*

*could imitate him."* [22] Thus Homer, as long as Letters shall be alive in the world, (and they shall live as long as the world does) shall remain in the praises of the letterati as illustrious, just as that adventurous Argo, from the tempestuous seas it sailed before all other ships, found its port in Heaven where now it is studded with as many stars as the heroes of yore it once carried,

> *It first ploughed the seas,*
> *And is celebrated worldwide for serving its noble passengers*
> *Raised to divinity for serving divinities.* [23]

Thus, after a thousand others, in our own day we have Galileo, a truly lynx-eyed leader of the Academy. [24] Both by the eye of his Wit and by the tube of his telescope he has rendered the commerce of earth with Heaven so familiar that the stars which before were hidden from sight no longer disdain to be seen and those, which before were visible, reveal to us not only their beauty, but even their flaws. At the foot of the sepulchre of this most acute Lincean we could carve as a lament what the poet said in derision about Argos,

> *Argo, you are buried; the light you had in so many eyes is put out*
> *A single night is cast over a hundred eyes.* [25]

In addition, there is Christopher Scheiner, [26] who from the motions of the Faculae, and the Maculae of the Sun, has found for astronomy and philosophy celestial lights of such noble, rare and authentic verity, for example, the double motion of the sun, that in the fashion of a top, firmly revolves around itself, and around the poles of its axis that move in two circles contemporaneously, ordinately curving it and causing the various appearances that the spots make on it. And beyond the very reasonable conjectures drawn from the conception, birth, increase, the occasional recurrence and absence of

---

22 **Velleius Paterculus, *Historia* 1**, 5: *Neque ante illum quem imitaretur, neque post illum, qui eum imitari posset inventus est.*
23 **Manilius, *Astronomica* 1**. 413/5:
> *- Mari quod prima cucurrit*
> *Emeritum magnis mundum tenet acta procellis, (ante periclis)*
> *Servando Dea facta Deos.*
[24] The Lincean, of Rome, a prestigious scientific society of great distinction.
25 **Ovid, *Met.*,** 1.720/1:
> *Arge jaces: quodque in tot lumina lumen habebas*
> *Extinctum est, centumque oculos nox occupat una.*
26 (1575-1650), German Jesuit, physicist, astronomer, rival of Galileo, author of *Rosa Ursina, sive Sol* (Bracciano, 1630) on sunspots.

the spots, he has defined the substance and nature of the sun itself—and so enriched the world with the loftiest discoveries, that if every century brought forth as much, it would take few for astronomy to become absolute mistress of all the Heavens, as in our day geography has become of nearly all the earth.[27] With Pliny, I say: "*Your powerful Wits have made you interpreters of the Heavens; you can read in the book of nature, and find themes that put you above gods and men.*"[28] Like that ancient Methon, who left carved on a column as a legacy to posterity the outlines in correct proportion of the changing course of the sun, in your name, Great Worthies, as the reward of eternal honor should be erected statues with golden tongues and underneath this inscription, **Ob divinas praedictiones**. (*For your divine prognostications.*)[29] Worthies; to whom Heaven should be given, not as once the Emperor Charles the Fifth gave the stars of the Southern Cross painted on canvas to Oviedo, the historian of the deeds of America, but Heaven itself, as a reward and her stars as a crown. And well do they deserve them since,

> *They moved our eyes to the distant stars*
> *And enlightened space with their ingenious Wit.*[30]

I have commemorated only these two; not to ignore all of them, for I could not speak of all of them. Only for us who come afterthem, I should remember with Seneca: "*Let us act like good fathers of our family: We should increase what we have received. This patrimony should pass greater from me to my descendants. There remains good work to be done. And much will remain, nor will anyone born after a hundred centuries be deprived of the chance to add to it.*" [31]

With this I do not mean to say that to become inventors of new things; we must make ourselves the masters of novelties,

---

[27] Despite his reluctance to do without so many of pseudo-scientific misconceptions, Bartoli affirms scientific progress as the mandate of his age.

28 **Pliny, 2.12.**55: *Macti ingenio este coeli Interpretes, rerumque naturae capaces: argumenti repertores, quo Deos, Hominesque vicistis.*

29 **Pliny, 7.37.** Not Methon, the statue of the Chaldean astrologer Berosus in Athens. On Methon, Vitruvius, *De Architectura*, 8.1.

30 **Ovid, Fasti** 1.305/6:
> *Admovere oculis distantia sydera nostris*
> *Aethereaque Ingenio supposuere suo.*

31 **Seneca, Letter 64.**7: *Agamus bonum patrem familiae: Faciamus ampliora quae accipimus. Major ista haereditas a me ad Posteros transeat. Multum ad huc restat operis; Multumque restabit, nec ulli nato post mille secula praecluditur occasio aliquid adhuc adijciendi.*

wandering without reason (especially in things that go beyond the purely natural) from those paths, trodden already for so many ages by the foremost Wits of the world holding in reserve for those who cross their confines, be it ruin or recrimination. To play the role of Diogenes pushing against the currents of all men, as if we alone were the sages, we alone were fishing at the bottom of the well of Heraclitus (Democritus) to pull up the truth.[32] To judge ourselves the Sun of the Wits of the world, not by the light of our greater knowledge of the truth, but by setting ourselves against the direction of the entire world. This is bragging as a boast what Apollo said by way of advice to his son Phaeton:

> *I head out in the reverse direction that undid others, but not me,*
> *With its impetus, as I ride against the fast-moving globe.*[33]

In his words we ought to hear that without danger of falling, we may not stray from the set pathways which are coursed by the Chariot of Light and marked with visible and explicit signs:

> *Here is the way: the wheels' clear markings you can see.*[34]

1. That the earth turns below the ecliptic in its yearly course, and every day's movement turns it from west to east; 2. That the moon, nay, all the planets, are habitable lands and have inhabitants of different natures living there; 3. That the universe is of infinite size, and in its immense spaces contains innumerable worlds, etc. These are opinions, that some moderns have fondly raised from their graves, calling them from the tombs; in the first instance, of Cleanthes and Phylolaus; in the second, of Pythagoras and of Heraclitus; in the third of Democritus and Methrodorus with whom for so many centuries they lay dead and buried in silence and oblivion.

This is not to enrich the world with new cognitions, but with old errors. It is not to make oneself the teacher of those to come, but the disciple of those long gone. The mercy of it is that these dreams of theirs, which the world did not receive with its eyes closed, will continue to sleep underground along with those of ours in their sepulchres.

---

32 *"Of the truth we know nothing, for the truth is in a well."* Laertius, *Democritus*, 9.72.
33 **Ovid, *Met.*, 2; 72/3:**
> *Nitor in adversum, neque me, qui caetera, vinci*
> *Impetus: et rapido contrarius evehor orbi.*
34 **Ovid, *Met.*, 2.133:**
> *Hac sit iter: manifesta rotae vestigia cernes.*

## 5.3 *How We May Steal from the Writings of Others in Good Conscience and With Praise*

But I see that I have set for myself too difficult an enterprise. I have been trying to shift our thoughts away from stealing by stealth from others, emphasizing our responsibility to enrich Letters with new contributions and the benefits we accrue by doing so. Perhaps it would be better for me to show how to steal in good conscience, without the need for restitution and with the accrual of merit.

Not all the thefts of Light taken off the wheels of the chariot of the Sun are punishable. Some (if I am not mistaken) are found in the books of the most famous Wits where the truth shines and triumphs. So not all offenders are condemned to the cliffs of the Caucasus and to the eagle of Prometheus. There can be impunity in taking, only we cannot take as the Moon does when it comes nearest to the Sun absorbing all its light in a perfect new moon and selfishly eclipsing it. Rather as one who, as in a glass of pure crystal, receives a ray of sun and does not lessen its brilliance, but rather by reflecting it back, intensifies its splendor. Just so, bees, equally ingenious and discreet,

*Busily delve among the resplendent white lilies.*[1]

So innocent is their rapine that without taking away from their odor, without violating their beauty, without disturbing the pistils of their flowers, with great abandon they gather wax and honey for themselves and for others.

The first way to take commendably is to imitate judiciously. If you are not a giant of great height, climb to the top of a high tower and from there learn the best roads and the safest way. If you don't have a theatre of your own ideas and of ideas well thought out in your head, then in line with the origins of painting in its simplest beginnings, take the outlines of the shadows of distinct and clear figures and compose your work upon these models.

When she was alive, Phrine, the Venus of Athens, as immodest as she was beautiful, served as the model for painters.[2] They took the proportions and the features of her face to portray, as best they could, the most beautiful and hence, the most godlike, Venuses in their

---

1 *Aeneid* 6.708/9: *Candida circum Lilia funduntur.*
2 **Clement of Alexandria, *Protrepticon*,** 4.48. The model for the Venus of Cnidos by Praxiteles. See Pliny, 34.19.

paintings. Just to see her was to learn. She served not so much as a model for the copies they were drawing of her, but as a shape of perfection for the idea they had in mind of a perfect proportion of parts, of the tempera of colors, and of poses from life. In such wise the compositions of the great masters of Letters stand before the mind of Wit. Studied with attention they imprint on the mind, little by little, a noble idea of like eloquence. Experience shows that a regular and attentive reader of works of noble sentiment and lofty style, as if inebriated by the same spirits, will seem incapable of expressing himself in any way other than nobly.[3] This happened to the nightingales that built their nests on the tomb of Orpheus— as if, from the ashes of that great musician and poet, they had also taken his spirit.[4] They proved more greatly inspired and gifted singers compared to the rest, heavenly sirens next to rustic buskers.

Such careful reading of the learned labors of others will stamp the mind with their manner of expression. It may well be that from this are born those mysterious miracles of imaginative power, such as we have seen in peasant mothers with plebian faces and unshapely bodies who bear children of angelic visages and features (like the lovely narcissus, a flower born of the homely onion) and this thanks to the perfect beauty engendered in their tender unborn babies by the expectant mothers while they frequently stood before and admired paintings of the most beautiful and exquisitely drawn faces.

Nor, even though the authors are superior and our Wits inferior, do we miss the benefits of looking at them and imitating them to make us more like them. The eagle before she thrusts her baby chicks from the nest, will fly in great circles and turn over and around them, poking them sometimes with her wings and pushing them to fly. The eaglets have no real heart to follow their mother above the clouds where one flap of their wings will take them, yet they are still moved to leave the nest and jump into flight and try out their wings on their own. It is natural for us to keep at what we like, especially, if the genius of our nature seconds the choice of our will. In this case, either our efforts become less strenuous or, as the toil of the work is subsumed in our enjoyment of what we are doing, the tedium disappears.

As we observe before us the sublime flights of congenial Wits, it will not only rouse and incite our desire to imitate them, but also

3 The gist of classical pedagogy: education by imitation.
4 Pausanias, *Description of Greece, Boeotia*, 9.30.

invigorate our thoughts, and strengthen our minds. The mind will feel more capable of things that without such a vision it would never imagine. And if we don't manage to reach Heaven and soar above the stars, at least we may rise above earth and leave the nest. We may not succeed in expressing with the adequate measure of eloquence the marvelous flights of the model we took to imitate. Nevertheless, we may at least follow the sunflower, rooted in place but mobile in its flower, that continuously looking at the sun, learns how to copy in its little gyre that ample circle which it draws from one horizon to another.

But to profit from the writings of others only by imitation is too paltry a benefit in the judgement of Quintilian, who treats extensively of this matter.[5] The second type of theft, which is not only lawful but laudable, is to take what we please from others, but making it better with what we have of our own in such a way that it is no longer the same. A diamond that is pierced to its core in this manner, by a single ray of light, reflects a beauty so much greater, as if it were painted with a thousand changing colors—the sun itself is not so glorious, and the stars are outdone. Such theft, is it not that craft of taking some fragile sea foam to fertilize it with the heavenly seed of one's Wit? From what was base material of no value is born nothing less than the goddess Venus, forming a composition of extraordinary beauty.

The famous work of Phidias, Olympic Jupiter, a wonder of sculpture, and of the world, was made of whitest ivory. But the elephants could not therefore boast of that divine masterpiece as theirs, nor indict the sculptor for the theft of the beauty for which the work was so famous. The perfect proportion of the parts, the majestic features of the divine visage and whatever else made that statue unique in the world for its beauty and value, all came from the Wit of the sculptor, not from the merit of the elephant. Tertullian says, *"The hand of Phidias wrought a statue of Olympian Jupiter of ivory and it was adored. But it was not due to the ungainly tusk of the animal, but to the supreme artist of the age, not because of the elephant, but because of Phidias."* [6] Someone who in this way takes rough and formless blocks to work them into statues, cheap pieces of glass to change them into diamonds, drops of simple dew to make them pearls, he is no thief, but an artist. He is not indebted to

---

5 **Quintilian,** *Institutiones. Oratoria,* **10.3.**
6 **Tertullian,** *De resurrectione carnis,* **6**: *Phidiae manus Jovem Olympum ex ebore molitur, et adoratur. Nec jam bestiae, et quidem insulsissia dens est, sed summum saeculi Numen. Non quia Elephantus, sed quia Phydias tantus.*

others for the material, but the material is obliged to him for the honor of such a noble creation.

But we have a far livelier demonstration of this in the artifices of the famous fountains of Rome, of Tivoli, of Frascati, where the waters become playful in their constraints, and ingenious in their obedience as they change into more shapes than the Proteus of the poets.[7]

From the slime and rugged stone of vast niches they drip, drop by drop, into the finest rain, better than what the clouds distill. They imitate, as it were, the winds issuing out of the cave of Aeolus, the South with moist airs, Zephyrus with pleasing gales, Boreas with blustering and cold blasts. They spread so subtly and fan out so evenly that they seem transparent veils flung in the air. They divide into little drops and form themselves, as it were, into a dewy cloud which against the sun becomes a rainbow painting its colors to perfection. With their movements, they bring dead statues to life and cast them in changing poses. They squirt furtively from the ground and spring and sport in the air with high spirits. They sob, with grief; they roar, with fury; they sing, with delight. They not only bring back to the world the hydraulic organs that Tertullian calls **Portentosissimam Archimedis munificentiam** (*The most impressive munificence of Archimedes*),[8] but in their murmurs and trills, elaborate and artful passages, divisions and changes of melodious voices, they make a lifelike imitation of the nightingales; as if from their mouths it was not "*the spirit breathing in the torment of the waters,*"[9] that was singing, but the sirens themselves nymphs of the water. By works of such ingenious and admirable contrivance we take waters of an ordinary source, before art elevated them from their native lowliness to nobler use by transfusing almost souls and Wit inside them, waters meandering humbly on the ground, along muddy banks, used merely to slake the thirst of animals, whereas now they are the delights of princes and the glory of gardens. Is this not, through craft, to elevate the material by working it and making it our own? One who steals does much the same. Let him bury his theft of the matter in the art of working it so that, in what he has added of his own, what came from another is altogether lost.

---

7 An introduction to frame the descriptive word painting, or ecphrasis, of the Tivoli fountains that follows.
8 **Tertullian,** *De resurrectione carnis,* **6** (*De anima,* 14.4).
9 *Ibidem.* (*De anima,* 14.4): *Spiritus qui illic de tormento aquae anhelat.*

But this kind of improvement, when things are no longer what they were before and become ours, is well understood and misused by those able, indeed, to change, but not to improve. This makes them more to be condemned for the greater misdeed of ruining what is beautiful and disfiguring the finesse of a work of art, than just stealing one. To evade the infamy of thieves, they become homicides, taking the life from all the beauty they take as they take the whole apart and mess up the pieces with so disheartening a heartlessness that in a few strokes of the pen, they transform a Helen into a Hecuba and an Achilles into a Thyrsites. They do to others' works, unintentionally, what the Athenians did as retribution to the three hundred brass statues of the famous Demetrius.[10] For the shame and infamy of his name they smashed them to pieces and cast them into vessels of the vilest and most sordid use.[11] The wand of Circe and the pen of such hacks test each other's strength; the pen, through ignorance, transforms beautiful creations into the most horrid monsters, while the wand, through magic, can change the bravest knights into sordid animals. Similar treatment was given to the verses of an excellent poet by an illiterate comedian. He would imitate them with his poses and with what Cassiodorus calls the silent and loquacious speech of the hands, the age-old contrivance of mimics.[12] But he expressed so awkwardly by his gestures what the poetry had conveyed by its words that in the twol fables of Niobe and of Daphne, who suffer their metamorphoses, the first into a stone, the second into a tree, as Niobe he became a tree, and as Daphne a stone:

*The actor Memphis mixed Niobe with Daphne*
*His Niobe was wooden like Daphne, his Daphne was stone like Niobe.*[13]

In stealing from others, we should use that care and reverence with which the eagle snatched up and carried the boy of Ida, Ganymede, into Heaven, not hurting him with his talons or tearing his garments. Leochares captured this in bronze with judgment and art, *"He knew it was Ganymede he was snatching, and not to hurt him, sparing even*

---

10 Demetrius of Phalerus, Cf. Laertius, *Demetrius*, 5.75.
11 Chamber pots.
12 Cassiodorus, *Variae* 1.20; 5.4.
13 ***Epigraphia Graeca***:
*Saltavit Nioben, saltavit Daphnida Memphis*
*Ligneus ut Daphnen, saxeus ut Nioben.*

*his clothing with his claws.*[14] Yet this won't do, for discretion in robbing mitigates but does not remove the crime of theft. But how much worse is it to deform, to confuse, to mangle others' works in order to make them ours? Amnd they do become truly ours, namely ill-made, like that Fidentinus, of whom Martial said,

> *Your delivery of my words, Fidentinus, is a travesty.*
> *Your acting is so bad, they become entirely yours.*[15]

In the beautification of a work, as it were, by altering it with a more noble quality, the things can be happily changed (as I have said, this is innocent and commendable theft). To this I add in the last place the increase of the quantity, where a large body is formed from a little seed or a tree from a tiny branch.

Many things can issue from the pens of good writers that are said sometimes only as incidental matters, just pointed to with a finger. The reader's eye may inattentively glance over them. Yet they are a shorthand pregnant, now with lofty, now with noteworthy ideas and someone who knows how to unravel what they contain in a ball can make a lot out of nothing, take it for himself and make it all his own.

Of all the stars it has, Heaven has allotted their proper spheres to no more than seven and allowed them the space to wander through that liquid and transparent air that stretches from here below out to the firmament.[16] But if it had assigned proper cycles and spheres to every one of them, the cosmos with only seven spheres and still so vast, what would it do, had it separated so many thousands of stars into their proper circles, and corresponding spheres? The same thing is true for the best writers in putting together their books. To some defined themes they give space, and as it were, a sphere and cycle,

---

14 **Pliny, 34**.19: *Sentientem quid rapiat in Ganymede, et cui ferat; parcentem unguibus etiam pervestem.* See Martial, 1.7. The boy of Ida is valued by Bartoli perhaps more as cupbearer to Zeus, along with Hebe, than as the god's lover boy. Damon, the fair shepherd, summons the moody Thyrsis, in the poet Bartoli's *Pastorale Invito a cantare, Saggio di poesie morali*, 23/27, the dialogue of two rustics harmonizing, after the idealized shepherd couples of Virgil's *Eclogues*.
15 **Martial, *Epigrams* 1.38**:
> *Quem recitas meus est, ô Fidentine, libellus*
> *Sed male cum recitas incipit esse tuus.*
[16] Bartoli does without the crystalline spheres but keeps the seven planets circling the earth of Ptolemy: Moon, Mercury Venus, Sun, Mars, Jupiter, Saturn.

giving them as ample treatment as they intend. But they also will allow themselves to fire off here and there what I would describe as the fixed stars of their superior thoughts and marvelous insights, enough to fill a whole sky, if they find the mind and intelligence capable of developing them satisfactorily. He who steals from others after this fashion is the talented thief who takes little, adds much and makes it all his own. And this without injury to the author from whom he takes a spark to make a sun. It is to his credit that from a small abandoned seed he has grown a great tree. And it is to his great honor, for it is the character of a great Wit to develop from the few notes of some unadorned words the double counterpoints of a major composition. This means, from the simple footprint left by Hercules, being able to formulate, as Pythagoras did, the massive shape of his entire body, adjusted and perfectly proportioned in all its parts.[17]

---

17 Gellius, 1.1, "*Ex pede Herculem.*"

# 6          *LASCIVIOUSNESS*

## 6.1    *Unworthy Profession of Lascivious Poetry*

From his cave in Bethlehem that brave lion, Saint Jerome, made the roar of his voice sound throughout the world, intimidating heresy and terrifying vice. Nor did he fail to take the licentious lust of poets to task. They disguised the stars with lewd configurations and for this invidious slander they were a thousand times more criminal than the giants of Phlegra, for they hurled against the Heavens not batteries of boulders, but the crudest crimes of earth. *"We should not follow the fables of the poets, ridiculous and misleading lies which bring infamy to Heaven and grant a place among the constellations to heroes for their rapes."*[1]

To tell the truth, worthy of the ire of Heaven, and Earth are such,

*Whose poems about the heavens are nothing but fables.*[2]

The lustful escapades of Jupiter, were they not sufficiently clear to the world in other lights, not to shine among the stars? Was it not enough for them to be world famous in marble statues, in bronzes, in paintings, in the applause of the public stage, that they should also be given the Heavens as their theater, the stars as their characters, and the world as their audience? How then could they make you believe that Jupiter from on high would fire his thunderbolts against the earth for being guilty of those vices that had their textbook in the Heavens? Adulterous Calisto has the stars around the pole and she does double service as guide, for she navigates at sea, and shipwrecks on land.[3] While shining from above, her lesson to chaste women points to lewd indulgence, if a Jupiter can pay for adultery with the stars,

*Thus, Ariadne is added to the stars of Heaven,*
*She is awarded this prize of the dark,*
*Honored as strumpet to illuminate the celestial axis.*[4]

---

1 **Jerome, *On Amos*, 5**: *Non debemus sequi fabulas Poetarum, ridicula, ac portentosa mendacia, quibus etiam coelum infamare conantur, et mercedem stupori inter sydera collocare.*
2 **Manilius**, Astronomica 2.57: *Quorum carminibus nihil est, nisi fabula coelum.*
3 Jealous Juno made her a bear and she became the constellation, Ursa Major, turning around Polaris, rhe North Star, in Ursa Minor.
4 Prudentius, *Against Symmachus,* 1.142:

From such constellations of obscenity, what influences, if not lascivious, can descend to earth?

Archytas had to say a dirty word in a public speech. As it came to his lips, it seemed so distasteful to his tongue that, not to pronounce it, he took for his tongue a piece of coal as more suitable to material for burning and more blotting it out than writing it on a wall, he got it across. Oh! The golden tongues of the stars. As the night charms all the world to silence, to hear what they have to say, what are their instructions? They publicize with the language of light in Heaven misdeeds that on earth, for shame, search the cover of darkness.

If it were only the ancient poetry of the pagans so tainted by this and not outdone by the modern poetry of Christians! It is a victory won not by painting the stars with imagined configurations of bawdy stories, but by printing it in books, and worse, conspiring to seer into the mind the lewd acts themselves, so effectively, or rather, so harmfully.

The poetry of these times has no lack of its Ovids. They favor Mount Ida over Parnassus, myrtles over laurels, turtle doves over swans, Cupid over Apollo and transform the virgin Muses into public strumpets. For immoral poets such as these, an Augustus as their Mecaenas is in order, nor should the snows of Scythia, and the ice of Pontus be withheld to cool their overheated loves. Nowadays, this weakness is so prevalent that the occupation of lasciviousness springs almost directly from the call to be a poet. Antisthenes gave the measure of Ismenia the actor with an analogous conclusion, *"If you are a good performer, you must, therefore, be a bad man."*[5]

Wouldn't one have sworn that poetry in going from the pagans to Christians would act as Venus allegedly did in Sparta? After crossing the river Eurotas for her to enter their state, they made her break her mirror, remove her baubles, and discard her whorish garb.[6] And did she not only dress modestly, but even assume the soldier's armor and air, looking more like a warring Pallas, than a seductive Venus? Of course. But things are so far gone that the ability to write obscenity, once punished by exile, is now rewarded with honor and prizes. The

---

*Sic (Mox) Ariadnaeus stellis Coelestibus ignis*
*Additur. Hoc pretium noctis persolvit. Honore*
*Liber, ut aethereum meretrix illuminet axem.*
5 Plutarch, *Pericles*, 1: *Si bonus Tibicen est, ergo, malus homo est.*
6 Plutarch, *On Sparta.*

modern Orpheuses are raised to high Heaven and among the stars are worshipped the lyres that have opened up hell, not to bring back an imprisoned Eurydice, but to conduct a host of innocents there. Their books travel throughout earth and spread through every clime. They are citizens in every country and have been diligently translated to speak in every tongue. They fear there might still persist a part of the virgin world, unless they sow the whole world with their lustful impulses.

The titles of the great appear on the front of these books, dedicated to them by the authors and they circulate more freely under the aegis of eminent protection so that those who should be the censors are often enough the protectors of immorality, using their names and dignity for the worst ends, the way the wild warriors of Scythia, while engaging their lust inside their chariots, from outside, *"They hang their quiver from the harness as a sign not to interfere, not to be caught blushing in their armor."*[7]

Now let Hippocrates make loud complaint against the public laws that by fixing no punishment for ignorant doctors gave them the license to kill.[8] As that other writer said, *"They learn their art at our mortal peril, and finish off their patients with their operations. A doctor is free to commit homicide with complete impunity."* What can one say when a public distiller of poisons that become even worse for tasting even better, is not made to pay with his head, but crowned with honor.[10]

But if, after the fashion of Lucian who made us listen in anger and regret to the infamous tongue of his professional liar, the Pseudologist, and hear the unseemly uses to which he put it,[11] the murderous pens of so many lascivious writers could make the list of the sordid acts, one by one, they incited in the hearts of those over-avid readers of their poisonous writings, would there be anyone at all

---

7 **Tertullian,** *Against Marcellus,* **1.2:** *Suspendunt de jugo pharetras indices, ne quis intercedat: Ita nec armis erubescunt.*
8 Hippocrates, *Corpus.* The Oath enjoins "to abstain from doing harm and not to administer poison." Modern version; First, do no harm, *"primum, non nocere."*
9 **Pliny, 19.2** (29.2): *Discunt enim periculis nostris, et experimenta per mortes agunt. Medicoque tantùm hominum occidisse impunitas summa est.*
10 A pointed reference to Giambattista Marino, (1569-1625). His sexually explicit *Adone* (1623) is dedicated to Louis XIII who appointed the Neapolitan poet laureate of France in 1615.
11 **Lucian,** *The Pseudologist* (*The Ignorant Book Collector*).

left to shower them with generous rewards, to honor them with praises exclusively awarded to achievements of superhuman excellence?

Less criminal than these was even that viciously lewd Hostius who used mirrors to reflect the sight of abominable activities, *"They showed him things that the dark of night is not black enough to keep hidden."*[12] But this was just to show to himself, **sibi ostentabat.** Poisonous though they be, the dragons who stay in their underground lares are not considered to be so threatening that we go to hunt them out and slay them. But when they come outside to contaminate the air with their breath, no one who can slay them, will want them alive. Some set before the eyes of all the world, *"The things that darkest night is not black enough to keep hidden,"* with the damage even compounded when the pen that draws such things is finely skilled and artistically gifted. In the ancient painting of the Greeks bodies were portrayed, **Nihil velando** (*hiding nothing*),[13] and for those who continue to do so there can be no adequate punishment. So, when honors and awards are given for such things, does not this constitute a spectacular display of the stupidity, to be less harsh and not to say with greater truth, the malevolence, of mankind?

It is considered infamous for a man to take on the clothes and the traits of a woman. So, for a man to assume not just the fittings, but the trade of an old whore, pimping every sort of filthy lasciviousness, is this to be considered honorable? Is such a life worthy of statues, and laurels?

## 6.2    *Guilty Excuses of Indecent Poets.*

But let us hear the excuses in defense of their impure books, proffered by those who the fire of Cupid's torch has ignited into a frenzy that makes them more madmen than poets. Excuse number one:

That festive and merry poems (thus, *"For them all impurity is accounted urbanity)*[1] entertain by the delight of fables and by the

---

12 **Seneca, *QN*** 1.16.6: *ea sibi ostentabat, quibus abscondendis nulla satis alta nox est.*
13 **Pliny, 34.5.**

1 **Minutius Felix, *Octavius*,** 28: *Apud eos tota impuritas (impudicitia) vocatur urbanitas.*

sweetness of verse with thoughts of love that only arouse the reader's thoughts, so that the pleasure they give as one reads is all for the mind's imagination and not sensual.

For my rejoinder I call your attention first to the case of two unfortunate sisters. They were to first to read a famous tragicomedy of this kind, recently published in book form.[2] And they became such experts in lewdness that soon they were giving lessons and set up their home as a bawdy house and themselves as courtesans. Then there were many married women who heard this same pastoral on stage (and this has become an authenticated experience of long standing). When they arrived, they were chaste; when they departed they were chaste no longer. They took to practicing that loose license of loving whomever pleased them (as they heard in the play's precepts and saw in its examples). When their infidelity was discovered, they were murdered with their lovers, so from the licentious fictions of a tragicomedy, they took the true outcome of a tragedy. But through all of Europe and the whole world, as far as these books have gone, how many dramatic scene changes, how many tearful catastrophes have they caused? They had souls for the glory of virginal virtue and pristine purity in no way inferior to the angels. But after they drank from the golden cup of licentious poetry its bewitchment and its poison, for ever after they preserved in the guise of humans the morals of beasts. In the first reading they lost the virginity of their eyes and, as one whose name I know not, said in Plutarch of the dissolute: *"They turned their virgin pupils into whoring eyes."*[3] Next, their virgin souls were gone and after that, their flesh— as if it had lost its salt— went to rot

Saint Augustine complains of the progenitor of poetry's lies, Homer. Because he portrayed the gods— some as homicides, some as thieves, some as adulterers— such sins became identified as a property of the divine and were foisted on the world by him unintentionally: *"It was made to seem that anyone who did such things was not imitating humanity's failings, but the celestial gods."*[4] But our own, writers who put their tongues in the mouths of poetic figures, say that nature is too imperfect, being

---

2 Giambattista Guarini, *Il Pastor fido* (Venice, 1590; 1602).
3 **Plutarch**, *Moralia, De vitioso pudore*, 1: *Verterunt pupillas virgines in meretrices.*
4 **Augustine, *Confessions*, 1.16:** *Quisquis ea fecisset, non homines perditos, sed coelestes Deos videbatur imitatus.*

so susceptible to the pleasures of love.[5] If the law forbids the procurement of them, then too hard and unjust is such a law that opposes nature. To impugn the steadfast virtue of virgins they will remind them that beauty fades with the years and with beauty gone, are gone the allurements that will find them suitors, that wizened face will pine in vain for what fair youth refused; that for such a short life only one love will not do; that virtue is only the art of appearing virtuous, etc. Such pestilential doctrines, these, are poisons squeezed from the Wit, poured by the hand and spread from the pen of a Christian who, as Tertullian says, *"is born to have but one wife"*[6] *"and he may engage in the cupidity of procreation with one woman, or else with none,"*[7] in the words of Minutius Felix. What else are they doing but making it easier to sin by trying to argue that it is due more to the weakness, not to say the law, of nature, than to the failure of the will? Youth wants it, example teaches it, chance argues it, frailness excuses it, circumspection is all it takes to conceal it. Is such talk just the pleasant pastime of one's thoughts, sparking mere loves, platonic and theoretical, not Epicurean amours? What kind of scoundrel could utter such things? If it were not from Aelius Verus, with his idolatry for Ovid's *Ars Amatoria, (The Art of Love)*,[8] then it could only come from an animal schooled in Letters and skilled in poetry.

It is no good saying that such lessons and examples are offered by fictional characters. Persuasion derives not from the nature of the advocate, but from his argument, not from the speaker, but from the. issue. And what else are the figures of poetry, if they are not like mountain caverns ringing out echoes? The voice is the author's; while others can speak it, as a hand does the writing, while the paper serves to show it. Love, who took the form of Aeneas' son, Ascanius, ignited the passion of the unhappy queen, Dido, no less than had he appeared as Cupid in his true garb and not in disguise.

If we defer to experience, the great teacher of truth, for proof, she confirms the daily rule that while we are reading about the loves of other people, we are beginning to learn about our own. Compassion

---

5 *"s'ei piace, lice"*: Giovanni Battista Guarini (1538-1612), *Il pastor fido*, Act.3, scene 4. The celebrated and popular, *Faithful Shepherd*, quoted anonymously by Bartoli earlier and censured here.
6 Tertullian, *Apologeticus*, 46.10: *Qui soli uxori suae masculus nascitur.*
7 **Minutius Felix, *Octavius*,** 31: *et cupiditate procreandi aut unam scit, aut nullam.*
8 Aelius Verus, *Historia Augusta*, 5.9.

for the lovelorn, unhappily spurned, will ease the way for us to surrender in like cases. What we condemn in fictional characters as cruelty and hard-heartedness to a lover, will make us soft-hearted in similar situations. When the kindling is good and ready for the flint, all it takes is the spark of an encounter; of a hello, of a look, to light the fire.

Our own hearts melt in the heat of others' flames. We stamp our souls with the seal of the emotions felt by fictional characters. More than one Augustine has wept real tears for the poetic heartbreak of Dido in her abandonment.[9] Such are the usual responses that every day poetry engenders in its scenes, in its books. And though at times we may not understand why we fall in love with someone else's love, we are in love with something unknown they have about them, just like that foolish boy in the fable, who really fell in love with an unreal image:

*"He doesn't know what he is looking at, but what he sees stirs his passion."*[10]

I feel the shame with Clement of Alexandria of mentioning here the two Venuses, of Cyprus, and of Cnidos, the first made of ivory and the other of marble, lifeless statues in themselves, but for the lurid fantasies of others, far too alive. Just let me attach the epiphonema of his parting comment and apply to poetry what he said about sculpting such lascivious statues of nudes, *"So effective was this art in seducing men caught up in the pleasures of love and sending them to hell!"*[11]

Another defense of lascivious compositions: That such poems have nothing bad about them but their bark. These are the artifices of allegory that mask meanings of the purest moral philosophy, flavoring them with the honey of their fabulous adventures to make their nourishment more palatable. The ancient custom, framed in its laws by Crete, was for children to receive instruction by means of music. And a great part of God's law was put into verse by David, in the poems of the Psalms, *"So that while the grace of the poetry enchanted the ear the lessons of the divine word might likewise be instilled,"*[12] as St. Augustine said. So might their poems be prefaced by quoting Dante's tercet:

---

9 **Augustine, *Confessions*, 1. 13.**
10 Narcissus in **Ovid, *Met.*,** 3: *Quid videat nescit, sed quod videt uritur illo.*
11 **Clement of Alexandria, *Protrepticon to the Pagans*.** 5: *Tantum ars valuit ad decipiendum, quae homines amori deditos illexit in barathrum.*
12 **Augustine, *On Psalm* 2.**

*Ye souls endowed with sound intelligence,*
*Observe the hidden lessons that do lie*
*Veiled up in their mysterious poetry.*[13]

Consequently, the poets, for those who inspect them closely are very *"Philosophers under the name of poets, who by their art have been successful in making the people fully prepared for the hardest lessons."*[14]

Now have you ever in your life heard a fiction more poetic, a lie more barefaced than this? The destroyers of morality will be taken for its very preceptors.

*And they act like priests as they write like beasts.*[15]

Such a lie served Pompey well. In the theater he was building he had a small chapel dedicated to Venus built for the lewdest acts, so they would not tear the whole thing down on him. *"Making her by dedication the patroness for the whole theatre, he said, so that the name of the goddess was given to temple of those damnable and those damned while it foiled by superstition the imposition of the normal strictures."* [16] But nowadays the world is not so bereft of sense, not to recognize that certain allegories, applied by others (with their leave) to this poetry are allegories so far-fetched that they don't cover up the shameful things they show the reader. Such allegories were not in the design of the original poem and the author never gave them the slightest thought. They are chimeras— not allegories— useless attempts on the part of those would try to translate senseless lusts into meaningful mysteries.

The *Tablet of Cebes* is something quite distinct and requires the thread of an old interpreter to unravel its labyrinthine ways.[17] The stranger who admits he does not understand the enigmas of the sphinx will need him to avoid death where he was expecting profit. Something quite different are these modern poems. They take a sphinx to

---

13 **Dante**, *Inferno* 9. 61-63*: O voi ch'avete gl'intelletti sani*
 *Mirate la dottrina che s'asconde*
 *Sotto il velame de li versi strani.*
14 **Maximus of Tyre, *Sermon* 29**: *Philosophos, nomine poëtas, qui invidiosam rem ad eam artem perduxerunt, quae maximè populum demulceat.*
15 Juvenal, *Satire* 2.3:
 *Et simulant Curios cum Bacchanalia scribant.*
16 **Tertullian, *De spectaculis***: *Quasi morum lanienam, cui subijcimus, inquit, gradus spectaculorum. Ita damnatum, et damnandum opus templi titulo praetexuit, ac disciplinam superstitione delusit.*
17 Cebes (5 century BC) The Tablet attributed to him (1rst century AD) is the Greek *Pilgrim's Progress.*

elaborate their enigma, more than they need an Oedipus to interpret them.

Yet, I will not deny that there were some ancients who diverted the eyes of the crowd from the mysteries of their theology by concealing, like the treasure within Silenus, under the cover of their myths, the things they thought were true. Nothing remains of the mysteries of the Egyptian sages, but their images--- bats, monkeys, owls--- once learned hieroglyphics which have become today the forlorn survivors left on the ancient pyramids. Otherwise, as to the ancient theology of the Gentiles, nothing is left in the memory of the world but the adulteries, the abductions, the murders of the gods; images too degraded to use for explaining through them mysteries of divinity. But the poets of today have no reason for this, nor give it any thought. And if they had, they would be no less temerarious than wicked, by means diametrically opposed to their proposition, namely, to inculcate moral behavior with lewd fables that are more likely to corrupt the morals of the virtuous. This would be (as says Nazianzen the Theologian): *"To head to shore through the rocky shoals."*[18] Therefore, it is impossible to attempt to dress wolves as shepherds, or the lascivious poets as moral philosophers.

The third defense: They will say their writings mean no harm to others, and are only pursuing their own honor. That their books open with the declaration of Ausonius written in capital letters: *"If our entertainment is not pleasing, don't read it; if you do read it, then forget it; or if you don't forget it, ignore it."*[19]

In other words, he who falls must blame himself as weak—not the poet. He did not write the book or publish it to make the reader fall. Are the rocks at fault, if one made of glass goes crashing into them? If you can't handle a sword, don't carry one. If you're not a good sailor, don't plunge into water when a storm threatens. The reader must be like a bee, gathering his honey from inventive styles of writing by imitating their poetic expressions, not a spider, sucking the poison of lasciviousness. Even in Holy Scripture we read about the incest of Ammon, the adultery of David, the foul infamies of Sodom. The finger of God wrote them; nor are they to be condemned because

---

18 **Gregory Nazianzen,** *Oration* **3,** *against Julian: per scopulos ducere ad littus.*

19 **Ausonius,** *Preface,* **Cento** on Virgil: *Cui hic ludus noster non placet, ne legerit: aut cum legerit obliviscatur: aut non oblitus ignoscat.*

some may draw from them their sinful example, more relishing the deed than being chastened by the punishment. Therefore, if some debase their morals reading a book written only for the purpose of sharpening the Wit, this would be the fault, not of the innocent author, but of the unenlightened reader.

*What clever arguments human ignorance thinks it has!*[20] says Tertullian, in another such instance. Have you ever seen such sophistry, better couched in syllogisms? I was expecting them to try to persuade me by saying: What is not explicitly intended, cannot cause guilt, and the sin is no sin. They never make claims for the malice of the sin, but only for the pleasure or profit of the plot. Who taught them to say that they don't want it just because they say it, and all the while they conspire by every artful means to accomplish what, if their intentions were otherwise, others would not have perceived? If the goal of some poets were exactly this, to arouse, with the delight of fable and verse, impulses to lust in readers, could they have done it in a more accomplished and a more effective way? And when they were writing, were they either so stupid, or so blind, not to realize it? And is it possible to say that they did not want what by such impressive means they effectively were trying for? May it not be said about them, what Tertullian comments about women alluringly attired: "*What great danger are we? Are we liable for the lusts of others? Your beauty is his perdition, if he is aroused, you are the sword of his undoing.*"[21]

Even in the primitive ages of the Church certain Christians, before their baptism who had been sculptors by profession, wanted to be allowed, as before, to carve and sell statues of Jove, of Mars, of Venus. And in defense, they would say they intended no sin for others, but profit for themselves, to earn a living, not for others to fall, that their statues were worshipped was the evil of idolatry, not the fault of sculpture. We live according to the laws of Christ and work according to the precepts of our art, so how do we sin? Our poets, to defend themselves in a like situation would declare in their favor. But both the sculptors and their assistants Tertullian rightly condemns and indicts their hands as **Manus Idolorum matres**, (*Hands, the mothers of idols*)

---

20 **Tertulllian,** *On Spectacles*, 2.2: *Quam sapiens argumentatrix sibi videtur ignorantia humana.*
21 **Tertullian, *De culura foeminarum*, 1**: *Quid alteri periculo sumus? Quid alteri concupiscentiam importamus? Perit ille tua forma, si concupiscit; tua facta es gladius illi.*

and calls them **Manus praecidendas** (*Hands to be severed*). He made them guilty of sacrilege, the priests of idolatry, nay, more than priests. "*Since*, (said he), *through you the gods have their priests.*"[22]

## 6.3    *On the Good Use of Bad Books*

To prevent the Spartans from becoming inebriated Lycurgus, the lawgiver, in this case, the lawless, cut down and uprooted all the vines, but the remedy was much worse than the malady, as if, not to see our deformities, we were to pluck out our eyes. Rather, says Plutarch,[1] he should have had fountains for water near where the vines were growing, to correct Bacchus with the nymphs, a wild god with many sage spirits. The same applies to those who, in order to prevent all the evil that books do in the world, would remove from the world all of its books. These are extreme remedies which, as the father of medicine (Hippocrates) teaches, should only be used in extreme cases, when there remains no other remedy.

There are many books, in which, as in the head of the octopus (this is what Plutarch says of poetry), there is some good, and some bad. The danger is for those who are, as the ancient Cato, **helluo librorum** (*addicted to books*),[2] so hungry and indiscriminate, that they eat the bad with the good and later suffer the consequences. I give you leave, says Augustine,[3] to take your prey or booty from the books of bad writers, but in the same way the Israelites did in the houses of the Egyptians where they took the vessels made of gold, but not the idols, though they were made of gold. Sharpen, as the Hebrews did,[4] the scythe of your Wits on the whetstones of the Philistines, but do not sow in their fields and safeguard your harvest and your crops, for theirs have more chaff than wheat.

Someone with good eyes can find in the books of an ingenious author a great variety of things. Thus, once the astute Ulysses, dressed as a merchant, unpacked a trove of women's trinkets before the maidens of Skyros, with the happy ruse of a clever knight, in order to

---

22 **Tertullian, *De Idolatria*, 2**: *Cum per te Dii habeant Sacerdotes.*

1 **Plutarch, *De poetis audienda*** (*On reading the poets*).
2 Cicero, *De finibus*, 3.
3 **Augustine, *De doctrina Christiana*.**
4 **1 *Kings* 13.**

uncover Achilles and win him to the war. His fearful mother had hidden him among those maidens in women's dress.[5] Some of them ran to the mirrors, others to the brooches, to the bracelets, to the rings, but where did Achilles go? Coming into his true self, he took in hand a sword he found planted among the feminine trinkets. So, unmasked and, as it were, bested by Ulysses, he gave in and joined him as his companion in the Trojan War. Just so, when we read books, we should carry ourselves with a noble masculine spirit, disdaining and unaffected by whatever is womanish, so that we incline our hearts and set our hands only to the things worthy of us.

Even in this Alexander showed himself to be equal to his stature, a great man. When he was offered the lyre so often used by Paris to sing of the beauties of Helen and of his loves, he would hardly even look at it. Instead, he wanted the lyre that the great Achilles, in the cave of old Chiron, had played with his hands still stained with the blood of the lions and tigers he had just torn to pieces.

But it is not enough to read dangerous books with good intentions, if we haven't learned how to read them in such a circumspect and wary way, as one walking:

*On fires covered by a dangerous coat of ashes.*[6]

Saint Basil ingeniously explained it where he said,[7] we must never allow our minds, like the helm, to be in the hands of the author we are reading for him to twist us where he wants and steer us at his pleasure. Keep away from the string ray so that his poisonous icepick does not get you, otherwise he will tie you with it, render you stupid and senseless and take you prey. Herbs (pursues Basil) as sweet smelling as they are, may have hemlock and wolfbane mixed in. Flowers as lovely as they appear, may be hiding vipers and asps and should be picked with a hand more cautious, than curious. The more the danger is concealed, the more it must be feared. A laughing mouth and a charming face are the looks that mask betrayal.

Not only in the rings worn by Demosthenes, by Cleopatra, by Hannibal, but in books as well, the poison lies hidden under jewels, rings no less fatal for being so costly.[8] Wits, sublime as the Heavens, and star-studded with the wonderful and noble thoughts that shine in

---

5 Hyginus, *Fables* 96/8; Statius, *Achilleid* 1.675.
6 Horace, *Ode,* 2.1.3: *Per ignes suppositos cineri doloso.*
7 **Basil, *Homily of the utility from the book of Genesis*.**
8 **Pliny, 33.1.**

their writings, should never reassure us to the point that when we read them we forget to be cautious and wary. For it often happens with books, as with the Heavens, that the fairest stars form part of the most scandalous constellations. When we study them, we must heed the advice which the sun gave to Phaëton, to keep his eye always on the road and his hand fast on the rein, since even in travelling among the stars,

> *The way goes through danger and by the shapes of wild beasts.*[9]

To our purpose there is the alertness of the dogs of Egypt. They drink at the waters of Nile in haste, less keen to quench their thirst at a leisurely pace, than afraid to fill the hunger of the crocodiles. Also let me insert here the caution of the eagle, which, when it goes to hunt a poisonous dragon, does so,

> *Attacking from behind, so the beast can't turn to bite him.*[10]

All this applies when the books have good things and cautious readers can profit from them without damage. Otherwise, some deserve the words that Tertullian had to say about the ancient theatricals, *"The best part of them was the filthy language they so generously lathered up."*[11] And the rest are rife with poisonous doctrine and pestilential teachings. We ought not to wish (as the comic says), *"To be strangled on the branch of a beautiful tree."*[12] So what if this or that other lascivious poet had not written and published his poems? Without these could I ever be a poet, ever know how to be one? Shouldn't I use the words that Pompey said when he was sick? When his doctor put a turtle dove on his diet, adding (since it was out of season) that Lucullus could help him to one, as he kept them all year, said Pompey with a contemptuous look, *"What what? If Lucullus didn't not luxuriate, Pompey could not live?"*[13]

With books that can distill only poison and plague, we should do as Crates the Theban did with the money coming from the sale of his goods. He cast it into the sea and said, *"Away, I lose you, not to be lost through you."*[14] And just so Origen, and after him St. Ambrose, called

---

9 **Ovid, *Met.*, 2**.78: *Per insidias iter est, formasque ferarum.*
10 **Ovid, *Met.*, 4**.716.
> *Occupat adversum, ne saeva retorqueat ora.*
11 **Tertullian, *De spectaculis*. 7**: *Quorum summa gratia de spurcitia plurimum concinnata est.*
12 **Aristophanes, *Frogs*.**
13 Plutarch, *Pompey*: *Quid? Nisi Lucullus luxuriaret, non viveret Pompeius?*
14 Laertius, *Crates*, 6.87: *Ite: perdo vos, ne perdar à vobis.*

the harmful teachings of fertile Wits in the words of David, *divitias peccatorum*. *(The great riches of the ungodly)*.[15]

The songs of the sirens were quite sweet and melodious. The doldrums have no stronger hold on the ships they grasp in their jaws than the sirens with their enchantments, so that without dropping anchor or striking sail, they stood immobile, as if they had run aground,

> *The vessel plying the broad sea*
> *With the wind pushing the stern ahead*
> *Was halted by a single voice.*[16]

What then? After their siren's song came sleep, and after sleep came death. Thus, their only enjoyment was what it took to make them sleep and what sleep it took to make them die.

> *There was no pain, death was itself a pleasure.*[17]

The best escape from these perils was to stop the ears to their chants and enchantments with the famous wax of Ulysses. "*He contrived a most effective deafness to what he could not defeat by his intellect, overcoming it better by paying it no mind.*"[18] We must treat in like fashion these enchanting sirens of books. They are pleasant it is true, but for the most part harmful, so that both for their uselessness, and for their damage: "*Better not to know than to know.*"[19]

Her cups are made of gold and pearls, but who would drink Circe's poison from them? What great curiosity about seeing the head of Medusa on the shield of Pallas Athena could induce one to look there, if that look cost turning to stone? And for that, "*It is enough to look once?*"[20] How much damage to both morals and religion (without addressing here the unbridled liberty of bad people) derives from the trusting nature of the unsophisticated innocent? When aspiring to polish their Wit in the mirror of such books, mining for the riches of

---

15 *Psalm* 36.16.
16 **Claudian**: *Epigram on the Sirens*:
> *Delatis licet huc incumberet aura carinis*
> *Implessentque sinum venti de puppe ferentes,*
> *Figebat vox una ratem.*
17 ***Ibidem***: *Nec dolor ullus erat, mortem dabat ipsa voluptas.*
18 **Cassiodorus, *Variae* 2, Letter 40**.10: *Qui cogitavit felicissimam surditatem, ut quam vincere intelligendo non poterat, melius non advertendo superaret.*
19 ***Augustine***: *Nescire quàm scire meliùs est. (Melius est nescire quam errare) Enchiridion* 5.17.
20 **Claudian, *Gigantomachia*,** *The Battle of the Giants*, 94: *Satis est vidisse semel.* See *Aenied*, 6.487.

precious ideas from the treasures of learned authors, they are acting the part of those who, attempting to wrest the jewels from the heads of dragons, inhale their breath and their poison. As they go on their merry way, they get stuck in the mire. Thirsty for certain spirits to brace their minds, they swallow enough to be driven out of them.

Walking in the dirt or mud, even with the lightest tread, leaves some muck under foot. The stars, says Pliny, are the pure substance of Heaven, infused with light. Nonetheless, they are fed from the humors of earth, the unclean fodder they suck up from here below, and so are marked by spots and deformities. So, the good Pliny believed, though unreasonably, "*Spots are nothing but dirty clods of earth raise up by the humors.*"[21] But it is true that souls, while heavenly in vocation and being, if these souls feed their minds on unclean humors, imbibed from Petronius, from Apuleius, from Ovid along with many others, or from certain poets (and writers of novels)[22] in our language, who are the worst of them all, they will contaminate their hearts with filth, tempted to crave what they see, just as the sheep of Jacob at the sight of the many colored rods bore baby lambs spotted with the same pattern of colors.

Is there any dearth of books that Taste just as good to someone with a sound palate? Why play the flute, said Alcibiades, to see one's mouth contorted, and cheeks puffed out, when harp and lyre give greater pleasure, without such distortions? And with that he threw it away and no one in Athens would play one from then on. Books, which make you monsters and transform the beauty of God's image sealed in your soul into a beastly and brutish shape, why read them? If there are so many others of equal pleasure, and greater benefit, why drink the filth of the most impure authors, copying Galato who, with a clever ruse, painted many of the poetic imitators, or thieves, of Homer with their mouths open for whatever he was vomiting,[23] if we can find a sweeter tasting nectar with no dregs. More flavorful and satisfying than the wallowing pleasures of the senses are the pure refreshments of the mind, a music far more enchanting than even was heard at the banquet of the Tryian queen:

*By Jopas that new-Phoebus is expressed*

---

21 **Pliny, 2.9**: *Maculas enim non esse aliud quàm terrae raptas cum humore sordes.*
22 Added after the 1645 edition.
23 **Aelian 13. 22.**

*In Robes of Lovely yellow bravely dressed*
*(With charming Looks, and Sceptre of pure Gold)*
*Heavens Miracles, and Motions, which the old*
*World-bearing Atlas to Alcydes told:*
*He sings the Moon's obliquely Regular ways,*
*Which her become, and oft eclipsed Sol's Rays:*
*How men and beasts at first were made, and how*
*Raines, Winds, and Lightnings are produced now:*
*The subject of his song in the next strain.*
*Is of the Bears, Crow, Hyades, and Wain:*
*And why the Vernal days to the Ocean fly*
*So swiftly, and the nights so leisurely."*[24]

## 6.4    *Paraenesis: Exhortation to the Writers of Lascivious Poetry*

Hear me, O Lucifers of the earth. Did God endow you with a Wit full of lofty thoughts and acute understanding for you to turn its point in ingratitude against Him? Did he teach you to handle a pen with praise for you to aim it as an arrow and wound His honor? Did God endow you with the minds of angels, to have you become enemies as devils?

Don't tell me: 'We had our ingenious Wit just for this." To you I say what Tertullian said of the Israelites, *"You preferred garlic and onions to the fragrance of heaven."*[1] With the brilliance of your Wits which might have shone with the rays of benevolent stars, you have put fire to dead

---

24 Dryden's English, *Aeneid* 1.720/9, as rendered in the Italian translation of Annibale Caro: 1.1203/13:

*Coi capei lunghi, e con la cetra d'oro*
*Il biondo Iopa, qual Febo nouello,*
*Canta del Ciel le merauiglie, e i moti,*
*Che dal gran vecchio Atlante Alcide apprese.*
*Canta le vie che drittamente torte*
*Rendon vaga la Luna, e bruno il Sole.*
*Come prima si fer gli huomini, e i bruti,*
*Com'hor si fan le pioggie, e i venti, e i folgori.*
*Canta l'Hiade, e l'Orfe, e'l Carro, e'l Corno:*
*E perche tanto a l'oceano il verno*
*Vadan veloci i di, tarde le notti.*

1 **Tertullian**, *On Fasting*, 6: *Maluistis alium, et caepe, quàm coelum fragrare.*

122

wood, putrid with corruption. It might be true that you were no good but for poetry. But, to author lascivious poetry, was that the necessity of Wit or rather the vice of will? As Pythagoras did with a lascivious harpist, all you needed was to change the tune of your muse's lyre and switch out of the tipsy Lydian mode, into the sober Doric so that, instead of inciting the emotions of others with the impulses of lascivious passion, you might have put these to sleep.[2]

But, if the muse you got was a strumpet and tainted with what you call the genius or talent for lascivious versifying, I will say of you, with greater justice, what Lactantius had to say of the philosopher Leucippus, the first inventor of atoms and propounder of chaos: "*How much better to be silent than to use one's tongue for such wretched and useless purposes.*"[3] Is it not better to have no vein of poetry than to have a vein gushing toxin and poison? A prudent emperor would never consent that his wife should drink wine, though the doctors swore there was no other way that she, sterile, could bear a child. The wise prince held the remedy worse than the malady, saying, "*I prefer a sterile wife to a wine sop.*"[4] O how much better would this other saying sound in your mouth, "***Malo Musam sterilem quàm lascivam.***" (*Rather a sterile muse than a lascivious one.*) If I can speak no language but an animal's, I'd rather be a mute than a prattling beast.

And what does it profit you, when you waste your Wit and consume your years and life to publish to the world a work which may even be immortal, if for it you get applause on earth, and torments below, praises where you are not, and torments where you will stay for all time? The Horaces, the Catulluses, the Ovids, the Gallios, the Martials, (not to mention our own poets of a more sacred religion, but of a more profane poetry); how does it help them to bask now in the light of public fame, when in the meantime they are buried in the darkness of hell? So, for every jot of obscenity they wrote, they are tortured down there, while up here, unawares, they are pointlessly praised for it?

---

2 **Basil,** *Homily* **21,** *de libertate ethnicis,* **9** (*To young men on the right use of Greek literature*). See Porphyry, *Life of Pythagoras,* 30.
3 **Lactantius,** *De Ira Dei* ,10: *Quanto melius fuerat tacere, quàm in usus tàm miserabiles, tàm inanes, habere linguam.*
4 Emperor **Frederick** III (1415-1493), **Aeneas Sylvius** Piccolomini (1405-64) *De republicae Alphonsi,* (Panormita, [Antonio Beccadelli 1394-1471]), *Life of Alphonsus,* 2.7): *Malo uxorem sterilem quàm vinosam.*

Suppose after many years' study, your pen should send forth a work of immortal merit, even though, *"Few are they to whom just Jupiter has given his love."*⁵ Of that glory, which is the legitimate prize of the works of heroic Wits, you must expect nothing but the menial share, I mean, what comes from vulgarity or vice. Men of wisdom and judgement, to whose ears, *"The great solecism and vice is to tell a lewd story,"*⁶ will rather abominate you, as a canker of civil conversation and wholesome customs. Nor will the misused virtue of your Wits seem other to them than the indeed enormous, but wicked, strength of giants. These are not lauded for their strength, as they lifted mountains off the earth and heaped them one on top of another, but are condemned as wicked because they dared to storm Heaven to pull Jupiter off his throne.

But if nothing else will persuade you, watch as God descends to the discomforts of a stable, to the miseries of poverty, to the indignities of an obscure life, to the scorn of a misfit, to calumnies as a false prophet, to sale as a slave, to the condemnation of a criminal, to the death of a thief! All bruises under lashes, all blood amidst the thorns, all confusion in nakedness, all suffering on the cross! Now step forward and ask him, for whom he underwent so long a journey from points so far apart, as from Heaven to Calvary? For whom did he shed such copious blood, sweat, and tears? Had he, this noble merchant, in this, a plan for profit, for aught than for the profit of souls? Did he want from us, or ask from his Father, anything but to have us for his followers in life, and companions after death? Now put yourselves in comparison with God and look at the indignity of such a stark contraposition. He, for the salvation of souls, does all he can, you use what you know to send them to damnation. What prognosis can you make? How will you face your guilt before your judge, while against you rise up the hellish screams of that multitude damned because of you? And in the records of the centuries to come, how many after them will be listed who perish through your fault? What defense will you have for your own crimes, guilty of those of others? But they are not so much the crimes of others as yours, since it was you who set the stump for their fall, you, for those fruits of death, who planted the seed.

---

5 *Aeneid* 6.129/30: *Pauci quos aequus amavit Juppiter.*
6 **Jerome**, *Against Helvidius* 16: *Solecismus magnus et vitium est turpe quid narrare.*

There is no man living on the earth whom Lucifer eyes with greater regard and watches and preserves with greater care than one who toils to distill from his brain in the golden cup of a book of Wit, either the plague of errors or the poison of impure poetry. One of these will suffice to relieve half the devils of the business of temptation, for a bad book countervails a hundred devils. Here Behemoth sleeps *"on distant reeds of a swamp,"*[7] there is no call to make men fall where the very ground, slick and slippery, tricks the foot and gives no support.

Timon of Athens hated all men; he loved but one, Alcibiades. But to love him was to hate them all. For he read in his character that he would be the ruin of many; indeed, if possible, the downfall of all Greece. And those true misanthropes there below, if there be any men that they caress as friends and embrace as dear, it is these with their books of immortal status and of mortal affliction, who have battled against Heaven over many centuries in order to expunge the purity in many breasts and to increase their reign with more souls.

These truths, seen in the light of reason and faith by a famous poet (as I know from the recollection of someone on familiar terms with him),[8] would often make him shudder in horror, and almost faint in grief. They would carry him around with the book that he had written in his hand in order to admire it: *"As if he were Phaeton charioteering around the globe"*[9] (as Tiberius called Caligula). Then he understood it deserved a bolt of lightning and sentenced it to the flames. But even if he did he stretch his hand to the flames to throw it in and burn away with them that world on fire, he would pull it right back with the blind violence of compassion. His love for it brought to mind the long, cold night watches of seven years (that he spent working on it), the great labors of Wit through which he squeezed into it the very best he knew how to give, the price to his feverish health, enfeebled by the file of ceaseless study, not a syllable or line of verse that did not cost him a piece of himself, the desire of the public audience which dearly longed for it, the glory that the merit of the work (in that form of singular poetry, unique),[10] promised: Alas! These were

---

7 **Job,** 40.16: *in secreto calami, in locis humentibus.*
8 Torquato Tasso (1544-1595) and his *Gerusalemme Liberata* (1585). This is firsthand information, likely had from Bartoli's grandfather, a friend of the great poet at the Este court.
9 **Suetonius, *Caligula*,** 11: *Tamquam Orbis Terrarum Phaetontem.*
10 Later emended.

the magic spells that tortured his hand, paralyzed his arm, and changed his heart, so that suddenly of another mind, he condemned himself as credulous and cruel and almost in a gesture to implore mercy and pardon from his book, he kissed it, hugged it to his heart and as a consolation for the fright of the fire, he promised that it should very soon see the light of day.[11]

God forbid that you may ever be the father of such a book. Albeit you recognize its harmful character and infamous morals, yet to kill it by your own hand, to tear it to pieces, to reduce it to ashes by fire will be a challenge so hard to accomplish, as if you were with your own hand to slay a son, and to rip his soul out with your knife thrust in his heart. As indeed the teacher of Origen[12] said in his *Stromata*, "***Libri sunt filii animorum.***" (*Books are the children of the soul.*)

The knowledge and foresight that publishing it in print will be for the fall of many and your own ruin, as a man, as a Christian, will sometimes horrify the mind, and freeze the heart. You will sigh at having done what cost you many a sigh and many toils. But in the end, these will be the scruples of conscience of Caesar at the banks of the Rubicon. You will strive to win over yourselves and God, then proceeding despite the damage to others and to yourselves you will pursue with a resolute, ***Jacta est alea*** (*The die is cast*).[13]

As for myself, I entertain the choice between two scenarios I see before me. On the one hand is the aged Abraham, binding his only Isaac as a victim upon the altar with a hand as steadfast as his heart was intrepid, fire on the wood of the sacrifice, knife raised to plunge into the throat of his innocent son, neither a tremor in his arm, nor a pallid countenance, nor tears in his eyes gave witness to his sorrowing heart, concentrating with such intensity on his priestly office; it was as if he had forgotten he was a father, or if there were the feelings of a father, they were more of envy, than of compassion for his dying son, through whom he was victim and priest— for he was killing himself no less than him, in whom, more than in himself, he lived.[14] Then to look on the other hand at an excellent author of a pestilential book,

---

11 This cameo melodrama of the conscience-stricken Tasso dramatizes the moral crisis of the Late Renaissance as it came to grips with the scruples of the Counter Reformation.

12 Ambrose.

13 **Suetonius, *Caesar*,** 32.

[14] *Vittima, e Sacerdote*: Here Bartoli has reworked, "*Ultime parole d'Abraam nel sacrificio d'Isaac suo figlio*" from *Saggio di Poesie morali*, pp. 77/78.

overcoming the contrasts of his thoughts, of his friends, and of all the devils in hell, giving it magnanimously to the flames with that selfsame hand that had, syllable by syllable, both written and weighed it, throwing away in one stroke the labors of the years past and the glory of the centuries to come, and killing at birth himself in his issue, losing with a voluntary refusal, that life, which only makes us live after death— I mean, one's fame in succeeding generations. Of these two spectacles I know not which I should more willingly behold, and perhaps it would seem easier to me, at the express command of God, father of the unborn, and life of the dead, to slay a son begotten with delight and who may be raised again by miracle, than at the secret bidding of the mysterious voice with which God speaks to the heart, to burn a book, that in conceiving it, in bearing it, in raising it, cost more pains than it has syllables.[15]

What? The love of glory, and the hope of acquiring the name of an invincible spirit, did they not move Brutus to condemn his own sons to death as rebels to their country, enemies to the public good? He would condemn them as a consul, not free them as a father, *"And he had to quit being a father to act as a consul."*[16] His heart mourned to see them tied at the stake, youths of great beauty and, in a word, his sons. *"Here there was a moving scene, for Fortune made him his own executioner."* [17] But he could do no less. Who then so hardened his heart, or who removed it, for the time, while he both ordered and watched undaunted the death of his sons? *"Love of the fatherland prevailed and his immense desire for honor."*[18] Can love of glory be so great as to make executioners of fathers? But where at once are lost both the son and the glory which he promised, how much more heroic the deed to kill him, since from nowhere else comes the strength to do it, but from the love of virtue?

But the hope of ever seeing so blessed a spectacle is vain. Yet I would urge that the worst parts, those thoroughly brutal, may be removed, that the book may remain, if not good, at least not exceeding

---

15 Like Tasso, Abraham is rendered in a painterly tableau of the Baroque drama of conscience, later invoked in *L'huomo al punto, cioe l'huomo al punto di morte* (1669).
16 **Valerius Maximus**, *History* **5.8**: *Et exuit Patrem ut Consulem ageret.*
17 **Titus Livy**, *Ab urbe condita* **2.5**: *Et qui spectator erat amovendus, eum ipsum Fortuna exactorem supplicii dedit.*
18 *Aeneid* **6**. 823:
    *Vicit amor Patriae laudumque immensa cupido.*

bad. Yet, in this case, one hears that answer, heretofore given to the senate of Rome, when they had under discussion to reduce the Tiber, by branching it and diverting the affluent rivers that emptied there, to protect the city from the frequent inundations that flooded it, *"The Tiber may not to be deprived of its tributaries, not flow in diminished glory."*[19] They will not suffer their works to be a drop less, to be shorn of a single dot. In their eyes, they would appear monstrous truncated, as they are truly monsters in their entirety.

---

19 Tacitus, *Annals,* 79: *Ipsum Tyberim nolle prorsus accolis fluvius orbatum, minore gloria fluere.*

# 7 SLANDER

## 7.1 Inclination of the Genius in Some and Misuse of their Wit to Slander Others

Who would have thought slander so sweet, that one Taste leaves a lingering desire, as with lions that are, once they lick blood from their paws, always hungry for more? Just so, after savoring the first relish of slander, one often feels for it so longing a desire, that he becomes one who'd rather lose his tongue than his barbs and cease to live himself before he ceases mortifying others. Old age (when it comes) may often deprive the head of its sense, but not the sharp tongue of its pricks, like old thorn bushes— the cold of winter removes their leaves, not their thorns— their raiment, not their sting.

In this category, for the most part, are the sharp points of those Wits only meant for stinging. They never speak their best than when they say their worst. They never shine more than when they are burning. All the marks of their Wit are quips and clever pricks. And to acquire more bite, they work their Wits even more than that famous orator, (Demosthenes) despite his lisping tongue, worked to sound and shape the letter R, mordant and canine.[1]

To listened to them, as a Menippus, a Zoilus, a Momus crafting their witticisms with such Wit is to hear music, but the sort of music Pythagoras heard in the clanging and banging of hammers. Their quills are taken from vultures, not swans. Like the quill that belonged to the famous Demosthenes, they have ink on one end and poison on the other.[2] Indeed, even the ink they use is toxic. It envenoms the names it writes so that poisoned to death, they figure in such writings in black and blue. The sparks of their Wit which in others are innocent flashes of light, not of fire; for delight, not for offense— in them turn into bolts of lightning with flaming wings and death on their tips.

They have transfused in their heads the genius of Lucilius, *"Who first founded the sarcastic style"*[3] Their mouths speak with the tongue of the ancient epigrammatists, namely (as Martial defines it), **Malam linguam** (*a malicious tongue*).[4] Though their speech may be sweet, and

---

1 **Plutarch,** *Demosthenes, 29.*
2 Laertius, *Demosthenes.*
3 **Pliny, preface,** 7: *Qui primus condidit styli nasum.* Roman,180-103 BC.
4 **Martial,** *Epigrams 2,* **preface.**

copious, it can never be said of them, as was said of the darling Plato, that the bees put honey in their mouths, instead they contain a scorpion's egg, or a spider's venom. In truth, they hold in their hands the scalpel of the anatomist, rather than the pen of the writer, and the deeper they cut, the better they operate, leaving the living with wounds, and the dead in pieces.

Such men as these don't deserve to live among men, as they act like beasts (as was said about Cicero) and to score the point of a witty jibe, don't hesitate to lose a friend.

> *Just to get a laugh for himself*
> *There's no friend this one will spare.*[5]

Whereby they may be fittingly called with the comic, **Vulturii** (vultures) since, *"They devour and destroy enemies and friends alike"*[6] In inventing one of their conceits, they don't care if the party they attack is innocent and suffers. They are only training their eyes on a good hit, even if they resemble the eagle who dropped a tortoise on the poet's bald head (Aeschylus) to crack the shell. In another's sufferings, they have their pleasure, and their honor in another's disgrace. They take after (if he really did such a thing) Buonarotti, who crucified a man to paint a lifelike Christ on the Cross.[7] Or rather, they take after Nero, who set fire to Rome while he played his lyre atop the tower of Maecenas. As his city collapsed into real ruin, he was singing of Troy's fabled conflagration.[8]

Alas! Their barbarous ambition is to stand out, at the expense of others, as great Wits of sharp and nimble brain. To try the temper of their steel and the strength of their arm on the cadavers of convicts is the cruel custom of the Japanese.[9] How much worse is it under the pretense of playful sport, to plunge into someone's breast a dagger which is no less fatal to his reputation, than the thrust of a sword would be to his life? As Vegetius says, *"A good hit only a few inches deep is enough*

---

5 **Horace 1 *Satires*, 4.34/5:**
> *Dummodo risum*
> *Excutiat sibi, non hic cuiquam parcet amico.*
6 Plautus, *Mercator: Hostesne an Cives comedant parvipendunt.*
7 Bartoli suppressed this allegation in the second Rome edition (1650), but it appears in the numerous subsequent printings from Venice.
8 Suetonius, *Nero*, 38.
9 Bartoli would later pursue this detail in his history of the Jesuit missions in Japan, *Il Giappone* (1660).

*to kill.*[10]As you well know, the satyrs, fathers and masters of satire are more repugnant for being half-beasts than beautiful for being half-gods. As for your mordant taunts, your Wit pleases less than your malice displeases.

Can these be the sublime uses, the divine employments, for which Wit was bestowed on you? Would you make a travesty of Wit, transmuting it from the king that it is into a tyrant, and from a pillar of civilized life, into a murderer and a butcher? Apply to yourselves what a writer in antiquity said against the cruel Perillos. He justly excoriated this artist, who debauched the innocent art of sculpting the images of gods and heroes in bronze by forging a murderous bull, to be the executor, or the executioner, of Phalaris and his unspeakable life sentences, *"The profession of creating images of the gods and of heroes was perverted from a very civilized art. Was it the idea of its originators to make it an instrument of torture? If any work of this artist survives, whoever saw it would hate the hand that made it."*[11]

Their normal punishment is to be loved by none, shunned by many, hated by all and to acquire the infamous title of satirist, slanderer, snout. They could well have inscribed on their foreheads that ancient distich, taken from a Greek epigram,

*If my nose is set against the sun my grimace*
*Will cast its shadow across the teeth to mark the hour.*[12]

Diogenes, the lead dog of the pack of Cynic philosophers, had his palace or rather his kennel, in a barrel. This was the Heaven he turned around in; his intellect was truly worthy of such a sphere. This, the cave from which he delivered his oracles, had more the smell of wine than the odor of truth; this the chair, where teaching, he undertook to correct the immoral morals of others. It would have been a mighty wonder (had he succeeded) that a wine barrel should bring

---

10 **Vegetius, *De re militari* 1.12:** *Duas uncias adactae mortales sunt.*
11 **Pliny, 34.8** (19*): In hoc a simulacris Deorum, hominumque devocaverat, humanissimam artem. Ideo tot conditores ejus elaboraverant ut ex ea tormenta fierent? Itaque una de causa servantur opera ejus, ut quisquis illa videat, oderit manus.* (The trial run of the brazen bull of Phalaris, tyrant of Akragas (Agrigento), was the immolation of its creator, the Athenian sculptor, Perillos).
12 Attributed to Trajan, cited by Thomas More:
*Si meus ad Solem statuatur Nasus, hianti*
*Ores, ben ostendet dentibus hora quota est.*

some to their senses— that usually will drive others out of theirs.[13] Whatever was the lesson of his teaching, it was such that Plato called him, ***alterum Socratem sed insanum*** (*another Socrates, but insane*).[14] Nevertheless, because in that rotten and grubby barrel he mingled the wine of unadulterated philosophy with the mordant vinegar of a continual malediction, he drew not scholars, but scoffers. All Athens regarded him as a dog and shunned him as rabid.

And who would want to hug a thorny porcupine you can't touch carefully enough that it won't prick? Who wants the company of someone, like a scorpion, ***Semper cauda in ictu est?*** (*Whose prick is always cocked*).[15] Who wants to be friends with a lion? Even if he doesn't use his paws or teeth, his tongue is so scratchy that even when it licks, it draws blood. Better you honor them, not to have them as enemies and offer them sacrifices— as the Romans did with the Goddess of Fever, *Febris*— so they favor you by keeping far away, only remembering to let you permanently slip their mind.

It would be no great punishment for slanderers just to be shunned, if they were not also persecuted. Sometimes they try to keep alive by steering clear of those who can answer the pen with the sword and words with deeds and they remember with regard to these, they must be mute, if not blind. They can follow the example of certain wild geese from the north when flying by Mount Taurus. They will put a stone in their beaks and try not to awaken the eagles nesting there with their quacking. But rarely can they keep quiet and at one time or other, they automatically do what they always do, from habit or nature. So, either they make, as silkworms do, a binding around their mouths, or close them by biting on a scorpion. This should recall the truth of Pollio's dictum on Augustus, not to, ***Scribere in eum, qui potest proscribere*** (*scribble against the one who can proscribe you*).[16]

You can't always find someone with ready money to pay to shut them up, nor someone who (upon the advice of Alphonse, king of Aragon,) will throw the dog ***medicatis frugibus offam***, (*A sop of drugged victuals*) to keep it from barking— at least from biting. It was the singular case of that lawyer in Martial:

---

13 Sentence excised in 1650, but in many printings until Bartoli's final proofing in *Opere, Le morali* of 1684.
14 **Aelian, 14**. 33.
15 **Pliny, 3.25.**
16 **Macrobius,** *Satire* 2. 4

*Why are you such a loudmouth, Aelius, always bothering the barristers?*
*It can't be for free, as they pay you even to shut up.*[17]

Many times, **accipiunt, ut taceant** (*they are paid, to shut up*), but their pay might not be in kind, might make it so they are never heard from again. This was the reward of that notorious Zoilus.[18] He was either burned alive, or stoned to death, or crucified, so that with one of these three kinds of good currency, he collected the full wages of his slanders against Homer, the prince of poets.

## 7.2    *If a Writer is in Error, He should not refuse Correction; and One without Knowledge should not presume to Correct or Criticize Others*

No man  on earth has so clear and crystalline a Wit that standing in the light of Sapience, he doesn't cast some shadow--- more or less opaque and tenebrous— of ignorance. Our souls are in themselves purest fire, all light and clarity according to an ancient sage. But because they are linked to the gross matter of our body— which gives them life, besides their innate inertia— they are also clouded with vapid sediments; and as a flame mixed and mingled with smoke, they lose a good deal of their liveliness of motion and their clarity of light. Hence, we have difficulty in seeking and uncertainty in discerning the truth. And it so happens that, *"This lenience we have sought and granted many times over."*[1] Though we can sometimes miss the center, we are not immediately exiled from the circle of the learned, as with the moon, which may sometimes be eclipsed and dark, but not for this is it banished from Heaven.

Truly insufferable are those who tout their own writings or defend the writings of others as oracles of infallible truth— as being twenty-four carat gold with no admixture of error, with no alloy of falsity. As for their own writings, let them hear St. Ambrose, who compares them most aptly to our children. Our love for them blinds our judgement so that, where they are concerned, the better the father,

---

17 **Martial**, *Epigrams* 1.95:
>    *Quòd clamas semper, quòd agentibus obstrepis Heli*
>    *Non facis hoc gratis, accipis ut taceas.*
18 **Vitruvius**, *De architectura,* 7, preface, 8/9.

1 Horace, *Ars Poetica*, 11: *hanc veniam petimusque damusque vicissim.*

the worse the judge. *"At times, when writings fail, the author favors them. For as parents love even their disabled children, so writers will even be fond of their mangled works."*[2] With regard to the writings of others let them, besides many other places of Augustine, read his 111th Epistle where he says his custom was not to adore the authors but the truth; not their words, but reason, breaking from them when they separate from it. And, he says in conclusion, *"So am I with the writings of others, as I want my readers to be with mine."*[3]

For this reason, the wisest sages, before publishing their writings are wont to submit them to the examination and censure of a friend, who is both discerning and loyal, so that where they find them lacking they can say, as the ancient fencing masters to their cadets, **Repete** (*Repeat*). But if, only after publication, their defects come to light, the authors may correct them themselves. They can retouch them after the fashion of the ancient painters who did not insist their creations were works of total artistic perfection but would inscribe below them the **Faciebat** (a *work in progress*) of Polycletus and Apelles. *"As if they were begun and never finished, given the different views of critics, if the artist went back to his creation he could amend anything wanting, if he still could."*[4] The great Hippocrates gave an example of this when he was not embarrassed to retract certain things he had written about sutures of the brain.

Sometimes the writer will only notice errors he made unawares, after the text of his discourse has been printed and published. Or he may have others point them out and in the appropriate context furnish the antidote of a correction in their criticisms. In that case, if he is sufficiently experienced and a rational friend of his duty, he will not take umbrage or consider it an insult or get angry. He should not copy the early Romans who, when they were completely ignorant of mathematics, would schedule their public activities by a faulty and

---

2 Ambrose, *Works*, 8, *Letter* 63, to Sabinus: *Vnumquemque fallunt sua scripta, et Authorem praetereunt. Atque ut filii etiam deformes delectant parentes, sic etiam Scriptores, indecoros quoque sermones palpant.*
3 **Augustine** to Fortunatianus, **Epistle 111** (Letter 148).15: *Talis sum ego in scriptis aliorum, tales volo intellectores meorum.*
4 **Pliny, 1,** preface, 6: *Tanquam inchoata arte, et imperfecta, ut contra judiciorum varietates superesset artefici regressus ad veniam, velut emendaturo quidquid desideretur, si non esset interceptus.*
5 **Plutarch, Quomodo profectus in virtute** (*How a Man may be aware of his progress in virtue*).

unreliable sundial, *"For its lines did not coincide with the hours."*[6] The writer will not want his errors to disorder in this way the measurements of knowledge used in public. The great Augustine said, *"One should not love oneself so perversely that he will lead others into error in order to conceal an error made by him."*[7]

Truly, to be helped in undeceiving oneself— and the public moreover, from error— ought to be as dear to everyone, as the duty all have, to love the truth. And hear in his words, the sentiments on this issue, of the same Augustine, a man whose Wit was matched by his modesty. *"I do not hesitate to search for answers or to learn where I am mistaken. Whoever reads this, if he is as sure as I am, let him continue with me, and if he is unsure as I am, let him search for answers with me. Where he sees he is in error, he should return to me; where he sees I am in error, hw should correct me."*[8]

What I have said here concerns the modesty appropriate for the writer. It should apply to the reader as well. He ought not make a habit of just hunting for the errors of writers to bring them down— like vultures hovering by putrid carcasses or ravens waiting by carrion for their food. Moreover, they are so very keen, as if there were no other way to avoid error but by noting the errors of others. Yet the aphorism of Ambrose is very true, *"Often in issuing judgements the judge is more wrong than the wrongs of the one he judges."* [9] This is the discourteous manner of many, *"Who seek fame by criticizing the knowledge of others."*[10]

*Rods are the sad sceptres of pedagogues.*[11]
They hold a censorious brow, ever raised over the authors they read, to whip them, enjoying the whip more than others do the sceptre. From this spring the many controversies and rebuttals, not to say the duels and the tragedies of countless authors, some extraordinarily

---

6 **Pliny**, 7.86: *Non enim congruebant ad horas ejus liniae.*
7 **Augustine**, *Letter* **7, to Marcellinus**: *Nimis enim perversem seipsum amat, qui et alios vult errare, ut error suus lateat.*
8 **Augustine, *On the Trinity***, 1.3: *Non pigebit me sucubi haesito quaerere, sic ubi erro discere. Proinde quisquis haec legit ubi pariter certus est pergat mecum, ubi pariter haesitat, quaerat mecum. Ubi errorem suum cognoscit redeat ad me ubi meum revocet me.*
9 **Ambrose, 2 *Apology of David*, 2:** *Saepe in judicando majus est peccatum judicit, quam peccati illius, de quo fuerat judicatum.*
10 **Pliny, 1, preface**, 7: *Qui obtrectatione alienae scientiae famam sibi aucupantur.*
11 **Martial, *Epigrams*, 10.62:** *Ferulasque tristes sceptra Paedagogorum.*

learned, who have wasted much time in this kind of battling, and much sweat; but to what purpose?

*Waging wars from which there were no triumphs to be had.*[12]

This is a subject, methinks, not to be entirely passed over with a blind eye;. So, a few comments on the subject here.

First: A man with nothing but a tongue, and a belly (as Antipater said of Demades),[13] who sets himself up as an assayer of the golden writings of excellent men; to gage how much purity and how much dross they contain, criticizing what he can't understand, rejecting what he doesn't like, biting off what he can't chew. A vile harridan, instead of her spindle, took up a pen to attack the divine Theophrastus, charging him with ignorance and stupidity,[14] She thereby revived the ancient monstrosities of fable: such as the haughty Omphale in condemning the great Hercules from a bludgeon to a distaff, from killer of monsters, to a spinner of wool. Another was Demosthenes, the cook of emperor Valens— as if his kitchen were a school of wisdom and the dishware books— who weighed the theology of Basil the Great and rejectd it as a meal lacking salt and unsavory Sapience. One master, Juan Luis (Vives),[15] treated the most learned Augustine as an ignoramus and had the presumtion (**Sus Minervam**) (*a mouse to Minerva*)[16] to teach the true forms of logic to the great mind of Augustine, that Archimedes of intelligence. Against the enemies of truth and faith Augustine could throw as many thunderbolts as the arguments he made, when he took from principles as manifest, as the rays of the sun, his propositions and fed them though the forms of dialectic to the point of infallible consequences: such a ploy, isn't it like watching *"mice running out of caves,"*[17] as they run with a straw for a lance to tilt at the breast of a lion? To see swamp frogs not only muddy the water for Diana's bath, but to attempt swallowing all her beauty whole? To see beasts of burden with their horrid braying as noisy trumpets in an effort to terrify the Giants and put them to flight?

Seeing such men, and others of similar stamp, comment, refute and correct the writings of learned men, brings to my mind and almost

---

12 **Lucan,** *Pharsalia* 1.12: *Bella geri placuit nullos habitura triumphos.*
13 **Plutarch,** ***De cupiditate divitiarum,*** (*On the Love of Wealth*).
14 Leontion, See Cicero, *De natura deorum*, 1.33.93; Pliny, 29, preface.
15 Luis Vives, (1493-1540), in *Adversus Pseudodialecticos* (1520).
16 Cicero, *Familiares,* 9.8.2.
17 *Judith* 14.12: *mures de cavernis (exeuntes).*

before my eyes— that most indiscreet ass with teeth used to roots, stubs and thorny thistles who dared to tear apart and eat the whole of Homer's *Iliad*, bringing further disgrace and disaster to Troy (in the words of a poet) as once it was a horse that destroyed it honorably— and now, dishonorably, it was an ass.[18]

The Greek Aristides was dying, a man of martial valor, tested by more trials than one, because of the venomous sting of a small creature that bit him.[19] Death itself did not grieve the valiant man, but the vileness of this death did. For he was not torn to pieces by a lion, not trampled by an elephant, not clawed by a tiger, but bitten by a hapless creature. Similar, in my judgment, was the chagrin of those great universal masters, seeing they had been impugned, criticized, condemned— not by men excellent for Letters and Wit, but by a cook, by a woman, by a pedant. For had the stars (said Cassiodorus) seen in a sundial the immense expanses of their light imitated, and as it were mocked by the little motion of a shadow, they would be offended and in their disdain confound Heaven and the globe, and react with other movements, other cycles, *"They might change their direction not to undergo such mockery."*[20] What do you think that the multitude in every profession of Letters, oracles of wisdom, would do, if in the silence of their tombs they heard themselves defamed, some as blind, some as stupid, some as inexcusably ignorant? And this coming from some, not all them sages, indeed, not even men (if the mind be the measure) attempting win, among the ignorant crowd, the name and credit of another Hercules and another Samson, by plucking whiskers from the chin of already dead lions.

Secondly: Often it happens that it is our ignorance that makes us see error in others. We would do well to tell ourselves what many grave and holy bishops said to the apostate Emperor Julian, who had read and condemned a most learned apology of St. Apollinaris: *"You read it, but you didn't understand it, for had you understood it you would be making objections."*[21]

---

18 See Ammonianus, Suda, Adler, beta 1626.
19 Aristides of Locris, bitten by a weasel. Aelian 14.4/5
20 **Cassiodorus**, **Variae Epistolae 1.**45, Theodoric to Boethius: *Meatus suos fortasse deflecterent ne tali ludibrio subjacerent.*
21 **Sozomen**, [400-450] *Ecclesiastical history*, 5: *Legisti, sed non intellexistis; si enim intellexisses, non improbasses.*

The ancient Romans, in the exercise of wielding arms for which they kept their soldiers in training at all times, gave as the first rule of fighting with a sword, not to expose yourself to the sword of the enemy. For while you are warding off his thrust, he can wound you where you are unprotected before you can pull back the sword and go on the offensive. Vegetius said, *"To be mindful in this maneuver of a necessary caution: when the tyro goes to strike his blow he should not expose himself to be wounded."*[22] So also, the first rule for someone who takes up his pen against a writer ought to be, where one impugns another's ignorance, not to show his own. Otherwise, when you go inside a labyrinth for the person wandering lost inside, you have no thread to get back out. You will wind up the butt of Diogenes' jokes ridiculing those wretched grammarians, so concentrated on tracking the errors of Ulysses, that they were blind to their own.

We need not betake ourselves to bite others, until our wisdom teeth come out; and they (as Aristotle observes) only grow late. It is requisite to be doubly furnished, with Letters and with Wit, when you attempt to correct someone in error, for both the error to be certain and the correction to be impeccable. And, oh, how often it happens that for not grasping clearly enough the writer's real meaning, we strike like Mutius Scaevola, who thought he was killing the king, but slew his servant? We impugn as the other's words what he neither said nor dreamt, armed in desperation for a battle with phantoms. Short of eyes of our own able enough to see, had we used those of a discerning friend, he would have made us sheath our sword (as the Sybil had Aeneas do) so that we are spared vainly casting at shadows, with much exertion on our part and no damage to theirs.

Thirdly: You do not want to incense someone who is still living and think you can properly gage his knowledge from the writings he has published. When someone is incensed, outrage often sparks Wit, awaking his dormant spirits to step up, *"The oil in a lantern flows where the flame is."*[23] How many, with the golden veins of sublime Wit and precious knowledge buried in their breasts, once they have been provoked by the temerity of those who underestimated their store of Letters, have demonstrated their erudition to the world, leaving their

---

22 **Vegetius, *De re militari*,** (*On Military Matters*) **2. 12**: *In qua meditatione servabatur illa cautela ut ita tyro ad inferendum vulnus insurgeret, ne qua ex parte pateret ipse ad plagam.*
23 **Seneca, *QN*, 4**: *In lucernis oleum fluit illò ubi exuritur.*

critics much the worse off for annoying them? In like manner sometimes rocks pregnant with rich, but hidden ores, are blasted open by a thunderbolt and display in the crack samples of the riches hidden inside, so that they are known to be mountains of gold and silver where once they were considered hardly more than useless piles of rocks? How many whose brains seemed hard and cold as bracken ferns, pushed by a contest of pens, just as bracken ferns, when struck by lightning, emit not only sparks to bring light but flames and lightning to bring punishment? Is there a duller and more stolid an animal than an ass? Yet here we see the ass of Balaam, shaken more by outrage than reason, become in its own defense a Demosthenes. Chrysostom said, "*Balaam was an ass, of all animals the most defenseless, but it defended itself against the man who beat it, better than a rational being.*"[24] Moreover, do not even mutes (as is said of the son of Croesus )[25] in order to defend what nature has bestowed on them, untie their tongues and with the miracle of that natural love, for which nothing is a miracle, say things they had never learned how to say?

What a great number of men there are who, out of envy, out of rage for controversy, out of ambition to set themselves up on the ruins of others, as men of substance, will copy (says Theodoret)[26] that Shimei who gained his fame by stoning a king, and a king as holy, as innocent, as David. With the pricks of their over- sharpened pens, have they aggravated those they supposed to be lambs, proving to be lions, and then pulled back from the fray? But in vain, and too late, for

*Galeatus repents getting into a duel too late.*[27]

They have sown with Cadmus deadly words, like the teeth of a poisonous serpent, and afterwards have been frightened to see a host of armed men spring up so suddenly?

*A crop sown by its own farmer that quickly became warlike.*[28]

They have taken (as Archilochus told one who picked an unjustified quarrel)[29] the cricket by the wings and afterwards hearing its noise,

---

24 **John Chrysostom, *On Psalm* 47**: *Balaae erat Asinus, animal omnium hebetissimum; nec minus bene se defendit apud eum, qui ipsum pulsabat, quam homo praeditus ratione.*
25 Herodotus, *Histories* 1.85.
26 **Theodoret, in the preface to his *Dialectic*.**
27 **Juvenal**, *Satire* 1.169/70: *Galeatum sero duelli poenitet:*
28 **Ovid, *Metamorphoses*,** but Claudian, *On the consulate of Stilicho*, 1.321: *Messis cum proprio mox bellatura colono.*
29 **Lucian, *The pseudologist* (The mistaken critic).**

have wished that either they had no hands to take it, or no ears to hear it. They have competed, as Marsyas did, with Apollo thinking he was a shepherd when he was a god. Then, afterwards, as they saw themselves flayed like a steer, they begged for pity and made promises, but in vain.[30] For as the god wanted to take his skin, he wasn't taking words, nor would he be won by entreaties, as he was the victor in song. In short, how many have found themselves in the midst of vipers and asps, having no one to blame but themselves for rushing into the fray, tardy to take heed and whining to no purpose, just as that ill-fated Roman army, upon finding in Africa more monsters than human enemies to fight, declared,

> *I ask blame nothing on you, Africa*
> *Nor on you, Nature. Terrain full of monsters, devoid of men*
> *You spread it with with serpents....*
> *We have come to the land of serpents* [31]

One such was Ruffinus. He paid dearly for stinging and provoking St. Jerome when he chose rather to be his rival than his friend. But smarting afterwards from his adversary's hand, so handy to hit, so weighty to wound, he wanted to quit fighting, protesting that he was being punished for no fault, that it was the love of truth, not the passion of indignation that guided his hand while he was writing. Between Christians, between men of the cloth, strokes of the pen should not be inflicted as sword thrusts. To this St. Jerome replied, *"Granted you did not wound me on purpose, what difference is that to me whom you struck? I should not care, because you attacked me in good conscience? I lay here bleeding, the wound screams in my breast, my once white limbs are covered in blood. And you tell me not to let my hand point to the wound, so it doesn't show that you wounded me, ?*[32]

---

30 Pliny, 16.89.
31 **Lucan,** *Pharsalia* **9.854/6**; 859: —*Nihil Africa de te*
  *Nec de te Natura queror. Tot monstra ferentem*
  *Gentibus ablatum dederas serpentibus orbem....*
  *In loca serpentum nos venimus.*
32 **Jerome,** *Against Ruffinus,* 1.11.402: *Esto, me nescius vulneraris: quid ad me qui percussus sum? Num idcirco curari non debeo quia tu me bono animo vulnerasti? Confossus jaceo: stridet vulnus; in pectore, candida prius sanguine membra turpantur; et tu mihi dicas, Noli manum adhibere vulneri, ne ego in te videar vulnerasse?*

## 7.3 *Words of Advice on the Dangerous Business of Writing Against Others, and on How to Defend Yourself*[1]

Advising one of small knowledge and great ambition will take more than just repeating that a shoemaker by trade should not look **ultra crepidam** (*above the shoe*), not stand up to engage and criticize a face drawn and painted by Apelles.[2] For as he doesn't have eyes learned enough to understand such artistry, he should hold his tongue and not make bold to criticize. One should also add a few words on what the arguments between men of intelligence call for— as reasonable measures and adhering to the standards of equity— whether they are indictments of the writings of others or defenses of one's own writings.

As to writing against others: The love of truth should be the sole motive that puts a pen in hand and makes the writer her champion so to speak. Then modesty should be the tutor to teach the art of using it, to wield it not as the lance of a soldier but as the lancet of a surgeon, to emend against the error, not to offend against the author. Thereby one shows himself a good student of the divine wisdom, the Word, whose mouth in the *Song of Songs*[3] is likened, not to roses, whose color more than any other flower resembles the lips, but to lilies. This not only for their white candor, proper and natural to the truth spoken from the mouth of Christ, without paint or added embellishment and singularly resplendent (the ingenious gloss of Theodoret),[4] but also because the lily is a flower, as innocent as it is lovely, with no thorns or rough parts to make it pointed and prickly. St. Ambrose says of Christ represented in the lily, "*Sublime flower, immaculate, innocent, with no sharpness of thorns to do harm, but glowing with a halo of grace.*"[5]

The Stars, as they were fighting the Sifara, did not break rank, or forsake their posts, or waver in discipline in combat. "*Keeping in order*

---

1 Salusbury translates *pericoloso mestiere* as *nice mystery*.
2 Pliny.35.85. Ultracrepidarianism.
3 **Theodoret, *Song of Songs*, 5.**
4 **Theodoret, *Song of Songs*, 5.**
5 **Ambrose, *Book* 7 on Luke**: *Flos sublimis immaculatus, innoxius, in quo non spinarum offendat asperitas, sed gratia circumfusa clarescat.* See also his *Comment on the Canticle*, 2. 4.

141

*and line as they fought against Sisara."*[6] And such is one's duty in setting forth to write against others; a combat not without victory, though without blood. One should be careful in tilting the lance of one's reason, not to lose control of the bridle, nor to forfeit the reward of Wit through the defect of passion. Let him not stamp (on the glorious pride of Plato[7]) with the inglorious pride of Diogenes, and subject himself to condemnation by the very act of condemning another.

Convincing one of error is to put one's hand in the wound, reaching inside it is something to be done with exquisite delicacy, so that the cure brings no spasms where the wound brought only pain. The sollicitous Hippocrates orders that the eyes of the sick, being extremely delicate, be wiped with the finest linen cloths and their wounds cleansed with the softest sponges, and both with all possible dexterity and delicacy.[8] And before him the Archangel Raphael, the proto-medicus, ordered the young Tobias, as he treated the eyes of his blind father, before applying the gall for medicine, to give him a kiss for love: *"Kiss him and then wipe his eyes with this gall."*[9] Equal care should be prescribed to one who seeks to illuminate the eyes of the mind in error, the gall of admonishing another for his error (for just applying it in public is still a solution of great bitterness) is to be linked with a kiss and the kiss linked with love.

Carneades of the Academy, when he was preparing to write a tract against Zeno, the patron of the rigid sect of the Stoics, took a small dose of hellebore to purge his stomach against foul humors, especially against bilious gall, so that his Wit would not be murky in that important undertaking. *"So that nothing of the bad humors in his stomach should affect his equanimity."*[10] When one has cleared his brain and is sufficiently prepared on the issue of his argument, he should also be ready to purge his bilious humor so that his learning and his delivery are both flawless. Let him tune the affections of his mind to the music of reason so that the style in which he expresses himself, be neither harsh nor dissonant. Let him not enter the arena before he has sacrificed to the Graces, as the ever courteous Plato counseled the

---

6 **Judges** 5.20: *Manentes in ordine, et cursu suo, adversus Sisaram pugnaverunt.*
7 Reference later excised.
8 **Hippocrates,** *Corpus, On Injuries of the Head,* 13
9 *Tobias* 11: *Osculare eum, statimque lini super oculos ejus ex felle isto.*
10 **Gellius, 17.**15: *Ne quid e corruptis in stomacho humoribus ad domicilium usque animi redunderet.*

churlish Xenocrates.[11] Then let him go as those prudent and puissant Spartans who marched in battle not to the banging of drums, but to the sound of bagpipes and flutes, *"for a more comely and more modulated advance"* said Thucydides in Gellius.[12] Otherwise, a more dispassionate audience will witness your unruly behavior with nausea and disdain. What the poet Menander said to Philemon who took him to court— and through the ineptitude of the judges, won— they will also say to you: *"I ask in all sincerity, tell me: doesn't it make you blush to beat me?"*[13] Be aware, however effective you make your arguments, if you do not temper your skill with modesty, you will earn the title of that cruel surgeon of Rome, who cut with such brutality that he lost the name of surgeon for the name of butcher.[14]

To remain reasonable is far harder when someone is provoked, when he feels he may give freer rein to his resentment out of righteous indignation. This is a special category of storm which requires the figure of respect to be a strong helmsman with exceptional mastery over the emotions, to allay with skill and then to plunge forth with force through the fierce crashing and the impetuous assaults of the waves. That *"modicum of reasonable defense,"*[15] how far to go in self-defense, is a boundary difficult to reach without crossing it, as a man running down a steep mountain (more cascading than running) will have a hard time, to stop his feet and his body's weight where he ought to, and not be carried more than a few steps ahead.

If I hold my tongue, men will think I plead guilty by a tacit confession. If I do respond with alacrity, the dictates of innocent modesty may seem the remorse of a guilty conscience. If so, I am the laughingstock of the learned and in public disrepute, for even spiders will spin their webs over the face and beard of statues of Jupiter, unafraid because his thunderbolts are the hands of a god made of wood with no feeling. A rebuttal that leaves one's opponent's clothes in tatters and his face black and blue should be sufficient testimony for everyone else to be careful not to cut their pens too sharp against one who turns pens into arrows; answers ink with gall and stings with wounds, like thunderbolts from the clouds, *"Endangering few, but*

---

11 **Laertius**, *Xenocrates*, 4.2
12 **Gellius, 1.11**: *Ut modestiores modulatioresque fierent.*
13 Gellius, 17.4: *Quaeso te bona venia dic mihi, cum me vincis non erubescis?*
14 **Pliny**, 29.6. Archagatus, (ca. 219 BC).
15 *Moderamen inculpatae tutelae*, Roman legal term.

*terrifying many."*[16] One person is struck by lightning as his punishment, but all are frozen with fear, and the death of only one will teach any others to fear even the clearest Heaven, remembering how it thunders, when disturbed.

Withal, many will abandon themselves to passion and, to defend their rights, relinquish all reason. They are blind not to see that rage in a disputant ordinarily argues for weakness and is a sign of losing; just as a calm and a smiling demeanor is testimony to victory. So, the prince who was the friend of Sidonius Apollinaris decided he had won the dispute, when the passion of his adversary gave way: *"He forgets the emotion he had to overcame, feeling that he has beaten his rival when his victory is confirmed by the other's aggravation."*[17]

Moreover, each objection of every rival does not call for an answer. To wit, the excellent dictum of Xenocrates that tragedy deigns not to answer insults from comedy.[18] And every objection that calls for an answer does not require the same quality of reply. When arrows but graze the skin, to what purpose should a man be upset and take on, as if they had pierced him to the quick? Enough to imitate the elephant who undoes a hundred arrows with a slight jolt of his body and

*"With a shake of his hide, he sheds the spears."*[19]

Indeed, sometimes one is so manifestly in the right, it may help to show what might be said, without so much as deigning to say it. Is there is a creature better armed for its own defense, or better prepared against outside offence, than the porcupine?

*He needs no outside help and carries it all with him,*
*His, the bow, his, the arrow, he pulls the string,*
*A single animal holds joint he arts of war.*[20]

But when it is provoked, though all the bristles of its body are cocked arrows, he does not fire all of them— and for what one will do, it does not use two; and if threatening is enough, it won't strike:

---

16 **Seneca,** *On Clemency,* **1.8**: *Paucorum periculo, multorum (omnium) metu.*
17 Theodoric, **Sidonius Apollinaris**, *Epistle* 2.8. To Agricola: *Oblectatur commotione superati, et tunc demum credit sibi cessisse Collegam, cum fidem fecerit victoriae suae, bilis aliena.*
18 **Laertius,** *Xenocrates*, 4.10.
19 **Lucan**, *Pharsalia* 6.209: *Mota cute discutit hastas.*
20 **Claudian**, *In Histrice*, (*On the porcupine*) 9 (45). 41/43:
    *Externam non quaerit opem. Fert omnia secum.*
    *Se pharaetra, sese jaculo, sese utitur arcu.*
    *Unum animal cunctas bellorum possidet artes.*

# Slander

*It never wastes its arrows in anger*
*Cautious and satisfied to threaten.*[21]

It only raises its bristles and, as if putting them in the bow, it seems to be telling attackers, **Che si, che si** (*Come on, do*). This manner of defense served Tertullian as he wrote against the Valentinians. He said, "*I shall show how to parry but not inflict wounds. Even if some laugh, the real issues will be dealt with. Many issues are best fought this way and not to be dignified as serious.*"[22]

But when either the importance of the question or the insufferable acerbity of the instigator will not allow for silence, or dissimulation, then it is time to take up a defense in earnest and employ everything available to the ken and capacity of Wit, art, reason and eloquence. Bring on thunder and lightning, but don't allow the thunderbolts to stink of sulfur and infect the world. They should be made of purest light to illuminate the truth— spearheaded, not by uncontrolled fury— but justly delivered by reason. Let there be, as in Janus, the god of war, the face of a youth and of an elder, spirit and sense, strength and maturity, impulse and moderation. Let Chrysostom not lament, "*that sometimes we roam among adversaries like wolves, often not as winners, though had we as sheep followed the shepherd's guidance we might have won, for he is the shepherd not of the wolves but of the sheep.*"[23]

Letters would be happy if its teachers would conduct their rivalries and contests the way Protogenes and Apelles once strove in friendly contention. One would draw in the middle of a very thin line another line, even thinner, without the least crookedness. Happy if the acute and resplendent arms of Wit were as Cassiodorus said of certain others, "*the arms of law, not of fury,*"[24] rays of verity, not arrows of slander. But to conclude, experience shows that the controversies of Wit from civil as they ought to be, for the most part, turn criminal. It would be better in my judgement, when the interest of the public good does not stand against it, to convert the sword and spear into plowshares and

---

21 **Ibid:** *—Iraque nunquam*
*Prodiga telorum, Cautem Contenta Minari.*
22 **Tertullian,** *Apologia against the Valentinians*, 6: *Ostendam sed non imprimam vulnera. Si ridebitur alicubi, materiis ipsis satisfiet. Multa sunt sic digna revinci, ne gravitate adorentur.*
23 **John Chrysostom,** *Homily 34 on Matthew: Quod tanquam lupi in adversarios ruamus, saepe sine victoria, qui tamen vincerimus, si oves essemus à pastoris auxilio non recedentes, qui non luporum; sed ovium pastor est.*
24 Cassiodorus, *Works*, 7, Sermon 2: *arma juris, non furoris.*

pickaxes and to cultivate one's own Wits rather than warring against those of others. But if the urge to vituperate will only find peace and quiet when it is engaged in disquieting others, (as said Jerome to Augustine, eschewing a contest of Wits, and disputes), is there any want of public divulgers of error— heretics, atheists and politicians— to catch and convict? Let them leave the men and kill the beasts. Let them say with Entellus, when instead of Daretes, his enemy, he slew an ox.

> *Erice, I here to you this soul present,*
> *As being more worthy of this punishment*
> *Than that of Daretes. And victor, now useless,*
> *I lay by my art, and bow.*[25]

---

[25] *Aeneid* 5. 483/4, (Dryden): Caro's Italian Virgil: 5.e586/9:
> *Erice, a te quest'alma*
> *Piu degna di moroir offrisco invece*
> *Di quella di Darete. E vincitore*
> *Qui'l cesto e qui l'arte ripongo.*

# 8 *HAUGHTINESS*

## 8.1 *High Opinion of One's Own Knowledge and Low Opinion of Others'*

A man's head is not so small that it cannot carry, more than the fabled bladder of Ulysses, as many winds as vainglory and haughtiness can blow. And they are just as violent in turning land and sea upside down as the tornadoes that bring on storms and the exhalations in caverns below that make the earth shake with earthquakes. Equally disruptive in their way are those wretched letterati, so full or so empty of themselves, who issue forth with such estate, that they seem to careen astride a chariot in triumph. They are the Sauls, towering above others, *"head and shoulders"*,[1] not by a head so much, as by brain and mind. Such are the Olympians that the tallest mountain tops, the loftiest Wits, the broadest minds can scarce approach from below, to kiss their feet. They alone are the suns who enlighten all obscurity and obscure all enlightenment.

It is hard to know if they would more move Heraclitus to tears of compassion or Democritus to laughs of derision.[2] Well you may puzzle whether Alexarchus the grammarian was more apt for the philosopher's pity or the public's scorn, when he saw his school as Heaven; the rows of desks around him as the cycles of the spheres; his attentive pupils as stars; his lessons as the light; the nouns, pronouns, verbs, articles, etc. as signs of the zodiac; and himself as the sun.[3] Only so would he be painted, or portrayed, making it impossible to stare at him without squinting, as into the glare of the sun. Yet a title more suitable for him would be what Tiberius used for Appion, a grammarian like himself, and no less a braggart; someone devoid of sense and a windbag with the apt name *"Cymbal of the world."*[4]

What is there to say about the Remnius, (more puddle head, than Palaemon)? He would go up and down the streets bemoaning the world's misfortune; to go back, after he was gone, to how illiterate it

---

1 *Samuel*, 9.2: *Ab humero et sursum.*
2 Seneca, *De Ira* (On Anger), 2.10; Juvenal, *Satire* 10.28/35.
3 **Clement of Alexandria**, ***Protrepticon*** (*Exhortation to the Greeks*), 4: "assumed the character of the sun god."
4 Gellius, 5.14: *Cymbalum mundi.*

was before him, as the Letters born with him would die with him?[5] And indeed it seemed to be true for when he was dead, there was not even a single letter left to write his epitaph.

But far beyond the bounds of the ordinary human sense of superiority was the supreme idea that Alphonsus X, king of Castile, had of his Wit and knowledge. A man by profession astronomer (after whom still today the Alphonsine tables are named) yet not of such sublime intelligence, nor of such competence in this art that Atlas might have entrusted Heaven to his shoulders without danger of collapse. But he had such a high opinion of his own brain that he used to say, that had he been at God's ear when He created the Heavens and assigned their cycles to the stars, he would have taught Him how to dispose this work with greater order and with rules of more exact proportions.[6] Now let God go to ask Job as something transcending the capacity of our Wits, *"So, you think you know the order of Heaven and can teach it to earth?"* [7] As if God would go to school of Alphonsus in astronomy and bring along the volume of His Eternal Ideas, so that the king would erase and fix His model of the Heavens, and His pattern of the world in a more methodical contrivance.

Only madness could defend this idiot from the fulminations of the Heavens where *"He opened his mouth,"*[8] and, indeed, God dealing with him in his folly treated him with more compassion than anger and relieved his head of its pressure, as a madman gets a bloodletting from the middle vein of his forehead, by taking his crown away. He wanted him to understand that he was incapable of setting aright Heaven's revolutions in better form, by sending his kingdom a revolution which, with all the canons and rules of his calculations, he was never able set aright, so that he was thrown out of his house by his son and died in exile in a foreign land.

Men as mad as Alexarchus, as Remnius, though they may be less well-known, doubtless there are; as there ever were in the world. To describe them fittingly as they are, one might paint a great mass of smoke going up to the clouds; the more it rises, the more its size swells

5 Suetonius, *On Grammarians*, 23; not **Pliny, preface.**
6 Rodrigo **Sanchez** de Arevalo (1405-1470), ***Historia Hispaniae,*** 4.5
7 ***Job, 38.***33: Numquid nosti ordinem Coeli? et pones rationem ejus in terra?
8 *Isaiah, 49.1: posuit os suum (meum).*

and increases, and so we can apply Augustine's motto, **Quanto grandior, tanto vanior** (*The bigger it gets, the more futile it is.*)[9]

When we hear them vaunting themselves and disparaging others, we understand how well they deserve the salutation that Philip of Macedon gave in rejoinder to his vainglorious doctor, who had addressed him, **Menecrates Jupiter Philippo salutem**: (*Menecrates to Jupiter Philip, salutation*) His response: **Philippus Menecrati sanitatem**: (*Philip to Menecrates, sanity*), whereby he made himself the doctor of his doctor and sent him for the health of his brain, a dose of hellebore in salutation.

You may hear them brag that under their caps and gowns are lodged the loftiest and most profound cognitions, as under the bark of their shells and not elsewhere, can pearls be found, that their lectures are the charts of sure sailing, without which, in the sciences, there is risk of shipwreck or peril; that their doctrines are the ultimate bounds of truth, as the stars at the edge of the universe, so that,

*Higher than these there is nothing, these are the boundaries of creation.*[10]
Others are the springs, they the ocean: others are moles and they lynxes; others are butterflies, they are eagles; others fleas, they herons. "*O Doctors, relieve me of this madness!*"[11] or if he can't do it, at least let's try to open the door and let out the wind which so swells their wretched heads, and this we can do by bringing their eyes into the light of some crystal-clear truths, such as:

1. To everyone his own things, however small, seem big. Self-love is a concave mirror in which a hair becomes a tree and a mosquito becomes a Pegasus. With self-love as judge, one's own things loom large. A case in point was the Clitus who touted a battle at sea in which all of three galleys of the Greeks were beaten and sunk, as if he had put Xerxes to flight or set shackles on the sea. And from then on, he would only deign to be addressed by the mighty title of Neptune.[12]

The moon is forty times smaller in size than the earth. How can it appear to the judgement of the eye equal to the sun, which is

---

9 **Augustine, *On Psalm* 36.**
10 **Manilius**, *Astronomica* 1.534: *Altiùs his nihil est, haec confinia (fastigiia) mundi.*
11 Juvenal, *Satire* 6.46: *O medici, medium contundite venam* (*O medici, nimium pertundite venam*).
12 **Plutarch**, ***Oration* 2, *De fortuna Alexandri*** (*On the fortune of Alexander*).

itself larger than the earth by about a hundred and forty times?[13] Only because the vicinity of the moon to the earth makes it so much larger, the sun seems smaller, being at a much greater distance. Nothing, though, is closer than someone to the things he owns. That is why they seem incalculably huge and greater than the belongings of others—things outside our realm and sufficiently far away to be lost to sight.

2. If you compare grasshoppers to ants, is there any doubt they will look like giants? If you measure what you know, be it so little, with the knowledge of someone who knows nothing, you will think yourself absolutely, if only by comparison, most erudite. Those who would go to study in Athens, said Menedemus, arrived as doctors, lived as students and left knowing nothing.[14] This was not only because the more you know what you do know, the more you know what you don't know, but also because they were mixing with that most flourishing gathering of the noblest Wits on earth, matching their knowledge with minds that, by comparison, made them think they knew nothing.

This was the technique the great sage Socrates applied in his gentle deflation of the bold presumption of his Alcibiades. Wealthy from the wealth of his father and from amassing greater riches, he comported himself in the stately fashion of a great monarch, not as a private citizen of Athens. His teacher brought a mirror to his knowledge of himself with a world map wherein he found Europe; and on it Greece, and in Greece, with some trouble, Athens, *Now,* (says he) *show me here your house and your lands. They have, as you can see, no place on the world's map. And tell me why they fill your head with such contemptuous attitudes toward the world?* If you think your genius and Wit make you a star of the first magnitude, don't compare yourself with the smallest ones, but with the suns of the universe and in one and the same moment, you will see your light go out and your ambition shrink.

3. Someone who is great among others may long to be greater than them. To be in the first rank, but insist on being number one, is as insufferable an attitude as it was intolerable in that proud Pompey, *"Who, when he began his role in the Republic, would brook no equal and while he*

---

13 Forty times smaller, from Fontenelle to Voltaire to the nineteenth century, until modern astronomy made it 27% or less than 4 times smaller. The sun is 109 times the diameter of the earth.
14 **Plutarch, *Quomodo profectus*** etc. (*How a man may be aware of his progress in virtue*).

*should have accepted to be the first, he wanted to be the only one.*"[15] You may be outstanding in every branch of Letters, but that doesn't make you a lone phoenix, unique in all the world. You are no *Primum mobile* that needs no impulse or motion from a higher Heaven, to make the lesser spheres move and revolve.[16] Who is there so replete with knowledge, next to whom no one knows anything, for him to utter the insolent words of prince Caiaphas, **Vos nescitis quidquam** (*You know nothing*).[17] Nature was not so sterile that after making you, she could not find a comparable mold to make others. Nor was she so poor that, to make you rich in Wit, she had to let others go begging. When you look around you and see no one who stands up to you in command of knowledge, will you tell yourself in your insanity what Deucalion told his help mate, **Nos duo turba sumus** (*We two are a world in ourselves*).[18] Do you want to make your Wit into a Procrustes and command everyone to adapt to the measure of your judgment as the rule of truth? Would you want to chop off the feet of anyone who surpasses you, and stretch the feet of anyone who does not reach your height?

But even if you were for Wit and knowledge the first of the foremost, would it not reveal a base heart and a vile spirit for you to anoint yourself your own panegyrist and make a mockery of others? Hear how the torrents rumble and how they roar as they splash against the rocks. They seem not a flood of water, but a very sea, yet oft times they are but a few inches deep, though they stretch for a mile. Then there are the royal rivers, as deep as they are wide, with what, may I say, modesty, do they flow towards the sea? They give not the least murmur to betray how deep is their bosom, how ample their shores, how clear their waters, how rapid their currents, so silently and quietly do they flow. Those unable to reach deep below the surface (often in Wit, always in judgement) are most intolerably raucous and deafen the world with their self-praise and disparagement of others. They are unaware that they grow more contemptible, the more they inflate. As

---

15 **Velleius Paterculuis**, *History* ,2.33: *Qui, ut primùm Rempublicam aggressus est, quemquam animo parem non tulit, et in quibus rebus primus esse debebat, solus esse cupiebat.*
16 Aristotle, *Metaphysics*, 12.1072a.
17 *John* 11.49.
18 Ovid, *Met.*, 1.355.

the aphorism of Symmacus goes: *"In the spirits of the great there is no room for affected presumption."*[19]

It is characteristic of overweening Wits, not only to be haughty on earth, but also disrespectful towards Heaven. In the first instance, they are unjust to men when they arrogate undeserved superiority; in the second, they are sacrilegious with respect to God, whose being, whose actions, they would weigh by the scale and by the measure of their limited understanding. Therefore, on this subject, I offer you the following considerations.

## 8.2  *Two Great Misdeeds of Misbelievers:*
### *Pursuing Matters of Faith with the Curiosity of Philosophy and Believing Matters of Philosophy with the Certainty of Faith*

Geographers, when they make their map charts or globes of the earth, as they reach the confines of the known world, not knowing what lies beyond, are accustomed to draw some indistinct lines and outlines at random with fine dots and in the area left blank to write *Terra Incognita*. Of this practice of the geographers Plutarch made very apt use to excuse his pen when he began the lives of the heroes of remotest antiquity and could not speak in detail of the feats that had won them the greatness of their names and their glory as immortals. Antiquity and subsequent oblivion kept many lands unknown and many aspects of their lives occult and hidden. What Plutarch had to say about the feats of those ancient worthies is equally true of all the great complex of things which may be known by our intelligence.[1] Much is known, yet much is unknown— and not just unknown, but unknowable— until we make that school where the Word, the teacher who enlightens with a single glance, will teach us with indelible and crystaline signs all that our Wits, with the fruitless labor of their thoughts, strive in vain to penetrate. I mean the most hidden mysteries of belief. These are sure, if not transparent, and call for the submission of the faithful, not the inquisitiveness of the curious.

A man of the highest genius and greatest understanding possible, when measured against what he presumes to understand, is

---

19 **Symmachus, Book 10, Letter** 29; *In magnos animos non cadit affectata jactatio.*

1 Plutarch, *Theseus.*

hardly more than a shallow ditch to contain the ocean. Despite the lofty speculations and sublime thoughts with which the mind is elevated to the knowledge of the occult truths of faith, they come no nearer than the giants of Phlegra were to touching Heaven as they stood on top of Pelion, Ossa, and Olympus.[2]

The eye of a bat is not made to stare at the sun; eagles with their diamond-like pupils can scarce fix it in their sights. Fishing boats with a piece of sail and half a rudder are not made to navigate the ocean and discover new worlds.

Our intellects, attached to the weight of the senses are like ostriches, their bodies larger than their wings, unable to lift themselves a few inches from the ground or to fly except with their wings in the air, as their feet remain on the ground. But even if our wings were masterful, would that let us reach up to the clouds in flight, even to the stars? What mind, what genius of such lofty knowledge, exists that he can forego offering to God the sacrifice of his thoughts, upon that famous altar of Athens dedicated, *Ignoto Deo (to an unknown God)*.[3] He confesses his inability to understand what God conceals of his being and his workings and, so to speak, he will incline the winged auspices of his thoughts, as the auguries of birds in ancient rituals, so he cay say with Augustine, "*Better a faithful ignorance than the temerity to want to know.*"[4]

The water of a fountain will rise no higher than the head spring at its source and they say that water rises as high as it can fall. Now our judgement, does it not originate in the senses? And the senses to what else are they geared, if not to things perceptible within the bounds of nature? So how can we expect from this source, "*the fountain of waters springing up to eternal life*,"[5] which we understand to be our knowledge of things supernatural and divine?

Within the ranks of those we may call impiously curious, there are some who would presume to become on their own professors of subjects which heretofore have had no students. They whet the point of their Wits, despite the total impossibility of it, trying to penetrate to the very center of truth and see her in herself, unveiled and naked. They have scarce a mouth to suck the milk of faith, and already they

---

2 Ovid, *Met.*,1.151/62. *Gigantomachia*.
3 ***Acts of Apostles***.
4 Augustine, *De Trinitate*, 1.5: *Melior est fidelis ignorantia, quam temeraria scientia*.
5 ***John* 4.14**: *Fontem aquae saltentis in vitam aeternam*.

want to gnaw its bones, and ingest its marrow. They act as if they already understood what in nature is intelligible, so that they have nothing left to investigate but the occult mysteries of faith. They try to be Hercules. He had seen and conquered, the sea, the earth and Hell itself, and they say after him:

> *The earth tamed and the sea calmed,*
> *The infernal regions felt our strength,*
> *The heavens are untouched, but worthy of a labor of Hercules*
> *I shall approach the world's sublime space*
> *And dominate the ethereal region.* [6]

But as they stretch up on their feet to spread their wings and fly, it would be high time for someone to intimate the enormity of their challenge and the paltriness of their talent, someone to whisper in their ears, what the woman of Samaria said to Christ. *"Lord, you have nothing to draw with and the well is deep."*[7]

Before you take on greater matters, please answer me this question that St. Jerome has for you: Why does the elephant, a mountain of flesh, have only four feet on which to stand the enormous bulk of his huge body, while a flea, a living speck, has six? Do you have the nerve not knowing this, (and if you did, you would know nothing) to presume still to grasp what not even a man who understands everything cannot? At the first step I have made you take in the land of knowledge, like Thales, you fall into a ditch,[8] yet you make bold to see what is so far above the stars? A good lesson for you is the one Zeno the Stoic taught a brash youth. He had as little hair on his face as sense in his head and he wanted answers for things though he could hardly understand what he was asking. The philosopher put him in front of a mirror, asking in his ear: *"Do you think that the questions you have and the answers you want from me, are conceded to that wisp of a beard?"*[9]

Your Wit in comparison to that of the great Augustine is but as a grasshopper beside a horse. And you want to run the lance, and

---

6 **Seneca, *Hercules Furens*** (*Madness of Hercules*), 955/60:
> *Perdomita tellus, tumida cesserunt freta*
> *Inferna nostros regna sensere impetus*
> *Immune coelum est. Dignus Alcidae labor.*
> *In alta mundi spatia sublimis ferar*
> *Petatur aether.*

7 *John* 4.11: *Domine, neque in quo haurias habes, et puteus altus est.*

8 Aesop, Fable 40.

9 Laertius, *Zeno,* 7.19,

hit the mark, when he draws back and presumes not to try? He ressembled more the philosopher who threw himself into the sea, saying, *O abysse tu me cape, quia te ipse non capio (Grasp me, O abyss, for you I cannot grasp.)* [10] A hundred times in his writings he confesses he knows nothing, that he doesn't know even how to know, with the words: "*I don't know and do not blush to confess not to know what I do not.*"[11] How do you have the nerve to open your mouth and raise your voice to contradict and question what for sixteen centuries the pens of a world of learned doctors, the blood of a world of martyrs, the consensus of so many peoples, the proof of so many miracles have attested and ratified? With the taper of your little knowledge, do you propose to examine the light of the sun? Can the wisdom of God, your Master, not work in you what the wisdom of Pythagoras did for his students? "*For us there is no place for curiosity after Jesus Christ, nor for investigation after the Gospel.*" [12]

Others there are whose innate temperament (genius) is at once baser and more obstinate. Swearing *in verba magistri (in the teacher's words)*, they take the texts of some ancient philosophers for sacraments and their sentences for oracles and so agree to confess Christ, as long as they do not have to deny Aristotle or Plato. Thus, they hold balanced on a scale the equal weights of credence, the Gospel and Philosophy.

"*What has Athens to do with Jerusalem? What has the Academy to do with the Church? Our religion comes from the porch of Solomon: They should understand this those who want to confuse Stoic and Platonic dialectic with the dialectic of Christianity.*"[13] Even today the Church bewails and will lament to the end of time the damage done to her by the secular world's profane and idle teaching and by its ancient writers, the fathers of its darkness and teachers of its countless errors, to call them with the title Tertullian gave them **Patriarchas Haereticorum** (*Patriarchs of the heretics*)[14]

---

10 Aristotle.

11 **Augustine,** (*Confessions*): *Nescio, et non erubesco confiteri me nescire quod nescio.*

12 **Tertullian, *De praescriptione hereticorum*, 7:** *Nobis curiositate opus non est post Christum Jesum, nec inquisitione post Evangelium.*

13 ***Ibid:*** *Quid Athenis et Hierosolymis? Quid Academiae, et Ecclesiae? Nostra institutio de porticu Salomoni. Viderint qui Stoicum cum et Platonicum, et Dialecticum Christianum protulerunt.*

14 **Tertullian, *Adversus Hermogenes*.** (Farewell ancient wisdom, in this my wolrds are more orthodox than thou.)

What great damage did Plato do in the first centuries of the Church too much read, too much believed, and become, as the same Tertullian said, **Haeresum Condimentarium** (the condiment of heresy)?[15] For instance, and we pass over all the rest, since his example serves for all, we have the unhappy Origen. From an eagle keen to fix his eyes on the sun of Christian wisdom and to draw therefrom the light of the most sublime truths, he was transformed into a bat chasing a few sparks of light mixed in with many shades of ignorance and error. He became so great a Platonist that in the end he ceased being Catholic, losing truth to fables and faith to philosophy. The same man whose breast was kissed, *"just as a temple of the Holy Spirit and of heavenly wisdom,"*[16] was transformed into the master of a school of errors and the leader of the blind. What he said was so mad that as prior, **Ubi bene nemo melius** (*where good none better*) so after, **Ubi male nemo pejus** (*where bad, none worse.*)[17] What infinite destruction even today comes from that *"cunning chameleon of constructing and destroying,"*[18] Aristotle credited as the author of the mortality of the soul, as much as to say, the destroyer of the faith and father of those who without a human soul live the life of beasts? How many of his conspirators, *"who croak nothing else but Aristotle,"*[19] hold only those points of faith for certain that accord with the peripatetic oracles of the Lyceum, as if the Gospel were a grain of wheat, to be picked from the husk of human philosophy and not a bread of life come down from Heaven whose Taste, when savored, made us spit out the husks from our mouths, *"that have no marrow and no nourishment for instructing the folk, with the unsavory chaff of their contents."* [20]

Those are frogs, says Augustine, *"Frogs croaking in muddy swamps making noise but not inculcating the doctrine of true wisdom."*[21] Now, while the Heavens are opening to you, and you hear the Father, (pointing with

15 Tertullian, *De anima*, 23.
16 *tamquam Spiritus Sancti, et coelestis sapientiae templum.*
17 **Cassiodorus, *Institutiones Divinarum et Saecuarium Litterarum*, 1.**
18 Tertullian, *De praesciptione haereticorum*, 7: *Struendi et destruendi Artifex versipellis.*
19 **Cyril of Alexandra, *Thesaurus*, 11**: *Qui nihil aliud quam Aristotelem ructant.*
20 **Jerome, *On Jeremiah*, 4**: *Quae medullam non habent, nec possunt nutrire discentium populos, sed de inanibus stipulis conteruntur.*
21 Augustine, *Sermon 109: Ranae clamantes de paludibus limosis (quae) strepitum habere possunt, doctrinam verae sapientiae insinuare non possunt.*

his finger to the Word, his Son,) say ***Ipsum audite*** *(Hear him,)*[22] will you lend one eye to Christ, and the other to Aristotle, or to Plato? ***Coelum tonat: taceant Ranae*** *(Heaven is thundering, let the frogs be silent.)*[23] Where Christ teaches and reveals the truth, indeed, Himself the Truth, wisdom is silent and the philosophy of the world has no tongue, ***et philosophia nostra Christus est***. *(And our philosophy is Christ.)*[24]

---

22 *Matthew*, 17.5.
23 **Augustine,** *Sermon* **109**.
[24] **Peter Damian** (1007-1073), *Sermon* 57.

# 9              *LAZINESS*

### *Delusion of Thinking You Can Study Little and Know Much*

Not just from Hippocrates alone, nor only from Aristotle and Theophrastus, but from the tongues of the entire world we hear the public consensus and universal complaint: that Heaven, while it has been so prodigal with crows, with cypresses and with rock, has been most ungenerous with us in the allotment of time;[1] that our condition makes the mastery of art too long and too difficult in a life too short;[2] that our meagre viaticum is so very paltry for such long journeys. Lost are those forges of steel, those *Elixir vitae* (Elixirs of life) that embalmed alive men who once lived near to a thousand years of age and would decide to leave this world more from being tired of life than from having to die. We are like flowers, born yesterday, old today and dead tomorrow. Our life is so short, it seems we were born, but to die. What for the ancients was childhood; in us is old age, their pittance are our extraordinary riches; their overabundance, our treasures; and our white hairs are hailed with as much truth as Wit by Philo of Alexandria[3] and Tertullian, "***Haec est aeternitas nostra.***" *(This is our eternity).*[4]

If our knowledge that life is so very short could but persuade us to spend it according to its brevity, what seems a bane, would be a boon. It is an unreasonable thing to accuse Heaven of being niggardly with time to us when we are so foolishly prodigal in wasting it. We use our life as if its measure were the long span of many centuries, not the paltry handful of a few years. Who is there who does not exclaim with the father of medicine **Ars longa, vita brevis** (*the art so long to master, the life so short*)? Yet who has the determination to hasten to where even the most dedicated arrive but late? "*Who can reach wisdom? Who judges it worth knowing, unless in passing? Who looks on the study of philosophy or any liberal art, except on days when there are no games, or it rains, as more than a waste of time?*"[5]

---

1 **Seneca**, *On the brevity of life*, 1.
2 **Laertius**, *Theophrastus*, 5.41.
3 **Philo of Alexandria**, *Exhoration to the heathens*, 4.
4 **Tertullian**, *On the apparel of women*, 2.6.
5 **Seneca**, *QN*, 7.32: *Ad sapientiam quis accredit? Quis dignam iudicat nisi quam in transitu noverit? Quis philosophiam aut ullum liberale respice studium,*

# Laziness

Nature in her wisdom has placed man in the middle of the world as in the center of an immense theater. Cassiodorus calls him, says, *"A noble animal standing with his head erect for the most sublime deliberations,"*[6] so that not as a listless sojourner but as an avid spectator of this her incomparable creation; in such unity so various; in such variety so united; miraculous, with more wonders that adorn it than the parts it is made of. For those who see it clearly, it was nature's plan to place us not in the world, but in a theatre to admire, as in a school, and to learn. Therefore, she has enkindled in our hearts an inextinguishable desire for knowledge and set open before our eyes as many volumes as the parts of nature that comprise the Heavens and the elements, showing their clear interconnections and motivating us to find their hidden causes. What dynamic energy, what force of nurturing intelligence or of intrinsic power, turns the great framework of the elements with indefatigable movement? Are the spheres of the planets many Heavens, linked inside one another in a concave gyre and in a mutual embrace or is a single Heaven home to that whole great family of stars? Composed of what substance? Corruptible or immortal? Liquid as air, or solid and firm as diamond? Whence the sunspots, whence the bright faculae on the sun? Whence the darkness on the face of the Moon? What fire ignites the comets and new stars that of a sudden appear? What are they made of? Are they from elsewhere or citizens of Heaven? Indigenous to it, or risen up from here below? The irregular orbits of the planets, how can they coalesce in regular order? How to understand, how to predict the eclipses? How deep is the sky? What is the number of the stars? How fast do they move? What size are they? The winds, what makes them fly? What size are they? The spaces they move in, the forces of resistance, the quality of their workings, the regular measures of their time to be born, to last, to vanish? The clouds— who keeps them in air whatever their weight? How are the rains distilled, drop by drop? How from their womb, laden with water come flashes of lightning, which is fire? Who melts them into snow? Who makes them form hail? What ultramarine shells paint the rainbows with a uniform order of hues and a proportionate diameter for each? How do springs of water rise on the highest

---

*nisi cum ludi intercalantur, cum aliquis pluvius intervenit dies quem perdere libet?*
6 **Cassiodorus,** *De anima*, 11, *De positione corporis: Procerum animal et in effigiem pulcherrimae speculationis erectum.*

160

mountain tops? How in mountains of the same earth are there such different kinds of marble, such different tempers of metal? Who gives the sea its ebb and flow? Who keeps the rivers full, though their banks are always flowing out to sea? The interweaving of flowers and herbs, the workmanship of the diverse bodies of the animals, the birds, the fish, the tempering of mixed elements, the harmony of the ordinary elements with the arcane qualities. Finally, what exists, what is made, what is its being, how is it produced? [7]

To know all this in comparison to what might be known is to know nothing. And yet, is there anyone who can know this Nothing entirely? There is, then, so much to know and we have so little time to live and learn it. And do we think that only our surplus hours and bits of time are enough for us to study? Hear now what I have told you, perfected in the concluding parts of that precious slim treatise by Seneca, **De otio sapientis** (*On the studies of the sage*), *"Nature has endowed us with an inquiring Wit and aware of her arts and her beauty she has created us to contemplate her many wonderous works as spectators. She would feel deprived of the fruits of her work if such great, clear and intricately woven, such crystalline and manifold beauties were observed in solitude. And to let you know that she wanted us not just to look at, but to admire all this, look at the position she has placed us in… You were born to examine these things though you haven't much time, even if you dedicate yourself to it wholly. Even if you miss nothing out of superficiality or negligence, Man is born for immortal knowledge, but he is too mortal for it."*[8]

The sages, teachers of the world have left us for eternity, some the memory of their lives, others, the works of their Wit. So we must treat as the small diamonds what they treasured as precious, those minutest spaces of free time, which we can only worthily possess as misers. It was a miracle to see them while they were in the world and in this, as in their love of knowledge, they resembled the planet

---

7 This spirited incantation, or paean, catalogues the contemporary agenda in astronomy and natural philosophy, expressing the scientific curiosity of the generation inspired by Galileo.

8 *Ibid.* 5: *Curiosum nobis natura ingenium dedit, et artis sibi, ac pulchritudinis suae conscia, spectatores nos tantis rerum spectaculis genuit; perditura fructum sui, si tam magna, tam clara, tam subtiliter ducta, tam nitida, et non uno genere formosa, solitudini ostenderet. Ut scias illam spectari voluisse, non tantum aspici: vide quem nobis locum dedit…. Ad haec quaerenda natus, aestima quam non multum acceperis temporis, etiam si illud totum tibi vindices. Licet nihil facilitate eripi, nihil negligentia patiatur excidere, Tamen homo ad immortalium cognitionem, nimis mortalis est.*

Mercury, so very close to the sun that it can only be seen with great difficulty. The eyes of earth are negligible to those standing always in the eyes of the sun, these it watches not with an ineffective gaze, but with a large communication of light. In their perpetual study, they are like those falcons on the hunt near the north pole, where the days are shortest when the sun is in Capricorn. Then they become increasingly focused on finding, fast in following and energetic in marking and snatching their prey. Men, whose hair and whose thoughts were equally candid, were not ashamed to stop in the public byways, wherever they found some new knowledge. Diogenes, when scolded for eating in the public square, said, *"When I feel hungry in the market, why should I not eat in the market?"*[9] For them, something unknown was sufficient excuse to go and find it where it was. Furthermore, what the law of nature dictated for the body's sustenance, they allowed themselves from necessity, not for pleasure. It often happened that, either by voluntary abstinence they went without or sometimes, lost in the deep thoughts of their studies, at times they might forget. Thus, Carneades forgot that he was a man while he was all mind and all thought and was sated with the sweetest nectar of those noble cognitions with which he feasted his Wit. He might have let his body die of hunger if others had not forced him and revived him with food.[10] Thus, Archimedes seemed always outside himself, while he really was more than ever totally inside himself. Plutarch said, *"Taken from his desk, undressed and oiled for bath by his servants he would trace mathematical formulas on his skin."*[11] Thus, to pass over a hundred others, Demosthenes, knowing himself indebted to his noble Wit for his great success, made his house a prison, and shaved his head and he would not go out in public until he saw the hair on his head grown long and he had in his mind the sage reflections he was searching for.[12] We ought to be so much the more studious than they, since next to them our Wits are smaller. Are we doing not just enough, but even more than our duty, if from the comforts of sleep, from the business of our affairs, from the engagements of our interests, we take one or at most two hours a day to dedicate them to study? With so

---

9 **Laertius,** *Diogenes,* 6.58: *Cum in foro esuriam, quare in foro non edam?*
10 Valerius Maximus, *Histories,* 8.2.5.
11 **Plutarch, *An seni gerenda res publica,*** (*Should elders engage in government*) 5: *abstractus à tabula, à familis, spoliatus, unctus, super ipsa pelle sua Mathematica Schemata exarabat.*
12 Plutarch, *Demosthenes,* 7.

little study it would take the life a Noah, *"With the little nourishment we get, we keep death at bay, but we shall never develop to robust good health."*[13] Drops of water, continuously dripping, become chisels and excavate marble, it is true.[14] But because this is marble and they, drops of water, that it takes a hundred years before they can bore down a finger.

     Did you ever hear in an ancient comedy (be it by Aquilius, or by Plautus) entitled **Boeotia**, about a certain parasite complaining about the clever man who invented the art of making sundials, to the discomfort of stomachs? As they became the measure of hours and of the times that regulated public and private activities, no more could you eat when you felt hungry, but when it pleased the dial? Hear some of the verses given by Gellius.

*May the gods damn the one who first set the hours,*
*And came up with this sundial,*
*He has cut my day into pieces.*
*When I was a boy my stomach was my clock.*
*Now it won't get permission unless the sun allows it.*
*And now that sundials are in all places everywhere*
*Most parched folks are crawling with hunger.*[15]

So great a desire should you have to keep feeding your mind with the sweet honey of wisdom that your sleeping hours should seem like centuries, and the albeit necessary activities of sustenance, like torments. That same Demosthenes, I just mentioned, had such a great hunger to feed the mind that he weened his eyes from sleep and his mouth from food, so that, *"He was said to spend more on lantern oil than on wine, and to be at study before any early morning workers."*[16]

---

13 **Symmachus,** *Works* 1, **Letter** 23 *to Ausonius*: *Parvis nutrimentis quanquam à morte defendimus, nihil tamen ad robustam valetudinem promovemur.*
14 **Seneca, *QN,*** 4.3 (*Gutta cavat lapidem.*)
15 **Gellius, 3.3:**
*Ut illum Di malè perdant, primus qui horas reperit.*
*Quique adeo primus statuit hic Solarium,*
*Qui mihi comminuit misero articulatim diem.*
*Nam, me puero, uterus hic erat Solarium*
*Multo omnium istorum optimum et verissimum.*
*Ubi iste monebat esse nisi cum nihil erat.*
*Nunc etiam non est quod est, nisi Soli lubet.*
*Itaque jam oppletum est oppidum Solariis,*
*Major pars populi aridi reptant fame.*
16 **Jerome,** *Apologia,* **2 against Ruffinus**: *Plus olei, quàm vini expendisse dicitur, et omnes Artifices nocturnis semper vigiliis praevenisse.*

And it should be a law for you to follow, not to give to that greedy tax collector (as Clement of Alexandria called sleep)[17] the half of your life for surety. Their law permits the Sybarites, human animals, to banish all cocks from their city, so their crowing does not break the thread of sleep in the sweet hours.[18] You should use your beds, not to bury yourselves inside them, but to lay on top of them. Keep, as Pythagoras did, a faithful cock to wake you at dawn and raise you from the plumes to the pen, from the dreams of fancy to the contemplations of the mind.

You cannot expect what befell that fortunate warrior Timotheus whose good luck drew cities, castles, provinces into a great net and threw them in his lap as he was peacefully asleep.[19] In Letters, no fish are caught while asleep, because wisdom is not the gift of fortune, but the fruit of industry. Imagine that Cassiodorus is giving you his advice to certain others about the duty of their office: *"Keep steady watch with the night birds and keep your eyes open though the night, as they will find their food in the dark, so you can earn just praise."*[20]

These are the most precious hours of the day. Either it is a question of the privilege of particular influences of Heaven, as Ficino teaches,[21] or because thoughts are impressed on the clearest surface of one's spirits as their murky and gross parts are revived or digested during sleep. They appear unclouded in the mind's mirror where they seem the reflections of those Prime Ideas that are the forms of truth. Whatever the explanation, the experience of one who practices it teaches that Aurora is the mother of honey, when the finest pearls fall on the pages of a writer, as the dew congeals in their shells.

For one who uses it in this manner, sleep becomes not only what Tertullian called it, *"restorer of the body, reinforcing strength, guarantor of effectiveness, respite from work, balm for labor, to which the day gives way and the night sanctions, taking the color away from the world outside."*[22] But what he added further, the master of resurrection to a more blessed way of life.

---

17 **Clement of Alexandria,** *Paedagogia* 2.93.

18 **Atheaenus**, *Deiipnosophists, or Banquet of the Learned*, 12.

19 **Aelian,** 3.43.

20 **Cassiodorus, *Works*, 7, formula 8**: *Vigilia impiger cum nocturnis avibus, nox tibi pandat aspectus: et sicut illa reperiunt in obscuris cibum, ita tu possis invenire praeconium.*

21 **Marsilio Ficino** (1433-1499), *De Vita 1.*

22 **Tertulllian,** *De anima,* 43 (*de somno*): *Recreatorem corporum, redintegratorem virium, probatorem valetudinum, peccatorem operum,*

*Laziness*

The voice of an angel in the mouth of a beast is that excellent saying of Apollonius of Tyana, *"Who used to say* (according to Philostratus) *that a right living philosopher converses with God with the coming of dawn, speaks about God as day begins, and spends the rest of his time dealing with the world of men and conducting affairs.'*[23] For the workings of the mind, in whatever topic it is engaged, there is no time better than the first dawn of day. Then it seems, that by some mysterious consensus, the Wit lights up, as the day breaks to the world. Therefore, *"Blessed are they who keep constant vigil as the angels do."*[24]

And this ought to be the enterprise not of a few days only, but the regular rule of our lives, that in the division of the hours of the day, we dedicate the first and normally the most of that time to study. At least we should be able to say, as that great master of ancient painting, that no day passes, in which we have not, if not painted a whole face, at least drawn a line.[25] A light, a flame, while alive and kindled, is fed with little fuel, but if allowed to dwindle and die, it takes more to light it again. Let us not be like the Nile; the Tigris, and other rivers which before reaching the sea, often go buried underground and then rise again. They are, in truth, lost in hidden ways, in whirlpools, and then gushing out, appear once more. They have a hundred sources, spring a hundred times, are always themselves, yet never quite so. To stymie one's studies by a series of long interruptions, owing more to the inconstancy of inborn character (genius), than to the call of important affairs, this is to start big, to get nowhere and to finish never.

---

*medicum laborum, cui legitime fovendo dies cedit, nox legem facit, auferens rerum etiam colore.*
23 **Philostratus, *Life of Apollinaris* 1.12**: *Qui aiebat opportere rectè Phylosophantes, adveniente aurora cum Deo versari; procedente die, de Deo loqui, reliquum tempus humanis rebus, et sermonibus dare.*
24 Clement of Alexandria, *ibid: Beati qui seipsos assimilant angelis ita vigilando.*
25 Apelles, Pliny, 35.36. *Nulla dies sine linea.*

# 10                 *IMPRUDENCE*

## 10.1    *Thankless Task of Studying Contrary to the Inclination of One's Genius*

To make a happy start on the journey in the arts, in the sciences and in every profession of Letters, it is just as necessary for someone to consult his own internal genius and to take his direction from where it inclines as it is for one who is going to sea to observe where the wind is blowing; to dress the sails and tilt the rudder accordingly.[1] Nature is like the planets. Where they go retrograde, they make little progress. The one who pushes more and forces her will make less progress than the one who best intuits and seconds her; so that, operating freely in every undertaking, however challenging, with no less facility than felicity, she succeeds. She is like the celestial sirens who turn the great spheres simply with their song. But if she is met with violence, she does not increase her power by being forced, but rather, what was before its force, loses its power, as water is frozen by the cold— before it had movement, now all its strength is exhausted, and immobilized, as good as dead.

In the workings of the Wit, one contends not so much with the problems encountered in acquiring knowledge as with one's own genius and what that master of the Art called **Invita Minerva** (*the unresponsive Muse*).[2] Like someone swimming against the current where it runs fastest, he will swim hard, but not move ahead, until he is tired out and with diminished strength loses all determination, confirming the truth of that most natural of axioms: *Nothing violent is lasting*

This is manifest proof of the error of those who try to practice Letters and among them, either the speculative ones, or the practical ones or the mixed.[3] Where inclination, where talent (genius), where nature, does not lead them, it is just like trying to stop the rivers from flowing, to force them up mountains climbing up all the way to the top.

---

1 Salvator Rosa's etching, *The Genius of Salvator Rosa*, is analysed with reference to this discourse by Maria Rosaria Nappi, *Rosa Rame, Salvator Rosa incisore*, (2014), p. 164.
2 Horace, *Ars poetica*, 385.
3 For example, philosophy, science, and jurisprudence.

The sage Athenians considered the start of not knowing had its beginning in not knowing from the start how to learn what nature has placed before us. Before they sent their children to any course of training they tried to guess their bent. Ordinarily, the truthful interpreters of that were the things they were drawn to and they did so by letting them play with the tools of all professions. As Nazianzen says, *"So what they liked and ran to willingly, they would be set to learn."*[4]

They believed that Heaven was beckoning where by itself their inclination was leading them. And in that, they understood the mysterious Cebes, who in the first round of his tablet set the inborn genius whose call steers men though the sequence written out for them in life, *"It ordained when they came into life what they should be and showed what they should commit their lives to doing, if they wanted to have a successful life."*[5]

God, said Plato (covering the lymph of a most excellent truth under the bark of a fable) has linked the minds of men with different metals.[6] In peasants, iron; in princes, gold; and in all the others ranging between them he has mixed them proportionate to their status. So, from this come the various inclinations and varieties of talents. I would counsel every man, therefore, first by the essay of a good touchstone to test what the temper of his metal is and gain from it what it can offer. Let him trace (the Platonists also say) in the descent of his genius from the stars, as it was passing through the inner spheres, the seal of which planet it was marked by whether by a speculative Saturn, or by a lordly Jupiter, or a warlike Mars and let him confidently apply himself to the pen, to the sceptre or to the sword accordingly.

For certain, sometimes at school, it is a thing most disagreeable and awkward to see certain heads better suited to crack a tortoise shell, than to study.[7] Heads that have a mind so dumb and so ill-suited for the profession of Letters that they seem, contrary to Jove, to carry Bacchus in the brain and Pallas in the belly. Their intellect is heavy and gross, like the water of the Dead Sea (Lake Asphaltites) in which nothing sinks to the bottom. It creeps at a slower pace than the sloth,

---

4 **Gregory Nazianzen**, *Epistle* 227, *Basil to Eudoxius.: Ut qua quisque delectabatur et ad quam sponte currebant, eam doceretur.*
5 *Table of Cebes: Mandabat quid eis, ubi in vitam venerint, faciendum sit, et cui vitae se committere debeant, si salvi esse in vita velint, ostendebant.*
6 **Plato, *Dialogue on Justice*, 3. (*Republic*, 3.415).**
7 As a Jesuit regent at the Collegio dei Nobili in Parma (1630/4), Bartoli clearly knew the frustrations of teaching dullards first hand, while he was very popular with his best students. Some became lifelong friends and correspondents.

a remarkable creature of India, that when it is at its speediest moves half a pace in a hundred steps and a mile in a hundred days. No file can be found tempered hard enough to ruffle their brain, or at least to scrape off its rust. Let us lick (as bears do with their unformed cubs) with all the major tongues in the world,[8] they will never be able to shape on them the least feature of a man of Letters. Ammonanius the Grammarian would sooner make his ass a philosopher than try to teach one of them to learn the rules of grammar.[9]

To what purpose do you put such people in school, as in a stone cutter's workshop, if after all the hewing and chiseling they look more like a block than a Mercury? Why try to drill someone's head with Letters, where if Vulcan opened it, rather than a Pallas Athena, you would find a bat? Why find a teacher who is an eagle, if only to teach a tortoise to fly? One may be an oracle of wisdom, but why undergo the chore of instilling Letters in the head of one who lets all he knows fly out of his brain and can write no more Letters than cranes or storks make as they fly?

No use wanting pumices to be sponges, mastiffs to be greyhounds, and for oaks instead of acorns to make honey which can never be done despite all possible grafting. The foolish Sybarites taught their horses to dance and destroyed the warlike disposition of that generous animal with such an unmanly exercise. It is the same error to want one born for war to practice Letters, as it is wrong to try make an Archimedes out of someone who wants to be a Marcellus.

What then? We may challenge, but we cannot conquer nature. Sooner or later, when left at liberty, she will lead back to the place from where others violently abducted her. Achilles may for a time be hidden under a women's apparel. *"After being trained in the rocky, rustic and monstrous school of a savage tutor, he submitted to feminine dress. With his hair combed, he was made up to look in the mirror with necklaces and even pierced ears, so he looked like a woman".*[10] But all this cannot to be lasting in Achilles, as the genius of Achilles is better suited to the activities of a fighter than to those of a female. Therefore, the **Necessitas,** not of the Trojan

---

8 See Virgil, *Georgics*, 3.385.
9 See *Suda*, Adler alpha1639; Photius, *Bibliotheca*.
10 **Tertullian**, *De pallio* (*On the Philosopher's Mantle*) **4**: *Ille apud rupicem, et sylvicosam, et monstrorum eruditorem scrupea schola eruditus, patiens jam ustriculas, sustinens stolam fundere, comam struere, cutum singere, speculum consulere, colum demulcere, aurem quoque foratu effaeminatus.*

war, but of his genius, reawakened at the sight of a sword, *"He became a man again: the battle was sounding and the arms at hand. The sword's steel, he said, drew out his manhood."*[11]

Here I offer you in the matter of Letters only four out of a thousand who plied trades different from what the bent of their natural inclination intended and, after struggling in vain, they gave up the fight.

Socrates, training in sculpture, carved the three graces, but, I suppose, so gracelessly, that hell would not have accepted them as furies. He realized that at working marbles he himself was a stone. So, he broke the tips of his chisels and sharpened those of his Wit and gave himself to moral philosophy, where his genius led him. When he was an artisan, he was unable to turn his stones into statues of men, when he was a philosopher, he was able to shape his men, spellbound, into statues.

Plato gave himself to painting and seeing that he was turning into the caricature of a painter and that his paintings were no good except in the dark; he switched from indifferent drawings of bodies to the noble depiction of souls. He left the lies of the brushes and gave himself to the truth of the Ideas whose features he was the first to draw and whose image he brought to earth.

Augustus was ambitious to graft the poet's laurels upon his imperial wreath and to be an Apollo with the lyre, as he was a Jupiter with lightning. He composed his tragedy *Ajax* which, for the guffaws it earned, turned rather into a comedy, it was so poorly written. He still insisted, despite its lack of art, on a tragedy and this he got, for he gave it a tearful finale by tearing it to pieces. Capricorn, which he had in his ascendant, called him to rule, not to rhyme; not to the pen, but to the sceptre; not to private displays, but to the public theater of the world.

On the other side, Ovid was set by his father to litigation. He litigated more with himself than with anyone else. His genius as a poet and the most congenial influence of Gemini,[12] called him from the

---

11 **Tertullian,** *ibidem: reddidit sexum: De praelio sonuerat, nec arma longè. Ipsum, inquit, ferrum virum attrahit.*

12 In his *Astronomia Riformatata* (1666), Giambattista Riccioli, to celebrate Bartoli's brilliance, gives the exact degree of his ascendant in Gemini and assigns to him the discovery of the cloud belts of Jupiter on May 16, 1630. For this he put his student's name on a southernmost crater on the Moon. **Bartolus** is at the bottom of Riccioli's famous lunar map (1651), among a cluster of contemporary Jesuit scientists. Bartoli's crater was subsequently assigned to Jean-Sylvain Bailly (1736-1793).

frenzies of the forum to the retirement of the Muses and from the sword of Astraea to the plectrum of Apollo. So in the end, beginning himself with the changes of his *Metamorphoses*, he was transformed one day from a barrister into a poet.

See how genius is a faithful compass. It may be forced to turn elsewhere from its north, but it will never stay still, without some violent interference, until it gently works in us what the poet said of fate.

*The fates lead the willing ahead and pull the unwilling along.*[13]

But if it happens, that the interests of honor or of profit do not allow leaving off from what had a bad beginning, you can see as many monsters in academies of Letters as in African Libya: a poetic physician, a historian philosopher, a mathematician jurist. In them are mingled those innate seeds they bore in the womb of their mind's instinct with those acquired by study. Neither one nor the other completely prevails, so when one is both one and the other, one is neither one nor the other.

Therefore, if we will successfully apply our selves not only to Letters, but more to one than to another profession of Letters, we must seek counsel from our own genius which usually, for those with a good ear, makes itself heard in the language of those frequent desires, when it doesn't have what it wants, and by the Taste it experiences when it does. You must also say to your will, as Aeölus says to Juno,

*Command me to the work you choose, O Queen,*
*You word is my command.*[14]

Otherwise, when setting on the road to the Elysian fields, to strive against one's innate genius to achieve great success in any profession of Letters, is like trying to rip from its trunk the golden bough that is not always in nature's gift,

*No strength can win it,*
*No hard sword will let you seize it.*[15]

---

13 **Seneca**, *Letter* 107.11:
  *Ducunt volentem Fata, nolentem trahunt.*
14 *Aenied* **1.**76/7: *Tuus, ô Regina, quid optes*
    *Explorare labor, mihi jussa capescere fas est.*
15 *Aeneid* **6.**148/9:     *Non viribus ulli*
    *Vincere, nec duro poteris convellere ferro.*

But up to now I have more argued the need to recognize one's genius, than how it can be recognized. I do believe that its voice is so well known to us that it requires no interpreters to explain it, just ears to hear it. What I still must treat of concerns understanding the gifts and talents of others. These are the hallmarks and signs that help, conjecturally, to signal and identify a candidate's Wit. And these can be useful in helping us to guide the studies of those whom we have in our charge as directors, so that we don't err just as others, without understanding their own talents, may err in choosing for themselves a course of study against their own inclination.

## 10.2  *Signs of a Man of Wit from Physiognomy of little credit*

From the three Grecian orders— Doric, Ionic and Corinthian— the architects of antiquity, moved more by the laws of judgement than of art, when they built a temple to a god, would choose the one best suited to the nature of the god to whom the temple was to be dedicated.[1] Therefore, they used the Doric order, grave and severe, for their martial deities; Mars, Hercules and Pallas Athena, the Corinthian, soft and sensuous, for Venus; Flora, Proserpina and the water nymphs, the Ionic, in between, for Juno, Diana, Bacchus and such.

The very same law, as some Platonists and all adepts of physiognomy will have it, nature has rigorously observed in building bodies, the temples of the soul. Some souls are warlike, others cowardly; some vivacious and ingenious, others stupid and sluggish; many servile, others imperious, born to command. In conformity with their inner genius and temperament nature draws the outer features of the face and uses the architecture for the body that corresponds to the inclination of the mind. From these notions, the art of conjectural physiognomy has taken its principles, whereby what one sees in a face can show and indicate what lays hidden inside. From the quality of the features, whether good or bad, they gather many and diverse indications of character, often in contradiction with each other. Some are stupid and obtuse, some incisive and acute, with so many signs showing. It is as if someone of Protean nature could be known by the features of his face, rather than by the qualitiy of his Wit.

---

1 Vitruvius, *De Architectura.*

But many of these masters of divining focusing on the features and makeup of some few persons of Wit more than on its universal and mysterious origins, have made the faces of a few the common stamp for everyone; indeed, Della Porta,[2] as if he were the Alcibiades from whom to take the features of a true Mercury by copying himself, framed from his own particular markings the universal and almost exclusive conjectures of an excellent Wit. This accounts for the fallacies incurred by using the visage, the constitution and the lineaments of the body to prognosticate the vastness, the subtlety, the vivacity and the profundity of a man's Wit. I shall recite here, but with no attempt to counter them, the most common symptoms catalogued on this subject by the school of the conjectural physiognomists.

First: The Platonists deny that beauty of Wit and deformity of body can exist together in one and the same man.[3] The trine of Venus with the moon is the seal of the stars marking the most beautiful faces. Tuned by its numbers it tempers the soul and harmonizes it with the motion of the First Mind. Pythagoras, that soul of light, was so fair of feature that among his students, some called him— others believed him to be— Apollo in the guise of Pythagoras, or Pythagoras copied from Apollo. Nor is this saying without its reason. For beauty is none other than that special flower which in the earth of this body springs up from the soul like a hidden seed. And if a cloud should mask it, the sun shines through with its subtlest rays and makes it so beautiful that, no longer vapid smoke risen from the earth, sordid and dark, it resembles flaming gold, another sun. No otherwise a soul, that is a sun of light within the cloud of the body that covers and conceals it, shines through the body with the rays of its beauty rendering it also immeasurably beautiful. This is what Plotinus calls the dominion that form has over matter.

If it should be granted that souls come only into bodies resembling them and only tie this knot of tight amity where there is supreme similitude, who would not say that a beautiful soul cannot be tied to a deformed body?

But don't mention Aesop's name to them. He was born with his moon in the nodes and was as ugly, if anyone ever was, as Thyrsites. Forget Crates— not a citizen of Thebes but a monster of Africa. Forget Socrates so ill furnished with beauty, indeed, so grossly

---

2 G.B. della Porta (1535-1615), *De humana physiognomia* (1586).
3 **Plotinus, *Against the Gnostics and others*.**

featured, that Zophyrus the physiognomist saw him as the very idea of a stupid and blockish person. Alcibiades dubbed a him a Silenus, thereby calling him half beast on the outside, while inside he was more than a man. Theodorus is described in Plato's ***Theaetetus,*** as a youth of most engaging Wit. As he was discussing someone with this very Socrates, he ventured to say: *"He isn't good looking, he has your pug nose and bug eyes, though less exaggerated than you."*[4] Such people will not identify deformity in them as the intention of nature, but as the misfortune of chance; not as the defect of form, but as a fault of disobedient matter.

But if it does hold true, then women have the great advantage. To them beauty was given for a dowry and we see that nature's continual care is to work that soft and yielding earth for her to plant this flower there more successfully. And yet through the subjection to which they were condemned, they have as little an amount of judgement in their heads as they have a great amount of enchantment in their faces. Wherefore, of the most of them it may be said as the fox in Aesop said of the head of a marble statue with a very beautiful face, *"O beautiful head, but there's no brain."*[5]

And really, if experience teaches, it will be obvious that nature has not felt obligated by such a law, setting pearls only in gold, and placing Wits of highest intelligence only in bodies of exquisite beauty. *"A forceful and serene Wit may lie under any skin. A great man may come from humble circumstances. A misshapen and vile body may contain a spirit beautiful and great."*[6] Peasant features often clothe most discriminating Wits. Beautiful souls are found under a coarse hide, as the soul Hercules had under the rugged spoils of the Nemean lion. Galba the orator appeared a rough block of stone, but inside it, was a golden vein of precious and shining Wit. Mocking him M. Lollio used to say, *"Galba's brilliant Wit is poorly housed."*[7] Many others it would be too tedious to describe were so deformed, but so gifted with Wit, that it seemed in them, as in the magnet lodestone, that comeliness of mind and ugliness of body went hand in hand.

---

4 Plato in Tertullian; *Non est pulcher: similis tui est: simo naso, et prominentibus oculis, quamvis minus ille quam tu in his modum excedat.*
5 Predictably short shrift for the fairer sex, nature's gift to God's gift: Aesop, Fable 66: *The Fox and the Mask.*
6 **Seneca,** ***Letter*** **66**.3: *Potest ingenium fortissimum, ac beatissimum sub qualibet cute latere. Potest ex casa vir magnus exire; Potest ex deformi vilique corpusculo, formosus animus, ac magnus.*
7 **Macrobius,** ***Saturnalia,*** **2.6**.3: *Ingenium Galbae male habitat.*

Others again there are that measure the Wit's dimensions by the size of the head. They cannot believe great intelligence exists outside a great sphere. They do not see how a small head can conceive something great, as Jupiter did Pallas, how a giant Wit can fit in the narrow niche of a small skull.

They ignore that the mind is the center of the head and that the center does not increase by the size of the circle. The eye is no more than a drop of crystal, but in such small space does it not have so much room that, by the door of a pupil it can house with no confusion half the world?

*The tiny pupil can scan the whole of Heaven.*
*For the eyes in a little space can ponder the largest spaces.*[8]

It often happens, as a small heart can comfortably contain a great spirit, that in a head of small volume a mind of great understanding is housed.

Others argue from the pallor of the face, as from ashes, the fire of a lively Wit. Indeed, Nazianzen calls paleness: *"The fair flower of sublime minds."*[9] And reason would persuade as much, when the best part of the blood is consumed by the mind's exertions, it leaves the face colorless and strained. And so, the star of Saturn, father of profound thoughts, shows, with a near dead light, a meagre and pallid visage.

Many say that in eyes shining by day and sparkling by night, they can recognize the true owls of Pallas. Others there are, who in an awkward and flighty character can read a quick Wit. A head of thoughts that the ready flight of a pen in hand cannot match, may sometimes scribble letters illegibly, cut off words, and confound the sense. On the one hand, the swiftest animals leave behind the faintest tracks; on the other, the slow-moving ox stamps his steps with patience, marking, one by one, his phlegmatic footings.

But I have not undertaken to report, much less to refute all the signs for the presence of Wit is argued by these subtle diviners: dry and slender neck and shoulders, fleshiness, ample forehead, thin and delicate skin, middling voice, neither sharp, nor bass; hair not lankily long, nor fussily curled or frizzed, slender hands; thin legs, mid-sized physique, amiable coloring and what have you?

---

8 **Manilius,** *Astronomica* 1.927/8:
*Parvula sic totum pervisit pupula caelum*
*Quoque vident oculi minimum est, cum maxima cernant.*
9 **Gregory Nazianzen,** *Oration* 14: *Pulchrum sublimium virorum florem.*

Prognostications and conjectures are these, for the most part, with double faces and fallacious prospects. Yes, they are equally accommodating to contrary, not to say, opposite principles. At least it is certain, that in order to confirm them, the requirements are either experiments by the observations of men of Wit, or reasoning from the workings and application of the organs employed by the faculty of imagination and by the mind. The experience of one who has made such observations is that, out of every three cases, two prove to be false, that the workings of the internal instruments have no real connection with these external signs from which any significant--- not to say infallible—argument may be deduced.

## 10.3   *Origins of the Excellence and Diversity of Wits, and Sources of the Various Inclinations of Genius*

A directly opposite approach to the one above is taken by those who place all the energy of the Wit in the agency of the soul and posit its optimal function completely independent of the instruments of the body. They deny the possibility of theorizing from any sort of outward appearance about the quality or the quantity of Wit in others. Souls, they say, differ among themselves not only in their proper essence, but also by the degrees of excellence in their personal qualities that make one more perfect— or less— than another. The praise is due to that great Maker who creates them, and it is no less an accolade to the world's beauty that such variety of appearance exists in the faces of men. While they are composed of just a few features, to find two alike is considered a marvel; two of an identical stamp, a miracle. If the diversity of Wits is caused in this manner by the differing degrees of perfection in souls, then why look for signs of them in the body, as if (to follow the error of that great father of medicine, the proto-physician) the soul consists in nothing more than the consonance of qualities and the harmony of humors? To argue from the voice—from the complexion, from the features—acuity of Wit is like guessing from his paint brushes the excellence of the art of a great Apelles, or from his sword the valor of the arm of a mighty Scanderbeg.[1] An ox cut in half at one stroke, an Alexander painted, his arm raised with a bolt of

---

1 Albanian national hero, George Kastrioti, (1405-1468), *Life* by Marin Barleti (1508).

lightning seeming to flash out of the canvas, these are true arguments of art and ability. Wit itself can be known in no other way than in its works; it leaves no other hallmarks to tell its shape; it has no other shadow by which to measure it.

If this is not the case, then try to look at the diversity of Wits as stars of different genius and nature, variously inclined, and then, see if you can find an underlying principle behind it in the makeup of the body. Some have so quick a mind that their thoughts seem flashes of light, taking off, streaming and arriving at the same time. They are such fleet eagles that they are ahead of where their masters beckon, so that as Plato said of his Aristotle, they need to have their wings clipped so they fly not on impulse, but on reflection.

Others are the opposite, like Xenocrates, a Mercury with no wings on his feet or on his head, they are so slow and so listless that they must be spurred, not to run, but to move.[2] They are stars, but stars of that Great Bear so near the north star that they gyre slowly at a lazy pace, as if slowed by the northern freeze of the Septentrion.

Some have minds like the writing on water—no sooner is it formed than it disappears, minds as quick to forget, as to learn. Wits we can compare first to doves *"whose every movement shifts into new colors;"*[3] when one hue comes, the other goes. And to mirrors in which, *"Each image disappears as fast as it appears."*[4] On the other hand, some minds are like sculpting porphyry and rough stone. They receive no image without chiseling away with great patience, but then it is so lasting that neither forgetfulness nor time can rub it out. Cleanthes was of this sort, derisively hailed the Hercules of the schools, because to become a philosopher it took him no less mental exertion than it took the physical exertion of Hercules to make himself a demigod. Says Plutarch, *"The vessel with its narrow mouth took time to fill but always retained its contents."*[5]

There are those who as boys are all spirit; as men, all dregs. In their first years, the nightingales seem to sing in their mouths, as they did for the child Stesichorus,[6] but when grownups, they bellow like

---

2 Laertius, *Xenocrates*, 4.6.
3 **Seneca, *QN***, 1.5.6: *Quarum omnis inclinatio in colores novos transit.*
4 ***Ibid.***, 1.6.4: *Aeque cito omnis imago aboletur, ac componitur.*
5 **Plutarch**, *De recta ratione audiendi*, (*On reading*), 18: *Oris angustissimi vas difficilissime admittens, sed semper retinens quod admisit.*
6 Pliny, 10.82; Palatine Anthology, 2.125/30.

oxen. Just like that ancient Hermogenes, who was *"An old man among children, a child among elders."*[7]

In others, on the contrary, Wit gradually matures with years. At first, they seemed dead tree trunks, their buds hardly opening and gradually growing leaves, then in the end they bear more fruit than others grow leaves. Take the case of Baldo, a jurist, who, like a palm tree, took a hundred years before he bore any fruit, giving rise to the taunt he got from many when he was a student: *"You will be a doctor Baldo, but in the next century."*[8]

What shall we say of those, who in every branch of Letters have an equally perfect Wit? As the light to all colors, so their minds seem suited to all topics, lowly or sublime, to all degrees of width and depth. Few of them exist, yet they do exist. Of them we may use as an entire panegyric, those great words of praise,

*They are streams widely spread, but flowing together and mixed*
*in you, what they enjoyed as tributaries you gather into one.*[9]

Those blessed Wits have what Pliny found in a single tree, by itself a whole orchard, as it had the fruits of all trees grafted upon it.[10] This is what Ausonius saw in a statue of Bacchus. It had about it a semblance of all the gods so that he called it not a single god, but a pantheon of gods. This can be understood much more aptly, and in works of greater admiration and envy in such Wits. They are unique, but they are worth many, not only, but many of great excellence so that they deserve the description of the great colossus of Rhodes: *"His fingers are larger than several statues."*[11] They are singular but transform themselves into as many guises as Letters has professions. You cannot tell where they

---

7 Antiochus, *Sophists,* 2.7: *Senex inter pueros, inter senes puer.* See *Suda,* Adler, epsilon 3046.

8 *Doctor eris Balde, sed praeterito saeculo.* From an unidentified and mistaken source. Baldo degli Ubaldi (1327-1400), influential jurist, doctored at 17. This taunt is corrected in Pierre Bayle's *Dictionnaire Historique et Critique* (1697).

9 Claudian, *De consulatu Stilichonis,* 1.33/35:
*Sparguntur in omnes*
*In te mista fluunt, et quae divisa beatos*
*Efficiunt, collecta tenes.*

10 The Renaissance ideal of omnicompetent universal genius was important for the Jesuits' *cultura ingeniorum* and their humanist education *ad majorem Dei gloriam.* The contemporary polymath, Athanasius Kircher (1602-1680), a Jesuit wizard, became an outstanding contemporary example in Bartoli's day.

11 **Pliny, 34. 7**: *Majores sunt digiti ejus, quam pleraeque statuae.*

excel the most; as in everything they are equal to themselves and are inferior to none. You will sooner find them envied, than equaled. Finally, in whatever mode of understanding you ask of them, they will be able to say, as among the poets spoke the god Vertumnus:

*My good fortune is joined to my nature,*
*Turn me around in any direction you like. I shall be comely.* [12]

But then there are others, so focused on only one special area of study, that, not by choice of will, but by the promptings of their innate talents, to take them away from it would quite simply mean to take their Wit away from them. To see their excellence, one must observe them from one point, namely the one where all the lines of their knowledge unite as one; otherwise they have little stature, and indeed, they look like midgets.

These and many more reveal the characteristics and different varieties of genius and talent that can be noted among the Wits. Now, what mental makeup, what harmony of qualities, what disposition of humors so influences the soul that some people who are without gifts for mental exercise are most gifted and handy in simple and practical matters, while others are excellent in abstract things and useless in practical ones? How are they disposed, now to one, now to another, now to all, and now to none of the exercises of discourse, the workings of the Wit? If the activities of the soul's intelligence come from itself and are in its care, what is the role of the body, however it is tempered, or of the brain, however it is disposed? And if they play no part, then it holds true that the diversity of Wits represents different perfections of the soul, not various dispositions of body.

But if this be so, if the mind depends not on the organs to operate nor on the temper of the humors to operate well, how is it that some, either by an accidental blow on the head or by a strange disease, have suddenly or gradually lost their memory and lost their Wits? How comes it that their head, like Pandora's box, or Ulysses' deflated bladder of winds, stays forever after without spirit, and sense? How to explain the overheating of the brain, the disturbance of reason, the effervescence of impulses, disorder in discourse, delirium and madness? Why does a child who was quick of spirit and Wit sometimes grow over the years into a dimwit as dumb as he once was smart? Yet

---

12 **Propertius**, *Elegies*, 4.2.6:
> *Opportuna mea est cuncta natura figuris,*
> *In quacunque voles verte. Decorus ero.*

his soul is the same. Who then stripped his Wits bare, who uprooted his thoughts, who turned his spirit into something so different from what it once was?

Some countries are most fertile with great Wits. In Attica, that famous Athens, the nest and the nurse of the sciences, housed within its walls one great Parthenon, one single temple of Pallas, and a whole academy of literati. In contrast Boeotia was peopled, not by living men so much as by dead statues, in whom reason made no greater a show of dealing with others than among the animals the zoophytes show motion.[13] Do we not see great differences of Wits between city and city, even in adjacent territories? Some, as the Egyptian Alexandria, seem to have drawn their first foundations with polenta.[14] Others, placed upon the summit of Olympus have their feet higher than other cities have their heads. How could this come to be, if neither Heaven, nor the air, nor climate, nor the spirits, nor the humors they temper, had no effect on those actions proper to the soul as the origin of intelligent discourse, actions alone produced by the soul and imprinted on it.?

A more trusted explanation and surely an opinion more commonly held, is that the temperament of the different elements which compose the body is equally employed in the Wit and in the diversity of its genius. In the tempering of an instrument, it is the tuning of the strings and diverse chords of voices, intervals, tempos as well as the sequence of whole and half tones that determines the different harmonies—Phrygian, Doric, Lydian— and their different styles of music— grave, sensual, martial, melancholy, merry. So, let us study the various (so to say) tones, and modes of Wit.[15] They come from the various tunings of the primary elements, which were enumerated by Cardanus into nine kinds of human bodies.[16] Relevant also the proportion of eight parts of blood, two of bile, and two of melancholy that Ficino prescribed for the harmony of a great Wit and

---

13 Climatic determinism was an influential since the Late Renaissance, as articulated in the political philosophy of Jean Bodin, (1530-1596).
14 **Plutarch, *Alexander,*** 26.
15 This wonderful analogy introduces one of Bartoli's most elaborately worked and historically interesting disquisitions.
16 Girolamo **Cardano,** (1501-1576), **De aere et acqua. Lecture 9** on **Hippocrates.**

let each man take from it what he wants to think, even should he pay it no attention at all.[17]

This seems universally true that the workings of the Wit partake somewhat of fire, as the rapid motion of thought and the fiery spirits that Wit employs serve to demonstrate that those humors that are mostly fire suit it best, even as, contrarywise, phlegm will make it stupid and bring on a sort of lethargic somnolence. Therefore, the choler of bile which is hot in excess and dry is wholly suited to Wit. But even more apposite, (unlikely as it seems) melancholy, not that gross and nasty kind, which is more connected to phlegm as cold, than to choler as dry, but a certain scorched dose of sallow choler, cold and dry by nature as the earth but, if distilled and heated, quite susceptible to ignite (as the exhalations raised by the sun in a cold and dry earth) and produce a fire so vehement and forceful that it is like lightning in its power, though more durable and constant. From this sort of melancholy is born that fury and that alert frenzy of the mind that is totally borne outside itself and totally concentrated inside itself, giving it rapid motions and holding it steady and fixed, furiously emanating and furiously absorbing thoughts. Nor can blood and phlegm be missing, the one for nourishment of the spirits, the other for tempering, so that excessive dryness should not bring sterility, nor should excessive heat distemper the organ and make more smoke than light. The fiery must predominate, the rest in a mixture proportionate to its intensity.

And this, if I guess not amiss, is that very famous **Luce secca,** *dry light* of Heraclitus, that, *"Fiery energy and heavenly origin."*[18] Where this burns more brightly and is less turgid and clouded in the purified humors, it becomes there something more like Heavenly mindfulness than earthly Wit. This is that most rare Electrum that mixes Wit and judgement together. Wit the Mercury, all instability and motion, judgement, the chemical composite to fix it; Wit the lion and the dolphin, all fury, all speed, judgement, the bridle and anchor regulating the fury, restraining the motion; Wit the sail, judgement the ballast, one, the wing, the other, the weight— one, the face of Janus the youthful; the other the old and white-haired Janus.

Because the temper of the humors for the service of the mind is not one and indivisible, from its various compositions come the

---

17 **Ficino, *De sanitate tuendi,*** 1.
18 *Aeneid* 6.730: *Igneus vigor, et caelestis origo.*

abilities, the forms of genius, the talents which are geared to various professions of Letters. Some studies demand more patience and, as they say, phlegm; others call for greater alacrity of mind; elsewhere, a more solid imagination, otherwise more abstract theorization, here great memory, there the capacity to embrace at once the knowledge of many objects and to discern their interdependency without confusing them. The humors and their qualities are variously accorded and harmonized together, with more or less of hot, of cold, of wet, of dry. And so we are better fit with abilities for one or another profession of Letters, following the temper of the qualities that the instruments require for the successful disposition of their operation. And this ability of congenial potential for certain kinds of things is the foundation of what they call genius.[19] Everyone by instinct has an innate desire for knowledge. Nature does not err and is mindful that we may be drawn, as to our good, to what she may not have sufficiently equipped us to achieve. So, she plants in us the desire to accomplish what we are best suited for. The role of proportion which adjusts the potential to its object, together with the role of that desire which comes from the will to know, the first spurring the commission, the second leading it to execution, these engender that proportion and that sympathy which we may describe as genius.

Thus, it is not the disposition, the shape, the coloring, nor the dimensions of the parts of the body that we should observe as direct or truthful witnesses of Wit, when we select someone for a path in humane Letters. It is rather from their acts and deeds, the most natural testimonies of potentiality, that we can identify their internal makeup and temperament and find out to which of the arts or sciences their gifts are most appropriately disposed.[20] Thus, since honey cannot be culled from its true source in the stars (in Pliny's words), at least we should be busy with taking it pure from those flowers, which nature has chosen as best: *"There you get the best honey (rose hip) where the most fragrant flowers grow."*[21] Since knowledge may not be had otherwise than as dropped from Heaven into these earthly bodies, at least let the

---

19 Genius, then, is the individual's psychic endowment at birth and informs the development and balance of Wit and Judgement as its expression and character.
20 Discernment of leadership abilities was important among the Jesuits as they looked for the equilibrium of *ingegno* and *giudizio* in the candidates they recruited for Letters in their influential, endowed schools and for their order.
21 **Pliny, 11.**11: *Ibi enim optimus semper (ros mellis) ubi optimorum dioliolis florum conditur.*

commitment be to gather it from those whose makeup and temperaments resemble the celestial firmament, fiery and subtle, but stable and regulated, as best harmonized and most suited to Heaven.

HVOMO
DI LETTERE
DI FESO
ET EMENDATO
M DC LX
IN VENETIA

*Picini F.*

*Appresso Zacharia Conza*

**11**                          ***AMBITION***

### 11.1   *Folly of many who, wanting to appear learned, publish themselves as ignorant in print*

That insatiable urge, not to say, rage to publish ourselves to the world as men of Letters, would to God it could so shape and refine our Wits as it sharpens our pens, so that the world of knowledge might increase in size as books multiply in number.

Scarce in the nest of a school have we grown the down of the first feathers upon the brain than we take ourselves not only for eagles, but Mercuries with wings on our heads. Scarce do we have a spark of Wit than we aspire to shine as suns in print and, with strange ambition, try to appear as masters before becoming full-fledged students. Every thought that our minds conceive, we think worthy of bearing to the light. While often it is no more than a ***Ridiculus Mus*** (*ridiculous mouse*),[1] we nonetheless will bid the press to be Lucina, the midwife, to deliver it and foster not only its life, but its immortality. The gnats, moths and fleas in our heads, we want to be preserved like a bee in amber[2] and exposed to the sight and admiration of the world. Thus,

> *Many are afflicted with the incurable bad habit*
> *Of writing and grow old and bitter doing so.*[3]

Happy would Letters be, if books also had a winter and the leaves of the greatest part of them fell off, as the leaves of trees fall every year after autumn. The world would be so much the wiser, were there fewer masters of mistakes and oracles of untruths.

How many books do we take in hand which carry on their cover *"grandiloquent titles to make you drop everything?"*[4] In perusing the proud promises of their titles, you will call to mind either that verse of Horace,

> *What of worth can come from the boast of such a promise?*[5]

---

1 Horace, *Ars poetica*, 137.
2 *Apis nectare clusa suo*, Martial, *Epigrams*, 4.32
3 Juvenal, *Satire* 7, 51/2: *Tenet insanibile multos*
    *Scribendi cacoethes et agro in corde senescit.*
4 **Pliny, preface**, 6: *Inscriptiones, propter quas vadimonium deseri possit.*
5 Horace, *Ars Poetica*, 138:
    *Quid dignum tanto feret hic promissor hiatu?*

or that jest with which Diogenes mocked the great entrance gate to a small settlement saying, *"Shut this gate or else the town will run away and leave you without house or home."*

The eye and the hand run with impatience, one to turn over, and the other to read the pages, *"But Good Gods and Goddesses when you start you find it has no content inside!"*[6] Africa has the most beautiful coastline. Inland, it is just barren stretches of desert sands. The first sheet of such books is like that famous sheet of Parrhasius that seemed to veil a painting, whereupon Zeuxis deceived, *"insisted they remove the cloth to be shown the picture,"*[7] but in reality, there was no other picture than the sheet, tricking the eyes with the lies of the brush. This confirms that saying of Seneca, *"They appear impressive and great to observers, but when weighed, they fall short."*[8] Books many times deceive like the apples of Sodom. They are fair to look at; all they have is the hypocrisy of appearance. Inside they are ash and smoke and on opening they vanish into nothing, as Tertullian said, *"If there is any fruit, it is for the eyes only, to the touch they turn to ashes."*[9]

A man of Letters is much to be pitied as he sets himself avidly to study one of these books which have nothing but promise and show. He finds a paper cloud where he hoped for the riches of goddess Juno. Instead of finding the treasures he expected, he sees that the book costs him more for the time spent reading to no purpose, than for the money he paid for it. He fishes around day and night until with a ***Nihil coepimus*** (*We caught nothing*)[10] he puts it down. His Wit soars with curiosity in search of some fetching conceit, of some admirable piece of rhetoric, but as the birds that flew to the painted grapes of Zeuxis,[11] if he came hungry, he leaves unfed.

O! How many writers more than once have made the presses groan about whom we can echo the verse of Ausonius,

> *Time better spent sleeping, than wasting — sleep*
> *And lamp oil.*[12]

---

6 **Pliny, *ibidem***: *At cum intraveris (Dii Deaeque) quam nihil in medio invenies.*
7 **Pliny,** 35.10: *flagitavit, tandem remoto linteo ostendi picturam.*
8 **Seneca, *Letter* 66**.30: *Speciosa et magna contra visentibus, cum ad pondus revocata sunt, fallunt.*
9 **Tertullian, *Apologia***: *Si qua illic poma conantur oculis tenus caeterum contacta cinerescunt.*
10 *Luke* 5.5.
11 Pliny, 35.36.
12 Ausonius, *Epigrams*, 5.10:

The wretches have passed many a night to supply a book that puts to sleep all who read it, unless their pique at the author has kept them awake. How many books on the title page might also add the name a Spaniard, Doctor Zuazo, gave a little desert island he visited on his sea voyage to the Indies of America. On it he found neither grass nor any other sustenance, so he gave it this name, "*Nothing to eat here.*"[13] And yet (as Saint Ambrose ingeniously calls them) books are the harbors where the spirit recovers not only from tempests to refreshment but also from poverty to replenishment.[14] Then take here three of the many reasons, why it happens that so many useless books, empty of any good, are printed.

1.      Some think they've done nothing if they do just one book. They want to make by themselves a whole library.

> *This wretch, knowing no limits, will write thousands of pages*
> *on anything, more and more wasted paper.*[15]

A hundred volumes, a thousand pages each, issue of a single Wit, offspring of a single mind, drafted by single pen, this will make you step haughty and swell. Yet glory and fame are not given to books for their number, but for their content. How often in a stream of words, there is not a single drop of Wit, in a sea of ink, there is not one pearl, in a forest of papers there is not one branch of gold? All that writing, be it in a hundred volumes, sounds as the Echo of Ausonius:

> *Daughter of air and tongue, mother of meaninglessness,*
> *A tongue with no mind I move.*[16]

A rare miracle of patience in the reader would be, as he is throwing the book away, for him not to tax its author, with Martial's barb,

> *You blabber mouth, you get paid to be loud,*
> *How much would it cost to shut you up?*[17]

---

    *Utiliùs dormire fuit, quam perdere somnum*
    *Atque oleum.*
13 Gonzalo Fernandez de **Oviedo** (1478-1557), *Historia general y natural de las Indias* (1535): *Nolite cogitare quid edatis.*
14 **Ambrose**, *On Luke*, 4, preface.
15 Juvenal, *Satire* 7:
    *Hinc, oblita modi, millesima pagina surgit*
    *Omnibus, et crescit multa damnosa papyro.*
16 **Ausonius**, *Epigram* 32:
    *Aëris, et linguae sum filia, mater inanis*
    *Judicii, linguam (Indiciii vocem) quae sine mente gero.*
17 **Martial**, *Epigrams*, **9**. 68.11/12: *Vis garrule, quantum*

Books, as said Domitius Piso, cited by Pliny, "*should be treasures, not just books.*"[18] Every word should be a pearl, every page a jewel, so the reader may be enriched in an hour with what has taken us ten years to collect.

Alas! What has become of you, treasured usage and fortunate age, when the honey of the sciences was set in wax, inscribed there by custom with a stylus? As the instrument went slowly, resisted by the hardness of the wax the scribe had more time to think and to consider his material more carefully. Today, the pen conveys more fleetingly the words from the hand and the ideas from the head and both weigh less for being less weighed. The comic writer's vaunting soldier did say:

> *This sword I keep at my side as a consolation*
> *It won't lament or lose spirit*
> *For all the wounds it has already inflicted.*[19]

This captures the itch that many have to write, and write, as a sop to the unhappy pens idling in their inkwells without spitting out, in less than it takes me to say it, a book.

It is not quantity, but quality that bestows worth. Books are like souls. Their greatness is not measured by the body's bulk, but by the mind's nobility. How true rings the great Augustine's aphorism: "*In things that are small in size, their excellenge makes them great.*"[20] Mountain rocks may be enormous, but a diamond which is only (said Manilius) the **Punctum lapidis** (the tip of a stone)[21] outstrips them in worth, as they outdo it in size.

If you were in the position to address a congress of a hundred of the most learned men, Wits of the world, would you fill their ears with whatever lies on your tongue, indiscriminately, without correction, and, often enough, without substance and without order? Or rather would you not use your Wits to speak not only roses, as they said in the old days, but pearls and gold? Do you realize that through the press you are speaking, not to a hundred, or a thousand, but to all

---

*Accipis ut clames, accipere ut taceas?*

18 **Pliny**, preface, 4: *Thesaurus oportet esse, non libros.*

19 Plautus, *Miles gloriosus*, 5:

> *(Non) Ego hanc manchaeram mihi consolari volo*
> *Ne lamentetur, neve animum despondeat.*
> *Quia jam pridem feriatam gestem.*

20 **Augustine, *De trinitate*, 6.** 8: *In iis quae non mole magna sunt, idem est esse majus quod melius.*

21 **Manilius, *Astronomica*, 4.** 926.

the sages of the world as your reading audience? Follow Phocion's example. He was asked why he stood so long in thought. He replied that, as he was preparing a public address to the Athenians, he was selecting his words one by one to see if there were any he should leave out. **Laudato ingentia rura**, said the Poet, **Exiguum colito.** (*Sing of the great landscape but cull the small detail.*)[22] Respect the gigantic tomes of others, but worry less about matching their volume, more about superseding their stature. Write just one thing good enough to count for many. Just one, but one you can hold as Ceres held her only daughter,

*Out of the host of the damned Proserpina is her only concern.*[23]

2.     The other reason for a book's misfortune is when the choice of subject is unmatched by a sufficient supply of Wit. After I chance to write a stanza, or an epigram, I begin to hear the epic and tragic Muses calling:

*One really shouldn't think he's ready for the high seas*
*After venturing to launch a bark in a small lake.*[24]

Hercules may strive to storm the Heavens and for him to want to take them by force is no wonder. It is not his first attempt and he knows their power.

*He knows he has the power to defeat Heaven*
*As he learned from fighting it.* [25]

Likewise test your shoulders to the weight and where you can say, **Par oneri cervix**, (*the shoulder is equal to the burden*)[26] take up the task and you will do it. As St. Jerome said, "*Human prudence is to know the measure of one's worth and not to expose one's inability to the eyes of the world.* [27] You should unite Argus and Briareus. You must not have a hundred hands ready

---

22 Virgil, *Georgics* 2.412/3.
23 **Claudian**, *De raptu Proserpina*, 33:
   *Numeri damnum Proserpina pensat.*
24 **Ovid, Tristia 2**. 329/30:
   *Non ideo debet pelago se credere, si qua*
   *Audet in exiguo ludere cymba lacu.*
25 **Seneca, Hercules Furens**, 69/70:
   *Et posse caelum viribus vinci suis*
   *Didicit ferendo.*
26 Atlas, See Ovid, *Met.* 10.195:
   *Ipsa sibi est oneri cervix, humeroque recumbit.*
27 **Jerome, Against Vigilantius**, Letter 61.3: *Prudentia hominis est, nosse mensuram suam, nec (zelo diaboli concitatum) imperitiae suae orbem testem facere.*

to write, unless your mind also has a hundred eyes open to see. A large and promising field of noble argument should not so agitate your mind that your eagerness to launch into it can allow you to forget that you have neither the wings nor the strength for it. Lower such overweening plumes. They will bring you down before you can fly, so that you:

> *Like to the unfledged stork, that strives to fly,*
> *And being untimely hasty, fluttering leaves*
> *Its loathsome nest, and so a fall receives.*[28]

But of this I shall have to speak in another context further on.

3.      The third cause why there are more stillborns than babies is the impatience to give birth before full term. This ignores Horace's precept,

> *It should be given nine years,*
> *So there's time to make corrections*
> *Before the book comes out. Once out you can't take it back.* [29]

It is no wonder that mushrooms grow in one hour, and rot in the next. Our writings turn out, as Plato would say, like those famous gardens of Adonis, *"that suddenly appear, born in a single day and perish very quickly."* [30]

For the painter Agatharchus all the canvases of Greece, all the paints of the Orient were not enough. He drew his portrait pictures with more rapidity than the sun draws rainbows in the clouds. But so what? His pictures he hung in every sordid place, poorly displayed. Their lives were no longer than the men of stone sown by Cadmus.

By contrast take Zeuxis. He brought his works to term in more time than it took for the gestation of an elephant. Every brush stroke was subjected to critical examination. And he deserved that eternity of glory which was the sole inspiration of his painting. The sagest of men were always most severe with the works of their own Wits. The knowledge that they would be read and examined by men of great learning made them say with the younger Pliny, *"I am never finished. I think how important it is to deliver a work into the hands of my readers and can't*

---

28 (Salusbury) Dante, *Inferno* 25.10/12:
> *Si com'il Cicognin che leva l'ala*
> *Per voglia di volar, e non s'attenta*
> *D'abbandonar lo nido, e giù la cala.*

29 **Horace, *Ars poetica*,** 388/90: *Nonumque prematur in annum*
> *Membranis intus positis delere licebit*
> *Quod non edideris. Nescit vox missa reverti.*

30 Plato, *Phaedrus,* 276: *Qui subito, et die uno nati celerrimè pereunt.*

*be persuaded to do so without consulting several people repeatedly on the subject, for what you want is to be successful forever and with everyone."[31]*

And so, enough has been said here of those poorly furnished with Wit who try to write on subjects greater than their talents. Now I must not leave out certain others, who misusing their great gifts of Wit, waste their time and the attention of others on certain useless topics, what Arnobius called, *"things that add nothing to knowledge and which can be ignored as nothing."[32]*

## 11.2  *Ungrateful Toil of One Who Studies and Writes Things of No Use Whatsdoever*

Alchemists are men with more pluck than sense. In truth they have no sense, although on the great tree of folly, the branch they occupy may have the finest appearance, it is that branch of gold that leads to hell rather than to the Elysian Fields. But they are nonetheless fortunate, for they are searching for, as they call it, the philosopher's stone through the workings of their art, so in the end they do find it, and it is that golden ancient poverty, the true **Lapis Philosophorum** (*philosopher's stone*). Thus, they are left with nothing in the world and are free from the bother of keeping possessions and from the danger of losing them, both privileges of the true age of gold. They unwisely conspire to fix Mercury in quicksilver and perceive not that the god of thieves knows better how to take from others, than to give of his own. They want to transmute the moon into the sun. The moon never disappears more than when it is closest to the sun.[1] Most wondrous is the compellingly sweet charm of hope that deprives the heads of these foolish wretches of sense; their hands of money, their eyes of sleep, and their hearts of the love of the entire world. It blinds them, so they don't see what they are going through, that they live in torment. Then they are dulled by the minerals they work that make them dull to pain,

---

31 **Pliny the Younger,** *Epistles* **7.17 to Celeris Cherus**: *Nil est curae meae satis. Cogito quam sit magnum dare aliquid in manus hominum: nec persuadere mihi possum, non et cum multis, et saepe tractandum, quod placere, et semper, et omnibus cupias.*
[32]**Arnobius,** *Against the Heathens*, 2.61.1: *Quas neque scire compendium neque ignorare detrimentumn est ullum.*

1 **In the new moon.**

and imperviious to torment. Thus, you see them, like moths ever flitting around the little lamp that heats a hermetic burner, at the same time laughing in that light and tearful at that smoke. Finally, with the experiment finished, nearing the harvest of the living seed, they meet with a fine ***Ex nihilo nihil*** (*Nothing comes from nothing*). All their hope is volatile and only the dregs stay fixed. Fortune, that stood upon a ball of glass, now broken, has toppled. After everything they reach the conclusion that gold only grows when it is traded and that the veins or mines of it are only found in banks.

I have with two strokes of the pen roughly drawn the equally foolish and unhappy troubles of miserable alchemists who, with no other profit than the smoke that makes them weep, exhaust all that they have and all that they are. This, so that through them you can see the folly of many endowed with some talent of Wit, who waste it and time and effort, filing away their sanity and wracking their brains to dedicate their energies to the ungrateful production of certain books, whose contents serve only to waste the time of those who read them, as they waste the lives of those who write them.

I know that Favorinus, for sharpening the Wit when it has been blunted and dulled by long idleness, advises that an excellent remedy is to entertain trifling and humorous subjects.[2] And he did so in his praises of Thyrsites and of the quartan fever, as Dio Chrysostom did with a mop of hair, Synesius with baldness, Lucian with a flea and a hundred others who have taken up similar subjects.[3] But it is one thing to stir or restore the Wit with subjects that, while trifling are at least amusing, and another to wear yourself out with such endeavors and waste yourself and your time expecting to get from them all the glory of your dedication to unremitting study, as that other one who used to say,

*I rank second to none for my poetic trifles.* [4]

What do you think of Aristomachus, who with the most exact observations of every day--- not to say, of every hour, for sixty-two years--- continuously pried into the nature of bees?[5] So many years,

---

2 **Gellius,** 17.12.2/5.
3 These titles stand for an interesting and well represented genre of classical letters.
4 **Martial,** *Epigrams,* 9.1, to Avitus:
    *Ille ego sum nulli nugarum laude secundus.*
5 Pliny, 11.9.19.

such diligence, should, methinks, have achieved nothing less than the discovery of all the secrets of Heaven and the chart of all the movements of the planets.

Seneca loses patience with certain philosophers of his time who spend long watches of the night and implacable disputations of the day on certain childish questions. Were they more deserving of laughter or of a whipping? *"Mouse is one syllable, a syllable doesn't eat cheese, so a mouse doesn't eat cheese. What childish drivel! Are we are reduced to such inanities? Have we descended to such foolishness? Is this the sad and pallid fruit of our studies?"*[6] Men are wont to say that we are twice children, once when we come out of infancy and again in extreme old age when we become children once more, but one who passes, not to say, wastes his life in such conceited vanities: *"He is not, as they say, in his second childhood, but a child forever, the only difference is that he is playing grownup games."*[7]

To what end shall we pour our guts out studying just to weave webs to catch fleas? To what end should we, like Nero, cast nets of purple and gold, thoughts and animadversions of precious Wit, to fish for small fry?[8] Pliny, speaking of plane trees that provide nothing but shade, wondered, *"Who is not amazed that a tree for shade should be worth enough to seek it in exotic parts?"*[9] Is shade somehow so rare in Europe? Or is the shade from plane trees, because they come from far away, more beautiful to make us risk shipwreck in the remotest parts of the earth to procure the tree that produces it? Is there such a dearth of useless nonsense in the world, or is it sold so dear, that filling a thousand sorry sheets with it should cost you study, late nights, hard work and no small part of your life? If I can have thoughts of sublime Wit that soar aloft as eagles or falcons to catch new prey, why should I want them to be like the larks that seek no other gain from a tiresome ascent and hard flying than the silly music they chirp? Afterwards, they let themselves plummet to earth in one fell swoop, merry and content, as if they had given a music lesson to the sirens of Heaven.

---

6 **Seneca, *Letter* 48.** 6/7: *Mus syllaba est, syllaba caseum non rodit, Mus ergo caseum non rodit. O pueriles ineptias! In hoc supercilia subduximus? In hoc barbam demisimus? Hoc est quod tristes docemus, et pallidi?*
7 **Lactantius, *Divinae institutiones* 2.4, from Seneca**: *Non bis puer est, ut vulgo dicitur, sed semper: verum hoc interest, quod majora ludit.*
8 Suetonius, *Nero*, 30.
9 **Pliny**, 12.3: *Quis non miretur arborem umbrae gratia tantum ex alieno petitam orbe?*

There is (writes Oviedo) in the West Indies a great abundance of cotton, of alum, of salt and such like ordinary goods, of which that region is most plentiful, but no one will take them. They only anchor their ships to stop at port for cargoes of gold, silver, pearls and aromatics. A voyage so long, so difficult, so dangerous, (so it was in early days), they would not make for anything less. Oh! Brainless merchants! On your life's journey of which a considerable part is spent studying, the hard work of your writing might fill books with gold and pearls, while you only use them to enrich yourselves with what? Fables, trifling subjects, (my pen made to write, novels), love poems, redactions of ancient texts more often crippled than rehabilitated, capricious corrections, conjectures, vain imaginations, and what not? *"Why do you spend your money on vanities and not on bread?"*[10] So said Isaiah, and St. Jerome applies this to the unhelpful subjects of his day, how much more would he apply it to your completely useless present-day idiocies? Is Tiberius still alive to needle you to tell him whose daughter was Hecuba?[11] What name did Achilles go by when he was hiding among Lycomedes' daughters? What is the melody of the sirens' song used to bewitch seafarers? On which hand was Venus wounded by Diomedes?[12] On which foot did Philip limp? Is Domitian still alive to teach you to dedicate hours daily to his pointless fly swatting?

Heliogabulus, to show the world Rome's greatness, the idiot, had all the cobwebs hanging in its houses thrown together in one heap. He thought it would lay a solid foundation for a measurement of the grandeur of the queen city of the world. There is no sage who cannot laugh at this lunatic. But, is this not the same lunacy of those who prove their Wit to the public by raking together what amounts more to a heap of cobwebs than to the pages of a book, by writing of useless and vain topics? *"O that ye would be altogether silent, that would be the sage thing."* [13] The plaudits of foolish friends may magnify you all you want; they can never be more than the antic marvels performed at the festivals of Bacchus that Diogenes called, *"The great wonders of the demented."*[14]

---

10 *Isaiah*, 55.2: *Quare appenditis argentum, et non in panibus?*
11 **Suetonius, *Tiberius*,** 70.
12 **Plutarch, *Quaestiones conviviales*,** 9.4.2.
13 *Job*, 13.5: *Utinam taceretis, et videremini sapientis.*
14 **Laertius, *Diogenes*,** 6.24: *Magna miracula stultorum.*

But among the fruitless endeavors of Wits, (as those implicated may take umbrage) I only pick out the first place owned by what St. Basil aptly called *"Thoroughly venial balderdash."*[15] Astrology, I know not whether I should say forecasting astrology or foolish astrology, more in line for disrespect than for the aspects of the stars where she gets her lies to sell them at a higher price as celestial goods Her art is to erect twelve houses in Heaven by the help of men often without a hovel on earth, who, with hands that beg for bread to keep alive, dispense to some riches and dignities; to others misfortunes and catastrophes. You must not ask her (as Diogenes of one so garrulous about the Heavens) *"And when did you come down from Heaven?"*[16] For she pretends to know how to read in that great volume the fortunes of everyone, written with letters of stars and numbers of aspects, to know how to predict in the paths of those spheres the courses of everyone's life, to be able contain in trines and quarters and sextiles, as magical figures, the stars and the planets and to force them to tell the future events of thingss public and private; finally, to be a prophetess of truth. And all this by virtue of observations in kind, which never had a feature of the kind in Heaven. She begins with the exact point of birth, which she weighs on the scales of Hermes, by virtue of celestial figures, imagined by capriccio by others, observed by her mysteriously, by force of things with nothing of substance or reality, such as the two nodes and Fortune's role. Finally, despite a truth not discovered but encountered, not by means of craft, but only by the chance of a thousand predictions in one, she works to disguise the false as credible, and to promote the credible as true.

What does this profession merit, whose mission is to trick men on earth and to defame the stars in Heaven? Allot to it the Caucasus and the vulture of Prometheus if you deem it a far greater crime to make Heaven untruthful, the planets liars and the stars malevolent, than to take from the wheel of the sun, a spark of fire, a ray of light to bring to life the dead statues of Epimetheus and instill in their breast soul and sense.[17] I, so as not to pass judgment and damage someone, would put the case to the tribunal of that good emperor Alexander

---

15 **Basil**, *On Genesis: Negotiosissimam prorsus vanitatem.*
16 **Laertius**, *Diogenes*, 6.39: *Quandonam de Caelo venisti.*
17 One of the Titans, artificer of a deficient humanity, for whom his brother Prometheus steals fire and the arts. See Plato, *Protagoras*; Hesiod, *Theogony,* 511ff.

Severus, who punished Turinus, his favorite, for selling with false promises the favors of his master. He condemned him to die overcome in a cloud of smoke, as the trumpet blared, *"By smoke he is punished, for it was smoke he sold.*[18]

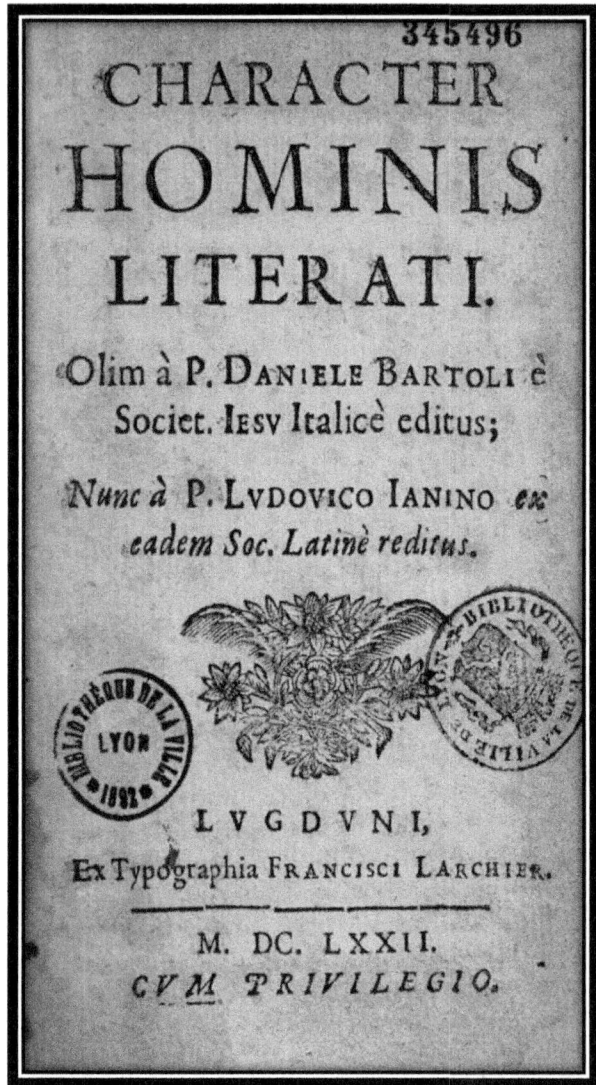

```
                                    345496
            CHARACTER
            HOMINIS
                LITERATI.
        Olim à P. DANIELE BARTOLI è
        Societ. IESV Italicè editus;

        Nunc à P. LVDOVICO IANINO ex
        eadem Soc. Latinè reditus.


                LVGDVNI,
        Ex Typographia FRANCISCI LARCHIER.

                M. DC. LXXII.
            CVM PRIVILEGIO.
```

---

[18] Aelius Lampridius, *Historia Augusta, Alexander Severus, 36.2: Fumo punitur, qui vendidit fumum.*

# 12       *AVARICE*

## 12.1   *Guilty of the Ignorance of Many is One who might benefit Many by Publishing and fails to do so*

No man is more unwillingly maintained by the world and sustained by nature than the man who ignores others and lives only for himself. He is a passerby, even in his own land, and solitary amidst others. He has the features of a man, but is a wild animal among men, undeserving to be born of others, as his only care is to live for himself.

Among these are doubtless to be numbered certain most miserly Wits whose generous endowments of golden talents in the sciences and the arts they would rather bury together with them in their tombs, than leave for the profit of posterity with their printed works. And this, were there no other inducement to do so, when there is the great boon of that honored memory, by which after death one lives in immortality,

*Who would want to recuse having merit in the mouth of the public*
    *and leaving poems worthy to be stored in cedar,*
    *not meant for wrapping fish or fueling incense.*[1]

And not only this allurement may, but a reason stronger should persuade him to do so and that is the public interest, not to be gainsaid by the excuse of one's indifference. Moreover, since knowledge does not come from Heaven as a gift to be lost with us, but as a loan to be conveyed to our successors and to do so is not so much liberality as, in a way, justice. It is received as air receives light from the sun, to be shed on earth and not to be kept unseen by others, and of little use to us.

Why over the course of so many centuries have our ancestors, solitary, pallid and besmirched, spent their long nights and spent the hours of their days, the days of their lives, digging out from the mines of their Wits with the heavy pickaxes of the most obstinate studies golden veins of new truths and new discoveries in knowledge? And have they generously shared them and made a public inheritance of their private patrimony so that, ungrateful to our forefathers and

---

1 Persius, *Satire* 1.41/3: *An erit qui velle recuset*
    *Os populi meruisse, et cedro digna locutus*
    *linquere nec scombros metuentia carmina nec thus?*

envious of our descendants, we should bury what belongs to them and to us below ground? The man who puts himself between our forefathers and those who come after us and considers the example of the former and the welfare of the latter, I do not see how he can have the heart to deny, either dedication to the first, or assistance to the latter. For if only seeing the images commemorating those who in the public guidance of peace and war have acquired the name of great men, our hearts are compelled, and our desires are drawn to similar deeds. In seeing through books, the living and breathing images of the Wits of those great souls bringing the life which in them still survives, still speaks, still teaches for the benefit of the world, can one who is unlearned not want to understand and can one who is learned not feel ashamed to keep covetously concealed what others have amassed only for the common good? *"Take up the list of philosophers. Just this will serve to awaken you, and when you see how many have worked for you, you will be motivated to be one of their number."*[2]

Philo says Sapience is a Sun and cannot be deprived of its splendor without destroying it.[3] Numerous Platonists perceived the souls of loftiest intelligence as symbols of nature together with fire, *"Whose existence is generative, even self-generating and will ignite from the smallest sparks."*[4]

If the example of our forefathers is not sufficient to persuade us, let us consider the welfare of our descendants to whom it would be doubly cruel to deny what it would profit us to give and it would benefit them to receive. Abolish this inviolable law, which we have not written in marble but stamped in our hearts, to entail our love, along with our possessions to posterity, and what have you? If you have not destroyed the world, you have made it barbarous and savage. Fortunate seem those who bequeath ample yearly revenues to the descendants of their blood and entail with their riches a happy fortune to their family line, but what more precious and more lasting inheritance can we leave than the riches of the mind, and the golden talents of our own Wit? These are revenues that do not diminish with use, that do not wear out

---

2 **Seneca,** *Letter* 39.2: *Sume in manus indicem philosophorum. Haec ipsa res expergisci te coget Si videris quam multi tibi laboraverint, concupisces, et ipse ex illis unus esse.*
3 **Philo,** *On Dreams.*
4 **Pliny**, 2.111: *Cuius unius ratio faecunda, seque ipse pariet, et minimis crescit scintillis.*

with time, nor disappear with public or private misfortunes. They are always alive, always entire, always at full value and uniformly pleasing. And from this the younger Pliny formed that forceful motive to persuade a young friend to leave for public benefit some fruit of his long and tedious studies. *"Create and shape something that will be yours in perpetuity. For the other things you possess will pass after you into other hands. But this, once you have created it, will always belong to you."*[5]

But hear what those sordid misers have to say in their defense: *"I am indebted to no man for what is mine. Let others work as I have and let them find by themselves what there is no honor in begging from others. This is piety, not rigor, love of Letters, not hatred of literati. Wits are bred to be slothful when they can find in others what they should draw from themselves. Necessity mothers Wit, and forces one who might want just to study others' works, to become a master who invents new works on his own. We do so to make Achilles of warriors by giving them whole, the bones of lions, to break them into pieces and eat the marrow. Similarly, to train swimmers, we put them in where the current is strongest, so that not by technique, but by necessity they learn survival."*

Why don't they see that Letters will never develop? If someone has spent many years in research and teaches no one what he has discovered, the person who comes after him and is also dedicated to research and keen to discover will know no more than the first, so how can learning grow? Yes, the knowledge others have found helps one to find what others did not know. What were consequences for others serve us as principles and we begin our research where the research of others left off. Sapience, said Augustine, is not conveyed as a slave, but as a spouse and wants successors and sons: *"This is the fruit of our Wit and the offspring of our minds we call not books, but progeny,"*[6] and if she doesn't have them, she weeps. Not in the words of Dido, *"perhaps a little Aeneas would be playing in my courtyard."*[7] but like the innocent daughter of Jephte who wept more for her virginity than for her death,[8] the true and only death being to die without issue to live on through. If a criminal miscarriage makes the mother guilty of homicide, *"And those who extinguish the future of the human race* (said Minuitus) *are*

---

5 **Pliny the Younger, *Letters* 1.3 to Rufus**: *Effinge aliquid, et excude, quod sit perpetuo tuum. Nam reliqua rerum tuarum, post te alium atque alium dominum sortientur. Hoc nunquam tuum desinet esse, si semel coeperit.*
6 **Augustine**, *Hoc est, ingenii fructus, et quosdam mentis partus, quos non tam libros, quam liberos dicimus.*
7 *Aeneid* 4. 327: *Saltem mihi parvulus aula luderet Aeneas.*
8 *Judges* 11/12.

*guilty of parricide before they give birth,*" then to kill in the womb of sapience what, pregnant with our thoughts, she conceived, to kill it stillborn, is not this parricide? Is it not, *"an anticipated homicide to prevent births?"*[10]

Others there are whose defense is age. Their excuse is that being old and hardly able to keep themselves alive, how can they produce for others? *For someone who has done so much, it would be cruelty not to let him shelter his wings in his nest and lower his sail in a snug harbor. Other times, other cares. Eyes that are readier for the sleep of death than for long nights of study cannot be leaders for others without putting them in danger of losing their way and falling.*

But, if I am not mistaken, these are not the words of one wanting to live out the few years that he has left, but who wants to die before death arrives, for death it is, if it is nothing more than only being alive. The studies of his extreme old age were the sweeter to M. Varro, the closer he got to dying, because he did not know a better way to live a full life than by using his remaining faculties of intellect, so he lengthened his life, as he followed his studies, and said to himself, *"While we are musing on these themes, we live on a while more."*[11] Indeed, Seneca, that noble Wit, taking old age as an incentive to work, where others might take occasion to rest, in the final years of his not entire life, he applied himself to investigate the occult secrets of natural philosophy and, surpassing himself, he said with his poet: *"We are inspired with great courage to create great things in little time."*[12]

Whence, as it were slapping his sides and spurring on the listlessness of frigid old age, he declared, *"Let us be diligent and continue the work which may not be completed, for it is still important and we'll face it without the excuse of old age."*[13]

Whoever saw (says Plutarch)[14] bees grow indolent from old age, craven and idle about their hives and not flying to the flowers to gather honey, as they did in their lively youth? Take from me my

---

9 **Minutius Felix, *Octavius***: *quam originem futuri hominis extinguunt parricidium faciunt antequam pariant.*

10 **Tertullian, *Apologeticum* 9.8**: *homicidii festinatio prohibere nasci?*

11 **Pliny, preface**, 4: *Dum haec (ista) musinamur pluribus horis vivimus.*

12 **Seneca, *QN*, 3, preface, 3, Vagellius:**
      *Tollimus ingentes animos, et grandia parvo*
           *Tempore molimur.*

13 **Seneca, *QN*, 3, preface**, 4: *Festinemus et opus, nescio an superabile, magnum certe, fine aetatis excusatione tractemus.*

14 **Plutarch, *Should elders be in government*.** (*An seni gerenda respublica*).

writing, said Gellius, and you have taken away my life. All I ask from life is to be of service to others. *"I want to be granted the space to live for only as long as I am equal to this capacity for writing and commenting."*[15]

Let the structure of life for one whose profession is Letters be that of the ancient Vestals of Rome in three well-measured parts.[16] In the first they learned the rites and ceremonies, as pupils of the elders; in the second they practiced them, among those in full career; in the last they tutored the beginners. Thus, the leaves brought out the flowers and the flowers, when they fell with a lovely finish, were tied into the fruit.

## 12.2   *Felicity Beyond Compare of Good Authors Who Publish*

The will to live has found hundreds of ways to not die. Medicine has neither the herbs of Medea against old age, nor the ambrosia of Jupiter against death, and too true, indeed, are the words of Sidonius, that many doctors, *"neophytes and quibblers, equally learned, and sufficiently experienced, will quite professionally be the death of many patients."*[1] So we have resorted to the art of painting canvases, sculpting marbles, casting bronzes, erecting arches, mausoleums, and theatres, and  while a man's life cannot last long, at least it makes possible a man's likeness on a painting, or his image set in the inscription of an arch, or on the epitaph of a tomb. But there is nothing among our resources, as I have already indicated, so able to keep us alive after death as the procreation of children through which nature provides for the continuity of our common species, and for the private desire of each of us. *"The father has died, but yet is not dead, for he leaves his offspring after him."*[2] But as true as it may be that the father transmits himself into the son he begets, so that dying he does not die while he still lives in him, nonetheless, children can often betray not only the looks, but

---

15 **Gellius, *Attic Nights*, at the end**: *Neque longiora mihi dari spatia vivendi volo, quam dum ero ad hanc facultatem scribendi, commentandique idoneus.*
16, **Plutarch**, *ibid.*

1 **Apollonius Sidonius, *Book* 2. Letter 12 to Agricola**: *assistentes, et dissidentes, parùm docti, et satis seduli, languidos multos officiosissimé occidunt.*
2 **Ecclesiastes, 30.**4: *Mortuus est pater et quasi non est mortuus, similem enim reliquit sibi post se.*

the genius and the probity of the father. Often it occurs, as with Apis, god of the Egyptians,[3] that the father is lightning, and the son an ox, because the disposition of the offspring does not obey the will of the author, but the nature of the creature, for children are formed not as one will, but as one can. Books alone are the children of our minds, the heirs of the best we have, the living images of ourselves, in them alone we have as much of life as we can enjoy after death. Cassiodorus said, *"Often someone will sire a son with no resemblance, as unlike in speech and behavior as it is possible to imagine. This is really the only way to guarantee one's progeny."*[4] These are our immortal children who make dying only a respite from misery, our introduction in them to a life of glory, just as Hercules, upon leaving the earth, was received after his labors into Heaven and began to shine among the stars, after his life was consumed in the flames of his pyre and seemingly reduced to a handful of ashes.

What stronger mainstay, what more stable foundation can the great souls have for the memory of their names and the glory of their merits that equals the eternal term of their books? Look at the ruins left by time of all things, flattening some and slowly eroding others. Rocky cliffs, decrepit and weighed down by the heavy burden of age, do they not bend towards their burial? As they crumble to pieces, with their shards, their bones, strewn here and there, do they not seem to implore the valleys for a tomb? Rust-eaten, even iron is turned to dust by the blasting file of time. Once great edifices become old carcasses, the naked skeletons, not of structures, but of ruins. If there remain a few fragments of dilapidated wall, more supine than standing, still on their feet, are they not more the trophy of time than the testament of their former greatness? Where there once were temples of the gods, royal halls, assemblies of senators, academies of literati, now hardly owls can nest, and thieving wolves keep their coven. In the meantime, among the ruins of all the most stable and durable things of earth, how do the trophies of the great Wits stand up? With the death of all things, even things without life, how do books live; or rather how in books do their fathers and writers stay alive? Let the truly sage Stoic of Rome have the word: *"Some will conceive to build a stone marker, and a marble*

---

3 See Herodotus, *Histories* 3.28.

4 **Cassiodorus, *Variae*, preface** 1.10: *Contingit dissimilem filium plerumque generari, oratio dispar moribus vix unquam potest inveniri. Est ergo ista valdè certior arbitrii proles.*

*monument, or an earthen tumulus piled high, but they are setting out on a short-lived project, for these will be buried in time. But immortal is the memory of Wit.*"[5]
And let the poet Martial have his say,

> *Messala's tomb has a fig tree growing out of it*
> *And the bold muleteer laughs at the broken horses of Crispus.*
> *But Letters are untouched by thieves and span the ages,*
> *Only they are imperishable monuments against death.*[6]

We may well deem fortunate that Metellus who was borne to his sepulchre on the shoulders of four sons, of whom two had been, one was, and the other was to be not long afterwards, consul of Rome. The pomp of this funeral procession was so superb that the historian proclaimed in admiration, "*This is the summit of glory, to leave life in felicity, is hardly to die,*"[7] but, in the end it was, **de vita migrare**, and his sons, though with grandest ceremony, were carrying him to the grave. Books uniquely, not just by four sons, but by as many as the press produces, bring their author back from death, and from the grave, and carry him alive everywhere they go. They put him, not in the hands, but in the eyes of those who read him, into the minds of those who understand him.

How frequently a man living in his country, unknown or neglected, who could hardly draw the eyes of some few as a man of Wit, has, through his books, enchanted the hearts of everyone. Like the famous lyre of Orpheus, on earth, says Manilius, it cast its spell on the trees, on stones, on savage beasts, in Heaven where it was conveyed, it enchants the stars in its trail.

> *Once enchanting woods and stones, now it leads the stars.*[8]

Bearing witness to this is that sweet desire we have to learn the faces and the features of those who have impressed on paper such a

---

5 **Seneca**, *Consolation to Polybius*,18: *Caetera, quae per constructionem lapidum, et marmoreas moles, aut terrenos tumulos in magnam eductos altitudinem, constant; non propagabunt longam diem, quippe et ipsa intereunt. Immortalis est ingenii memoria.*
6 **Martial**, *Epigrams*, **10.2**:
> *Marmora Messalae findit caprificus et audax*
> *Dimidios Crispi mulio ridet equos.*
> *At chartis nec furta nocent, nec secula praesunt,*
> *Solaque non norunt haec monumenta mori.*
7 **Velleius** Paterculus, *History* **1**: *Hoc est nimirum magis feliciter de vita migrare, quàm mori.*
8 **Manilius**, *Astronomica* 1.329: *Tunc sylvas, et saxa trahens nunc sydera ducit.*

beautiful image of their Wits and the impulse to possess their portraits, indeed to conjure up what they looked like, even when from the oblivion of antiquity their faces are unknown, *"Now not only do we have busts in our libraries of gold or silver, or even of bronze, of the immortal spirits we commune with, but we even go to the point of fashioning the features of those unknown to us from the desire to see the face of someone we have no likeness of, as in the case of Homer. So, I would judge nothing a higher testament of someone's success, than that all people will always want to know what he looked like."*[9]

And not only this, but how many times the unsettled mind, unable to untie the knots of the intricate difficulties that bewilder its thoughts will entertain the wish to see alive the only ones who might serve as the Oedipus to solve their enigmas. Once the magnanimous Macedon received a herald from abroad with some happy announcement that showed in the joy of his face and even before he could speak, *"What is it?"* (said Alexander) *"What news do you bring? Is Homer risen from the dead?"*[10] This alone was the sweetest news that there could have been for that great ruler whose spirit and desire were the match for an empire of infinite worlds.

Even today, if a majority of the greatest sages were asked what wish they might have beyond the ordinary, you would hear their desire to see returned to life, some Plato and Aristotle, others Hippocrates and Galen, some Archimedes and Ptolemy, others Homer and Virgil, some Demosthenes and Cicero, others Livy and Xenophon, some Ulpian and Paul the jurist, others Chrysostom and Augustine.

With respect to how we miss them in our day, their lives were not long enough, too short for a world that needs them. Hence, always a bitter loss is the death of a man who cannot die without detriment to the public, as he lived only for the public good. The Consul Pliny said most finely, *"I always find bitter and premature the death of those engaged in creating something of lasting value. For those who live for pleasure wind up living from day to day, while those with their minds on posterity preserve their memory*

---

9 **Pliny, 35.2**: *Non enim solum ex auro, argentove, aut etiam ex aere, in bibliothecis dicantur illi, quorum immortales animae in iisdem locis loquuntur: quin imò etiam quae non sunt, finguntur pariuntque desideria non traditi vultus, sicut in Homero evenit. Quo majus, ut quidem arbitror, nullum est felicitatis specimen, quàm semper omnes scire cupere, qualis fuerit aliquis.*
10 **Plutarch, *How a man can know his progress in virtue*,**16. 85.

*through their writings. For such as these, no death is not premature, as they always leave behind something incomplete."*[11]

The rays of sublime Sapience of these Suns of the world enliven the sciences, illuminate the centuries and embellish the whole earth. Do they not deserve the place of honor held by light at the beginning of creation? The light made by God was worthy of the first word of praise he gave from his mouth to any work of his hands. And not because it is beautiful in itself, but because it makes beautiful all it sees, therefore, *"(Light) found its spokesman (God), who was the first to praise it, for through it the world's other parts also become praiseworthy."* [12]

Such is the nature, and such are the merits of the sages. Seneca would honor them on the day of their birth, kiss the earth they trod, mourn the hour of their death, hailing them as **Praeceptores generis humani**, *(teachers of mankind)* and if this were not enough, **Deorum ritu colendos** *(to be revered by divine offices.)*[13] And why not? Vitruvius would add, *"When considering the many gifts bestowed on men by the prudence of the great writers, I think that not only should they be given palms and crowns but celebrated in triumphal processions and seated among the gods."*[14]

---

11 **Pliny the Younger**, *Letters* 5.5, **to Maximus**: *Mihi autem videtur acerba semper et immatura mors eorum, qui immortale aliquid parant. Nam qui voluptatibns dediti quasi in diem vivunt, vivendi causas quotidie siniunt: qui verò posteros coglitant, et memoriam sui operibus extendunt, his nulla mors non repentina est, ut quae semper inchoatum aliquid abrumpat.*
12 **Ambrose, Hexameron, 1.9**: *Tantum sibi praedicatorem potuit invenire, a quo jure prima laudetur quoniam ipsa facit, ut etiam caetera mundi membra digna sint laudibus.*
13 **Seneca, *Letter* 64**.9.
14 **Vitruvius, *On Architecture*, Book 9, preface:** *Cum enim tanta munera ab scriptorum prudentia (privatim publice) fuerint hominibus praeparata, non solum arbitror palmas, et coronas his tribui oportere, sed etiam decerni triumphos, et inter deorum sedes eos dedicandos (iudicari).*

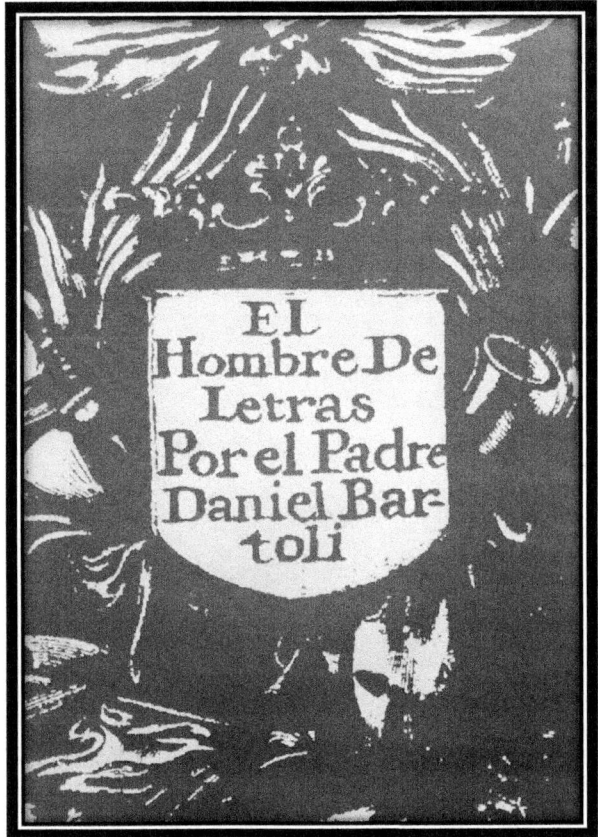

# 13          *OBSCURITY*

## 13.1   *Ambition and Confusion, two principles of Obscurity, Affected and Natural*

Widespread among the people in olden times, in direct opposition to the truth, it was believed that the fixed stars are mothers and keepers of souls and that, up in Heaven, everyone has his own star and brilliance of the first, medium, or lesser magnitude, corresponding to the place in society which determines one's relative standing. If this were so, certain obscure souls, certain Cimmerian minds, where could they come from, if not from those cloudy and turgid stars which give so little light mingled with so much smog that, as stars, they seem more like smudges than stars?

Such are those unfortunate Ethiopian souls who draw their darkness from the sun, the father of clarity, and learn confusion from wisdom, the mother of order. In the fire of Palladian Athena's sanctum, their Wits shine brightly, but the more they burn, the more they show only obscurity and the blackness of coal. They scorn eagle eyes for an owl's and so think they are the true birds of Athena that dwell in the night.

In vain would the very sage Socrates make his usual conjecture about them. He knew that speech gives a living image of the mind, so to know who someone was he would say to him, **Loquere ut te videam** (*Speak, so I can see you.*)[1] Their speech, their writing, is like an anamorphic drawing with certain monstrous figures of faces so misshapen, with features so distorted, that no eye will discern in them lineaments of human likeness, except by looking at a cylinder of polished steel, and seeing them in their reflection.[2] Unhappily dimwitted Wits,. Dedaluslike, they are contrivers only of labyrinths so twisted, so complex, so confused, that even they can hardly find by themselves the thread that will deliver wthem out.

But all obscurity is not of the self-same nature, nor has it only one origin and source. One kind is artificial, another natural, the first

---

1 Apuleius, *Florida,* 2; Erasmus, *Apophthegms*, (1540)
2 Anamorphic images reflect the century's experimental sensory imagination and its fascination with unusual and illusory visions. Anamorphosis and *trompe l'oeil* became Jesuit curiosities, notably in the art of Andrea Pozzo.

affected from ambition, the second from defect of Wit, meriting compassion, while the former merits censure.

It is a received opinion among the common people that all obscurity argues for Wit, that the extent of profound knowledge can be measured as the ancients calculated the height of Mount Athos, by judging from its shadow's length of the nine hundred stadia, and that nature in the darkness of the night has provided the stars and wisdom for the obscurity of Wits; that God himself casts a cloud over his oracles and that the excessive light of his abode, where he is visible, is described as shadowy for the way it reveals and conceals him; that this was the way of the sagest of the ancients whose sublime minds, whose high-flying Wits were like lofty mountain tops, with their heads almost always lost in mist and clouds so that their writings stood at a greater distance from pilfering, the obscurer they were, and that gems and diamonds of the firmest and brightest truths were best revealed among the thickest shadows.

Thus, the common folk are fooled by a false appearance of truth. They always admire most what they least understand. They care nothing for what is limpid and clear, since they can see it with their own eyes. They judge a few inches of turgid water an abyss of wisdom because they cannot see to the bottom. So likewise, in letters:

*White privets are trampled; while dark hyacinths are picked.*[3]

And so, some, from ambition for Wit, will affect obscurity, and with the ploy of not making themselves understood will make themselves adored. They change into more shapes than Proteus, to escape those who grasp them, so they may not be known for what they are. They invent more hieroglyphics than Egypt knew, to make believe there is a kernel of solid truth under a husk of feigned mysteries. Every one of their sentences is a Gordian knot that promises an empire to the one who can untie it. They scatter their words, more than the leaves of the Sybil were scattered by the wind, and leave the baffled unfortunates poking behind their oracles to misconstrue meanings that never entered the writer's mind.

Other times they expose their conceits, as the gods in a theatre, wrapped in a knot of clouds. They unveil the smallest bit of some well-ordered argument, so they can claim credit for what otherwise disappears in a wash of confused thoughts. Reading their books is like

---

3 Virgil, *Eclogue* 2.18:
    *Alba ligustra cadunt, vaccinia nigra leguntur.*

fishing for squid— very crafty fish— who to escape eye and hand, trickily muddy the water by squirting a cloud of the black liquid they contain. Thus, their pen is like these fish,

> *The very trick, which she knows how to use, enhances her nature*
> *And guides her ingenious strategy.*[4]

Oh! How often there is nothing there, where some think great mysteries lie hidden? Since it is their usual practice to cover, as the painter Timanthes did, with a veil, what they have neither Wit, nor art sufficient to express.[5]

They seem the newest versions of Heraclitus, (*"Whose obscure texts gave him the name,* **scotinon**, *the obscure philosopher."*[6]) What Pythagoras said about that philosopher's writings applies to them: *"It would take a Delian diver to reach that deep."*[7] They rank with the Apollonius at Delphi as reliable authorities, when, as he would , *"They neither speak nor conceal but just make gestures."*[8]

But the other obscurity more unfortunate than culpable, is a defect of nature, not a vice of the will. This, in some, comes from poverty and paucity of Wit. Their creative power, too cramped in its womb, cannot compose without confusing and cannot position the parts without crippling the whole. In others, it is occasioned by too fervid a mind, whose fiery thoughts, as in sudden conflagrations, often breath more smoke than flames.

These are those truly fiery Wits, active and quick of understanding. In just one turn of mind, flashing thoughts like lightening, they entertain a thousand ideas and possess a thousand new insights. It would be happy for them if they could reinforce their flame and bridle their fire. They ressemble the fleetest animals that leave the only the vaguest tracks, wholly focused on what they see as they rush on, so they cannot grasp what, even if at times only in outline, is

---

4 **Claudian,** *de saepis,* 46.8/9:
> *Naturam juvat ipsa dolis et conscia sortis*
> *Utitur ingenio.*

[5] Famous for his veiled head of Agamemnon, discussed by Pliny, 35.36, Cicero and Quintilian.

6 **Seneca,** *Letter* **12.**7: *cui cognomen Scotinon fecit orationis obscuritas.*

7 Greek proverb for profound courage, *opus ibi esse Delio natatore.* Not in **Laertius,** *Pythagoras,* but, Laertius, *Socrates,* 2.22, and Crates, in Laertius, *Heraclitus,* 9.12.

8 **Heraclitus, in Stobaeus**, 5: *Neque dicant, neque abscondant sed indicent solùm.*

instantly understood. Incrimentally incap capable of organizing, as they grow more imaginative with their ideas, they issue, whether speaking or writing, not a delivery, but many seeds and when they finally are cooled down again and settled, (when judgement is most discerning), they are unable to reformulate their thoughts again, lacking the same luminous insight that was missing in their Wit when it was ablaze.

And these two are, in my judgment, both causes of the vice of obscurity, the first, the crime of over-ambitious intelligence, the second, the shortcomings of weakness or confusion in the Wit. But, there is a third sort of obscurity, and it is very real. It is the obscure Wit of the reader who does not comprehend, not the author's, who only writes or speaks to be easily understood by men of average understanding.

If we argue from certain chief universal maxims and derive from their true principles further subordinate truths until we focus on one particular subject, (which is the noblest and most sublime of all the types of sage discourse), we are following the falcons in their great climbs and gyres as they soar upwards and swoop down on their quarry from on high. If we deck out wisdom with fictive, but suitable ideas, which are fitted like garments that both clothe and display what to conceal we ought not, to reveal we should not, this is a usage which Synesius calls, **perantiquum atque Platonicum** (most ancient and platonic)[9]. If we sometimes lift the pen from minutely drawing every single detail and outline of some details so that they are mentioned, but not at length; if we write as Timanthes would paint where, *"in all his works more is always perceived than is painted with a consummate artistry that contains a genius beyond art,"*[10] critics will condemn this as obscurity and say with Tertullian that to understand and penetrate such things, *"it will require not just the rays of a lantern's light, but a burst of full sunlight."*[11] They don't see that it is not our writings that need light, but their eyes that need a clarifying solution. They are like Seneca's demented maidservant Arpastes, suddenly gone blind but confident that she could still see as before, *"said that the house had gone all dark."*[12]

---

9 **Synesius,** ***De insomniis*** (*On Dreams*), preface.
10 **Pliny**, 35.36: *In cuius omnibus operibus intellegitur semper plus quàm pingitur et cum ars summa sit ingenium tamen ultra artem est.*
11 **Tertullian,** ***De pudicitia****,* (*On modesty*) 7.21: *Non lucernae spiculo lumine, sed totius solis lancea opus est.*
12 **Seneca,** ***Letter*** **50**.2: *aiebat domum tenebrosum esse.*

So, since no more important remedy for obscurity, of the curable kind, can be offered than the essential precepts of distinction and order, the father and mother of clarity, I have focused on them under the following headings, writing, with perhaps too extended a treatment what the subject called for. Nonetheless, as it is neither beside the point nor without potential benefit, I have organized a few recommendations which go from the choice of the subject up to the final corrections that I thought would foster a more orderly, more simplified and more successful method of writing.

## 13.2    *The Subject Chosen should be equalled by the Wit of the Writer*

The first and most important job of them all is the invention of the main theme. The first law of Horace advises that if you are a pigmy, you should not assume the weight of a world on your shoulders, as if you were an Atlas.

> *Ponder at length what your shoulders will not carry*
> *and what they will.*[1]

If your Wit has a weak and untried point on it, you should not work in porphyry, serpentine or marble, for they may prove much harder than your chisel. Measure your sail to the wind and your rudder to the waves and if you be but a small bark, do not act the mighty ship. Your ocean sea should be a lake, your Indies a little island half a day away:

> *Let others plough the high seas.*[2]

What would you do, if fishing for small fry you saw a large tuna caught in your net? Would you be so hungry for the catch, that you forgot the flimsiness of the net? You would fear to go for what otherwise you wanted with the knowledge that nets made of thin threads are no more fit for such a large catch than a spider's web is to trap a hornet.

Oh! How many wind up like the Icarus of myth who was neither a good bird in air, nor a good fish in water, since he fell from the air and drowned the water. His miserable father, seeing him go

---

1 Horace, *Ars Poetica*, 39/40:
> *Versate diu quid ferre recusant,*
> *Quid valeant humeri.*

2 *Aeneid* 5.163: *Altum alii teneant.*

beyond the bounds he set for him when he fastened the wings on his shoulders, was following him from afar, crying,

> *Ah simple, venturous Boy Farfalla fond,*
> *Why dost thou rashly soar so far beyond*
> *The flight I set thee? Why goest thou so near*
> *The scorching beams of sun's consuming sphere?*
> *Art thou so foolish as not to take account*
> *Thy wings of wax can never the fire mount?*
> *Why Icarus I say! soft! not so high!*
> *So ho! stay Icarus, and lower fly!*[3]

But what to do? If his delight outscored his danger and his eye outscored his ear,

> *Driven by the desire to go to heaven*
> *His flight led higher.*[4]

As the wax began to melt and his wings little by little lost their feathers, he fell from Heaven into the sea, and died there. Just so is someone who leaves his flight to whimsy and does not gage his ascent on high by the strength of his wings.

There may well be some subjects that seem to have the ambitions of the great Alexander. He would have no picture, statue or cast of his face except from the brushes of Apelles, from the chisels of Phidias, from the molds of Lysippus. They too will disdain a craft of any other style which is not the golden style. Alone among all the Wits, they want only the most sublime, in the manner of Jove, who over the whole earth reserved only the mountain tops for himself, and with good reason, because for the supreme god only should the summits of the earth be reserved.[5]

---

3 Salusbury's English. Ovid, **Met**. 8.203ff, in the Italian translation (1554-61) by Giovanni Andrea Anguillara:

> *Sconsigliato fanciul, sciocca farfalla*
> *Già del foco vicin tocchi la sfera,*
> *Ne ti sovvien, che debili a la spalla*
> *porti dentro le fiamme ali di cera?*
> *Icaro, oimè, tropp'alto Icaro sali;*
> *Ferma Icaro il volo, e bassa l'ali.*

The opening line is the first of six verses in *Della penna ad Icaro*, in *Saggio di poesie morali*, p. 28.

4 Ovid, **Met**. 8. 225/6: *Coelique cupidine tactus*
> *Altius egit iter.*

5 **Maximus of Tyre**, ***Dissertations***, 8.8

Aptly may we say about subjects what ancient sages said about one's fortune. As is true for articles of clothing, the largest is not the best, but what is the best fit and the most suitable.[6] The painter Pereichus normally painted only stables and horses; Seraphion only Heavens and gods.[7] But the Heavens of Seraphion reeked of stables, and his gods of horses, and conversely, the stables of Pereichus were a heavenly sight and his horses, through the excellence of his art, had about them something divine. It is not the subject, but the technique that gives the artist his reputation and the object its value. If you have a pen like the brush of Pereichus that can treat ordinary matters with extraordinary skill, do not choose to be a Seraphion, who, tempted by more lofty subjects, would make the beautiful misshapen, where he could have made the misshapen beautiful.

The world has never seen a more admirable creation than the sphere of the divine artificer, Archimedes. Making, as it were, a compendium of the world, by shrinking the large, by reducing the great, by slowing the swift, by lowering the sublime, within the narrow space of a globe, he knew how to compress it, and not to confuse it. He gave liberty to the planets, order to the stars, variety to their movements, proportion to the spaces, and disposed everything with such consonance, that if the cycles of great Heaven ever went awry, one could have fixed them by the revolutions of the small Heaven of Archimedes. But this noble creation, for which sapphires and diamonds would not have been precious enough for components, did he not make it of glass? With the fragility of imperfect glass, he imitated the eternity of the incorruptible substance of Heaven, without diminishing the worth of the work by the inferior value of the material. That great rock crystal which Mercator used to shape a celestial globe for Charles the Fifth, had encased in it bands of gold and the finest diamonds for stars.[8] He made it in such fashion, as was the Helen of that other painter, if not beautiful, then at least rich, but the artifact has hardly held the world's memory, much less its applause. The diamonds of Mercator were inferior in value to the glass of Archimedes, by the superior genius of his art and by his greater technical mastery.

---

6 **Apuleius,** *Apologia* **1**.19: *fortunam uelut tunicam magis concinnam quam longam probare.*
7 Pliny, 35.37.
8 **In the life of Mercator**

With this I do not mean to suggest that more common subjects are better to choose for being easier to do than challenging ones. I only advise whoever is not the swimmer that the great Delian swimmer was, not to swim great gorges but to ford lesser waters. If he has not the Wit, nor the learning, **Ubi consistat** (as required), let him not attempt, as could Archimedes, **Caelum, terramque movere**, (move heaven and earth) shouldering weighty matters and subjects of lofty intellect where neither the flight of his Wit, nor of his pen can reach.

Indeed, the finest part of a work is the excellence of its subject. One who works with his brain knows by experience that an appealing subject gives a wonderful focus to the Wit, so that a noble theme inspires worthy thoughts and nurtures a noble response. Maternus says in the *Dialogue on Oratory* of Tacitus, or rather by Quintilian, *"The spirit's force grows with the stature of the subject, you cannot deliver clear and brilliant oratory unless the subject merits that style."* [9] And, to tell the truth, on the rough texture of a coarse canvas rich designs of silk are ill embroidered, pearls and gold ornaments will disdain to show against such a background. Conversely, how grandly and stately (said a poet)[10] flow the waters of the Pactolus and the Tagus, because they run upon a riverbed of gold. They look more like diamonds than water, less precious a liquid and unbecoming to so noble a support.

Let him therefore, who can worthily discuss them, choose matters of sublime argument, so they may deliver noble compositions, otherwise he will be like the Spartan king, Archidamus, who took to wife a woman of such inordinately tiny stature that he was censured by the ephors about, *"breeding not kings, but kinglets"*.[11]

## 13.3   *The Partition and Skeleton of the Whole Discourse*

When a subject has been identified as suitable for the writer and worthy of his audience, he has to order it in skeleton outline and dissect the body in parts, so that this ingenious division  may cover

---

9 Tacitus, not Quintilian, *Dialogue on Oratory: Crescit enim cum amplitudine rerum vis ingenii, nec quisquam claram, et illustrem orationem efficere potest, nisi qui causam parem invenit.*
10 *Aeneid,* 10.141; Juvenal, *Satires,* 14.208; Ovid, *Amores,* 1.15.34; *Met.,* 2.251.
11 Plutarch, *Agesilaus,* 2. Quoting Theophrastus: *tanquam non reges, sed regunculos procreaturus.*

what there is to be said on the subject. This is one of the most important tasks of a writer. For as with the proportion of the parts of the body, so also with the division of parts in compositions, they have that beauty which comes from symmetry, and that clarity which proceeds from order. Therefore, one's judgement must conceive the design of the complete shape altogether, and from that, as love out of chaos, it has to distinguish, to organize, to compose part by part, and then join them together and unite all the parts.

The truly great quality of a superior work is that it can present many and diverse matters, but with such union of all the parts, that observing, now the foot, now the hand, the breast, and then the face, they are the same body with the whole understood in each of its parts,

*Let the middle not be disjointed from the beginning, nor the end from the middle.*[1]

And this, of all the excellencies of Heaven, is what, more than all the others, makes it wonderful, that in it the discord of so many motions is so harmonized and the wanderings of so many stars are so governed, that not only is there no disharmony in their variety, nor confusion in their multitude, rather the planets do communicate among themselves and, as it were, instruct each other in measures of sextiles, quadrants, trines, aspects diametrically opposed, all perspectives by which they do not so much feature one another, as display their mutual correspondence to the star gazer. So said Manilius:

*Nothing is more marvelous in the great universe*
*Than the order and the laws that rule it all*
*Nowhere is there disturbance, nothing in its parts is errant.* [2]

For, if the correct division of the parts is missing and with it, proper order, just as one who has given the first form to a statue of marble in a crippled and defective shape, however much afterwards he may polish it and work on every detail, it will not cease to be a monster, only monstrous, more or less. And it has no benefit for a disordered discourse to be full of lofty speculations and fascinating ideas, with

---

1 Horace, *Ars poetica*, 152:
  *Ne primo medium, medio nec discrepet imum.*
2 **Manilius *Astronomica*, 1**.485:
  *Haud quicquam in tanta magis est mirabile mole,*
  *Quam ratio, et certis quòd legibus omnia parent.*
  *Nusquam turba nocet, nihil his in partibus errat.*

solid reasoning and with ancient and modern erudition, so that it has the sparkle of many lights and the beauty of many decorations. An aphorism left in the writings of Hippocrates about an unhealthy body pertains to such compositions as these, *"The more you feed it, the more harm you do"*.[3]

One should, therefore, do as in their wisdom the bees do. First, they work their wax into honeycombs, and partition the hive. This is their first business and they dedicate considerable time and industry to it. Then they leave in search of honey, and in a few days, they have filled their empty combs.

## 13.4  *Preparation of the Material, called the Sylva*

When the subject is found, and the parts disposed, after comes the writing, to cover the bones with flesh and from a skeleton to make a body. And here is, at the onset, a normal mistake. Whoever brings to such work just a white sheet of paper, a pen and his own brain is attempting all at the same time to Invent, to Order, and to Compose, aiming his attention together to the Matter, the Order, and the Method as if he were the sun painting a rainbow in a cloud, with no irregularity in the circle, with no disorder in the colors, All you have to do is to look at it and by applying the brush of a sunbeam, in the same moment it is drawn and colored.

These, while chewing on their pen, looking up at the ceiling and buzzing like beetles mutter to themselves and put on paper beginnings without endings and so wind up at the end of the work at the beginning. How timely might one whisper in their ear as a joke, and a reminder, that familiar axiom which says **Ex nihilo nihil**. *(from nothing comes nothing)*. You are asking for gold to rain down from your head without any mine of it there and what's more you want it minted as good coin and struck as legal tender. So, in one and the same time, you are playing the alchemist, the assayer, the coiner, the treasurer, the prince, everything. This is the way straight to nowhere, *Not by lying down*

---

3 Hippocrates, *Aphorisms,* 2.10: *Quo plus nutries, eo magis laedes.*

*and looking up at the ceiling and mouthing the murmur of a thought can we expect something to materialize.*[1]

Look at making a book like building a house. It is not enough to have a blueprint and a plan, if stones, plaster, beams, and metalwork are lacking  So, *A thick crop of information and ideas should be prepared: it is from the knowledge of these things then that the composition takes form and beauty.*[2]A writer must have in his head a living library, collected with long study from all kinds of history, sacred, secular, natural, and civil, from political teachings, from ancient rites and laws, from grave and authoritative sayings of the sages, from fables, from hieroglyphics, from proverbs, above all else from natural and moral philosophy, from mathematics, from jurisprudence, from medicine, and from a requisite amount of theology; otherwise, it must be from dead books that he has got to search for and gather what he needs.

It matters little to conceive a noble subject, if when you are ready to deliver it, your breasts are not full of milk to nourish it, so that it perishes of sheer famine in your hands. Stasicrates wanted to make a sculpture of Alexander by making a super gigantic statue of him out of Mount Athos. He did not reckon that the city which he designed to put in one hand, without fields around it for planting, would thereby be inhabitable. This was what Alexander had his eye on above all. *Humored by this proposal he insisted on asking if there were fields in the area for the crops necessary to feed the city.*[3] And when the answer was no, with a polite smirk he pushed aside the offer of the unthinking sculptor: *Just as a new born cannot be nourished without a nurse's milk, nor be brought up to live and grow, so with a city, etc.*[4] Just so, whatever theme one chooses, if it cannot be nourished, it cannot grow or be sustained. Like a seedling

---

[1] **Quintillian, *Institutiones oratoriae*, 10**.3.15: *Ne igitur resupini, respectantesque tectum, et cogitationem murmurare agitantes expectemus quid obveniat.*

[2] **Cicero, *De oratore* 3**,27. 103: *Sylva rerum et sententiarum paranda est: ex rerum enim cognitione, efflorescere debet, et redundare oratio.*

[3] **Vitruvius, *De Architectura*, 2**, preface: *Delectatus enim ratione forma, statim quaesivit, si essent agri circa, qui possent frumentaria ratione eam civitatem tueri.*

[4] ***Ibid.***: *Ut enim natus infans sine nutricis lacte non potest ali, neque ad vitae crescentis gradus perduci, sic civitas, etc.*

sprung up in the dry sands of the Arabian desert, no sooner above ground, it goes without moisture, and without life.

Hence, it is prudent for someone, before selecting a subject, to see if he has, or can access, material sufficient to compose it. In this way experienced architects, says St. Ambrose, when designing all their buildings, pay primary attention to locating the lighting that every space will need. *Before he lays the foundations, he studies where it will be filled with light, for that is a building's most important feature, and if it is missing, the whole house is cursed as deformed and uninhabitable.* [5]

One must have ready familiarity with many books. His judgement must be at least competent in the selection of them and even more discriminating in the use of what he has found in them. And so, in the appropriate context, you may furnish the words of Wit and charm with which to express what you have to say. In this, the surest observation is that everyone, according to that personal genius which is behind the words he uses, comes up with what gives his thoughts their most congenial expression. And as *"The finest Wits disdain low and sordid subjects and are attracted to themes of the greatest order which they celebrate."*[6]

There are some who leave their diamonds with the cock of Aesop. As if their brains were yellow amber, they can only gather up worthless strands of straw. From flowers, some get only the sight, some only the smell, others the sketches they draw of them, others the essence distilled from them, while the bees take honey that is all of the same sweetness and quality, though they take it from flowers of different kinds and flavors. With books, meadows of sweet smelling herbs and flowers, it is the same for the nourishment of Wit. There are some who only take from them the sight, in the enjoyment of reading them, others imbibe some fragrant essence to enliven the brain and refresh the Wit. There are some who take their herbs in bundles,

---

[5] **Ambrose, *Hexameron*,** 5.9: *Antequam fundamentum ponat, unde lucem ei infundat explorat, et ea prima est gratia, quae si desit, tota domus deformi horret incultu.*

[6] Tacitus (Quintillian) *de eloquentia dialogus,* not **Seneca, *Letters*,** 39: *Neminem excelsi ingenii virum humilia delectant, et sordida, magnarum enim rerum species ad se vocat, et extollit.*

.

gathering what first comes mindlessly to hand, and some who more selectively pick only flowers for weaving wreathes and garlands. Some squeeze juices, others squeeze waters. Few, from a great multitude of objects different one from the other, know how to gather honey of the same taste, and employ them to speak all to the same purpose, as they give the delight of variety, notwithstanding the unity of meaning. These diverse manners of choosing and using are subject to judgement and judgement follows the genius of each to articulate, after his own style, the true idea of his mind. Therefore, things taken from books can be compared to dewdrops. When they fall inside a shell (as some believe), they change into pearls, but if they land on a moldy log, they become toadstools. Now, in gathering material for a book, I have a final caveat, that having too much may be as harmful as it is to have nothing. The writer need not be so restricted in his choice that his work should prove thinner than an emaciated Aristarchus, a Philetas of Cos, a living skeleton, where the bones, the veins, the nerves, the muscles, the pulses of the arteries, if not the very soul itself, are visible. Nor should he be so prodigal, so as to fashioni a man so corpulent that he looks not like a man, but rather like a large sack of potatoes. One who creates excessive bulk, unless he be that **Magnus Deus,** *(the great god)* [7] as love was called by the ancients, that brings order out of chaos, will be unable to distribute it, since massive quantity is ther reign of confusion.

    Furthermore, having collected so much, after selecting the best of what we have, we are most reluctant to throw out the rest as useless, though it far exceeds what we have picked. It goes against good judgement as wasteful to discard with so many other things the time and effort spent amassing them. They are all so appealing and appetizing that they get stuffed into books, as into a glutton's belly more from frenzied feeding, than for the purposes of digestion. Such superfluity of corrupt humors engenders indisposition of the body, lack of energy, paleness, and a hundred maladies, *So in the things that provide sustenance to our Wits we should see to it that what we have absorbed does not remain whole, and extraneous, but should be digestedt.* [8]

---

[7] **Plato, *Symposium*,** 2.195; *Phaedo*, 178b.

[8] **Seneca, *Letter* 84.**6/7: *Idem igitur in his quibus aluntur ingenia, praestemus, ut quaecunque hausimus non patiamur integra esse, ne aliena sint, sed coquamus illa.*

Thus, let us be aware that with respect to books, as with respect to bodies, we should not include whatever they are capable of holding, but what they are capable of assimilating and digesting. Now the subject found, the parts organized, the material collected and set in order, it is time to begin writing.

## 13.5 *Discouragement of Those with Problems getting started*

In every art and enterprise, more difficult than all the rest is getting started. The first steps require the greatest strength and constancy; after them, as for one scaling up a steep mountain, the way on is ever more level and practicable. All the arts may say of their beginnings, what Apollo, instructing Phaeton, said of his journey,

> *The onset of the journey is arduous, hardly matched*
> *By the strength of the fresh horses at daybreak.*[1]

As with money-making in merchandise, the hardest part is leaving poverty behind. As the Stoic says, "*It takes a long time to make the money to leave poverty behind as you' are crawling out of it.*"[2] Lampis, a very rich man, was asked how from the beggar he began as he had become so welathy.[3] "*My first meagre profits I made working constantly, day and night. The big money I now make while I'm sleeping, even days. I would sweat more in the beginning for a penny, than I do now for a fortune, so being rich now costs me no more than the pains I first took to get out of poverty.*

This fails to be understood by those unfamiliar with the craft of writing. At the outset their thoughts are sterile, their juices dried up, and their Wits are devoid of ideas. They give up, either cursing themselves as destined to fail or entirely forsaking their struggle for an art too difficult to learn. They do not keep in mind that from the darkness of night to the brilliant light of midday there is no immediate passageway. Beforehand come the first glimmerings, dim light in much haze, thencomes the dawn, less dusky and whitening on the edge of the horizon, next sunrise, richer with light and more colorful, and

---

1 **Ovid,** *Met.,* **2.**63/4:
> *Ardua prima via est, per quam vix mane recentes*
> *Enituntur equi.*

2 **Seneca,** *Letter* **101.**2: *Pecunia circa paupertatem plurimam moram habet, dum ex illa erepat.*

3 **Plutarch,** *An seni gerenda res publica* (*Should elders be in government*), 6.

finally, the sun. In its first appearance above our hemisphere it is hazy, vaporous, oblique, weak, and unsteady, but rising at length above the horizon (as someone gasping to climb a rocky cliff) little by little it ascends to the zenith point of heaven. They forget that a man must be a child first and crawl on the ground before he can start to run, standing warily on his feeble feet, with his tender arms up, tottering and falling at every step. No good at talking, after the long time he never spoke at all, he begins with gurgles, then his tongue stutters and stammers and his words come out at first choppy and twisted until he can try to say Da and Ma. Then he takes from the mouths of others the syllables and words one by one, and begins to utter, like an echo, the bits of phrases, more mimicking, than speaking.

Great men are not made at one casting like brass statues, formed whole and entire at once. They are rather wrought like marbles, by the point of the chisel little by little. Men like Apelles, Zeuxis, Parrhasius were great masters of art. Their paintings hardly seemed to need souls to seem alive, as they seemed to be alive even without souls. When they took in hand their brushes and began painting, is there any doubt that half their sketches were tossed or that under their paintings they wrote what the subject was, for a lion not to be taken as a dog? It is the opinion of Pliny that nature herself, (notwithstanding she is so great an artist and mistress of the most excellent workmanship) before she set herself to create the lily, a work of great art, prepared by making, as it were, a rough draught and model in the morning glory (convolvulus), a white and simple flower, he termed, *"almost a rough draft of nature, studying to make the lily"*.[4] If you pictured the Capitoline Hill of Rome with the Temple of Jupiter there, studded with the spoils of the whole world, would you recognize it as it once looked, when

> *The whole of Jupiter could hardly fit in the cramped space*
> *And the lightning bolt in Jove's right hand was made of clay.*[5]

From such an insignificant seed sprouted a mighty woods, thick with as many trees as the triumphs witnessed from the Capitoline. This accords with the law common to all things— first come springs of paltry origins and humble beginnings— then streams, next rivers— and at last, the sea.

---

4 **Pliny, 21**.5: *veluti naturae rudimentum, lilia facere condiscentis.*
5 **Ovid, *Fasti* 1**.201/2:
> *Juppiter angusta vix totus stabat in aede,*
> *Inque Jovis dextra fictile fulmen erat?*

It may well be true in some instances, after the ancient proverb, that royal rivers are navigable from their head waters, and that someone destined to prove, in some profession of Letters, excellent beyond the ordinary, will show extraordinary signs of this from the very beginning, after the example of Hercules,

*He was slaying monsters before he could recognize them.*[6]

He was strangling dragons as a baby in his cradle, as a prelude to the Hydra, and as a first proof of his strength. Nevertheless, however true for a few, this does not apply as the law for everyone. For the felicity of first works counts more than their facility and express the Wit's imaginative ability more than the artist's technical mastery.

Therefore, let us not forsake the enterprise, however unwieldy its beginnings; not abandon Proteus if he manages to burst the first nets we set him for him; and not try to be masters, before we are students. We should bear in mind that beginners do enough if they begin. Take for encouragement some verses of the king of poets, as they apply to your purpose,

*As when a dove her rocky hold forsakes*
*Roused in a fright her pounding wings she shakes*
*The cavern rings with clattering as out she flies*
*And leaves her callow cares and cleaves the skies*
*At first, she flutters but at length she springs*
*To smoother flight and shoots upon her wing.*[7]

Just so shall it be for your Wit. For now, you have to beat your wings with all your might and start to fly with everything you have. It will not be long before it takes no flapping of wings or beating of feathers to soar in flight most happily. And that will come along with the habit of writing, so that to do what you want to, all you need is to wish it, and it is done.

## 13.6  *We should use Various Styles, According to the Variety of Subjects under Discussion*

---

6 Seneca, *Hercules Furens*, 2. 219:
     *Monstra superavit prius, quam nosse posset.*
7 Dryden's translation, *Aeneid* 5.213-7:
     *Qualis spelunca subito commota columba,*
     *Cui domus, et dulces latebroso in pumice nidi*
     *Fertur in arva volans, plausumque exterrita pennis*
     *Dat tecto ingentem: Mox aïre lapsa quieto,*
     *Radit iter liquidum, celeris neque commovet alas.*

It now is time to show what style, what form or, as Hermogenes called it, what idea of style ought to be used by the writer.[1] Concerning this it should be known that in the style of developing any subject one wants, the foremost consideration comes down to Quantity and Quality. In the first, length or brevity are the measure; in the second, it is the effectiveness or weakness of the discourse. Because in both one and the other of these two categories you have two extremes and between them the mean, hence it follows— that under quantity come the lengthy, the middle and the brief— and under quality come the sublime, the middle, and the low. The three kinds of Quantity have been made use of by different peoples; the very lengthy, by the Asians; the very brief, by the Spartans; the middle by the those in Attica. In the second threefold category of Quality, there have been orators excellent, on the word of Marcus Tully Cicero, in each of these forms of speaking.[2]

The pure Asiatic is diffuse and talks at will, with the habit of saying, as that Albutius mentioned by Seneca, *"Not whatever one should, but whatever one can."*[3] A style, in Scaliger's words, murderous to the ears, which in a sea of words, has not a pinch of salt,[4] *"Without a certain impetus, it runs along with inflated and unconnected words. This way of speaking, it was appropriately decided, comes from the mouth, not from the heart."*[5] It would be miraculous (as Aristotle said to an importunate drone) that anyone with feet to walk away should have ears to stay and listen. Have you seen the first letters on the titles of legal documents written on parchment? How many pen strokes, how many figures and arabesque flourishes crowd together to produce them? And in the end, they are no more than an A, or a B, like any letter in plain writing. This is the true image of the Asian style. In a world of words, it tells you no more than others would say in a single sentence.

---

1 Hermogenes of Tarsus, rhetorician, late second century, wrote *On types (ideas) of style,* in 2 books with seven categories and sudivisions. See p.178.
2 **Cicero, *Oration to Brutus, De oratoribus eminentis.***
3 **Seneca the Elder, *Controversies,* 7**. Preface: *Non quidquid debet, sed quidquid potest.*
4 Joseph Justus Scaliger (1540-1609), historical scholar and arbiter of classical style.
5 **Gellius, 1.15**: *Nullo enim certo pondere innixus verbis humidis, et lapsantibus diffluit. Cujus orationem benè existimatum est in ore nasci, non in pectore.*

The pure Laconic style uses hieroglyphics instead of words, and in it as I have said concerning the paintings of Parrhasius, *"More is perceived than is painted."*[6] *"He strives to express several things with the fewest words,"* as Dionysius of Halicarnassus said of Thucydides.[7] It packs three lengthy sentences into a single line. Three lines are nothing short of a complete oration. Every word of it, rather every syllable, is how Demosthenes described the words of Phocion, the blow.of an axe[8]

The mean between these two, as the gold compound or electrum that is tempered and compounded of both, is the Attic. Without the insipidity of the Asian, without the obscurity of the Laconic, it has the clarity of one and the effectiveness of the other. As in a well-formed body it is neither all nerve, nor all flesh, with one part for strength, and the other for beauty. If you take away or skillfully change one word of it, you are still taking away, as with Plato **De elegantia** (elegance), as with Lysias **De sententia** (meaning).[9] It has what Seneca the Elder in his *Controversies* calls **Pugnatorum mucronem** (the punch of pugnacity),[10] that is missing in the Asiatic, but employs it with other more secure and appropriate ways of fighting than the Laconic, which in every pass makes a thrust, and closes in, only using (as Regulus said of himself) short strokes, and all at the throat of the matter but always with the danger that, *"He strikes the knee or the heel where he aims for the throat."*[11]

The different styles under the category of Quality have not as the aforesaid, the worst in the extremes, and the best in the middle, they progress in goodness one above the other, as one is superior to the others in perfection.

To explain their nature more clearly, I will recall what was taught by Aristotle and Marcus Tully.[12] That the art of persuasion has three most potent means by which it may achieve its goal— to teach,

---

6 **Pliny, 35.10**. *Plus intelligitur quàm pingatur.*
7 **Dionysius of Halicarnassus, *De iudicium Thucydidis*:** *Studet enim ut paucissimus verbis plurimas res comprehendat.*
8 **Plutarch, *Praecepta rei republicae*** (*Precepts of Statecraft*),7.
9 From **Gellius**, 2.5, quoting Favorinus: *Si ex Platonis oratione verbum aliquod demas mutesve atque id commodatissime facias, de elegantia tamen detraxeris; si ex Lysiae, de sententia.*
10 **Seneca the Elder, *Controversies*,** 2.2.
11 **Pliny the Younger**, *Letters* 2.20.15: *Ne genu sit, aut talus, ubi jugulum putat.*
12 **Aristotle, *Rhetoric*,** 1.1; **Cicero, *Brutus*.**

to delight, to move. And because each of them has a purpose quite different from the other, each of them uses different characteristics and styles, the simplest to teach, the middle to delight, the sublime to move.

As for the most basic level, here are the terms used by the father of Latin eloquence to describe them, *"To the point always informing, explaining rather than amplifying, worked into an adroit and pithy expression."*[13] In it the principal things are distinction, clarity, order, the choice and propriety of words, not metaphors, that are expressive and meaningful. It does not come with the flashes, the thunder, the lightning botls , nor does it have those ample and magnificent flights of eloquence with which great oratory flourishes.so majestically

The Mean, *"Decorous and ample, colorful and polished, where each word and sentence is gracefully linked. Its purpose is not to disturb minds, rather to calm them, not to persuade so much as to delight. He searches for elegant phrases more than for logic, can wander from the topic and make up stories and wordplay, as a painter will use a variety of colors. He compares similar things to one another, and often puts opposite ends against each other, etc."*[14]

The sublime all majesty, all imperial, has a most welcome violence that resounds in the minds of its hearers, it transforms all their affections and leaves them willingly ravished. It summons the maximum of lofty sentiments, of forceful arguments and of masterful order; of substance in the sentences, of efficacy in the words that can be marshalled. It is ample, eloquent, magnificent. A torrent, but crystal clear, a lightning bolt, but harnassed, with supreme variety of figures and with a sequence of emotions displayed without disorder. It is like a cloud which at the same time issues water and fire, lightning and rain. For this form of speech, I borrow the image by Quintilian, *"Which rolls down rocks and 'disdains a bridge' (*Aeneid 8.728*) and makes its own banks, a mighty torrent, against it a judge can offer no resistance drawing him to go where it rushes. It can bring the dead to life and can make citizen patriots raise their voices*

---

13 **Cicero**, (*above*, to Brutus), but *Orator*, 5.20: *Acutum omnia docens, et dilucidiora non ampliora faciens, subtili quadam, et pressa oratione limatum.*
14 **Cicero**, *Orator*, 27.96: *Insigne, et florens est, pictum, et expolitim, in quo omnes verborum, omnes sententiarum illigantur lepòres; 19.65: ne que enim illi propositum est perturbare animos sed placare potius, nec tam persuadere quan delectare. Concinnas igitur sententias exquirit magis quam probabiles; a re saepè discedit, intexit fabulas, verba apertius transfert, eaque ita disponitit pictores varietatem colorum. Paria paribus refert, aduersa contrarijs, saepissimèque similiter extrema desinit, etc.*

*and cry out in response. It magnifies and elevates its oratory and exalts it by the force of its expressive technique. It can involve the gods themselves in its audience and make them speak, etc."*[15]

These are the characteristics of the forms of speech here designated in their pure essence, but not described. The masters of this art which it is their profession to detail, can completely satisfy those desiring more plentiful instruction. My aim was to cover the articles necessary as the premise for the points that follow here. Namely, that the style should be varied suitably to the variety of the matters discussed by the choice of different voices, as the different shades of lighting on colors, as they constantly shift. You cannot use the same scenery for tragedies, comedies, and pastorals. This last requires fields, and woods, the comic, a general collection of city houses, for tragedy, princely palaces, and temples. The place must reflect the action. Likewise, oratory should suit its subject, sublime themes with no common style and common matters with no sublime eloquence.

In fine, we should employ in the choice of styles that insight and intelligence of the ancient statuaries at their forges They did not use every metal for their statues of the gods, but fitting their different natures, had different alloys, making them smooth or crude, horrid or comely, bright or dark. On the topic most praiseworthy was the judgement of Alcon who made a Hercules all of iron, *"induced by the god's constancy in his many labors"* said Pliny.[16]

We ought not, though, use the same uniform style dictated by the character of the main theme we are treating. In every composition change should come frequently to vary, as often as the things it is made of change. And, as in tragedy, the scene may change to a woodland, to express some aspect either of ancient satire or of modern pastoral, so a given work may call for things from a genre different from the main argument, and to give it decent expression there should be a change of register, appropriately, as Seneca noted, *"Grandiloquent in tragedy, simple in comedy."*[17]

---

15 **Quintillian,** *Institutiones oratoria* **12**.10.61/2: *Quae saxa devoluit, et pontem indignatur, et ripas sibi facit. Multa, ac torrens. Judicem vel obnitentem contra ferens, cogensque ire quà rapit. Ea defunctos exitat. Apud eam Patria clamat, et alloquitur aliquem. Amplificat, atque extollit orationem, et vi superlationum quoque erigit, Deos ipsos in congressum quoque suum, sermonesque deducit, etc.*

16 **Pliny, 34.**140: *laborum Dei patientia inductus.*

17 **Seneca,** *Letter* 100.10: *Aliquid tragicè grandè, aliquid comicè exile.*

Moreover, the parts of one and the same discourse, require various manners of oratory, as varied as narration is different from discourse, and discourse different from persuasion. *"The orator will make use of all forms of speech, not only in the body of the whole work, but in the details of its parts."*[18] Thus, one who studies a work of some size shall find no less variety than there are in a scene's progress where many persons of different classes and functions figure, for,

> *There is much difference between the speech of the servant and a hero,*
> *The experienced polish of the older man and the passion of fervid youth,*
> *Between the doughty matron and the indolent nurse,*
> *The voluble merchant and the farmer of fields,*
> *The man from Colchis and the Assyrian,*
> *the bred Theban, and the Argive.*[19]

and in the variety of these persons, the variety of their emotions should also be observed, and therefore,

> *Sad words are called for by a suffering countenance.*
> *An angry man is full of sthreats,*
> *The unwitting man speaks venal words,*
> *The severe man has a serious dictum.*[20]

So, in proportionate terms, for the prose that we use to write on a variety of things, we should variously accommodate our style..For, after the extensive quest for him made by Cicero, the only perfect— the only true Orator is he, *"Who knows how to speak on simple subjects carefully, important ones seriously and ordinary matters temperately."*[21]

---

18 **Quintilian**, *Institutiones Oratoria*, **12.10.29**: *Omnibus igitur dicendi formis utatur orator, nec pro causa tantùm, sed etiam pro partibus causae.*
19 **Horace**, *Ars Poetica*, 114/7:
> *Intererit multum Davus loquatur, an Heros.*
> *Maturusne senex, an adhuc florente inventa*
> *Fervidus. An Matrona potens, an sedula Nutrix,*
> *Mercator ne vagus: Cultorne virentis agelli,*
> *Colchus, an Assyrius, Thebis nutritus, an Argis.*
20 *Ibid.*, 105/7: *Tristia moestum*
> *Vultum verba decent. Iratum plena minarum,*
> *Ludentem lascivia, Severum seria dictum.*
21 **Cicero**, *Orator*, 29.100: *Qui et humilia subtiliter, et magna graviter, et mediocria temperatè potest dicere.*

## 13.7   *On the Style they call the Modern Conceited Style*

I suspect that some may think that in talking about the finer styles, I might have forgotten the very finest of all. Up to now I have not talked about what they call the conceited style, currently being used by many, with no small applause for their ingenious Wit.

This (say they) is the style exclusively granted to Wits enriched with lofty thoughts. Everything is a distillation of pearl and spun gold, the progeny of sublime souls, because, as the bird of the Indies, called the bird of paradise, it never sets foot on earth, never lowers itself and floats through the purest air in the serene sublimity of the Heavens. It portrays things with a precious mosaic of the thousand ingenious conceits it conveys, emulating that great Pompey, who in his triumph, albeit, **Veriore luxuria, quam triumpho** *(more truly opulence, than triumph)*[1] paraded the image of his face composed only of diamonds, rubies, sapphires, gems and pearls with so successful a contrast between the outlines and the colors that it was hard to know what to prefer, the subject or the workmanship. The *Venus* **Quam Graeci Charita vocant,** *(Whom the Greeks called Gracefulness)*[2] that Apelles said was slighted by every brush but his own is wronged by every pen but that of the conceited style which captures her features with the expression and liveliness befitting her vivacity. The world is not now what it was when men, born among oak trees, ate acorns as delicacies. Its taste in Letters has nowadays become so exquisite, that not only does the nectar imbibed by the ears (which are the mouths of the soul) have to be precious, no less precious must be the cup in which it is served, so that both the content and the service are not lacking in distinction and, as served up in this very witty style, "*We drink from cups made of a host of gems and of emeralds.*"[3] That ancient, otiose style of delivery in a speech of many hours spreads a great table. It may seem to feed you, for it has you listening, but it leaves you in the end, as in the beginning hungering, just as Tantalus,

> *In the jaws of the serpent, the thirsting old man*
> *Stands in the waters. No drink did he get*
> *Often deceived by his efforts*

---

1 **Pliny**, 37.6.
2 **Pliny**, 35.36.
3 **Pliny**, 33.2, preface: *Turba gemmarum potamus, et smaragdis teximus calices.*

*As the water pulls away. The fruit only make his mouth water.*[4]
They may well promise fruit but you get just the fronds of words, your ears are filled, but your mind gets no sustenance. The modern style puts a great variety of plentiful delicacies before you and takes them from you after a first tasting, then presents other new ones. It keeps you ever sated, ever hungry, echoing the ancient rule of the finest feasts in which, *"After tasting all the food, it is taken away and other and better and more ample fare takes its place: This is held to be the summit of fine dining."*[5] Just because the style is beautiful and winsome, it is not necessarily softly feminine or ineffective in its efforts to persuade. Grace does not vitiate its force. It can make the same vaunt as the soldiers of Julius Caesar who proved *"Even perfumed, they are good fighters."*[6]

Ajax may carry his leather shield, unadorned and in terrible condition, Achilles has his covered with gold, and studded with diamonds, but it is no less strong, for being more beautiful.[7] Imagine an Alcibiades, equally generous of heart and fair of face. He delights to dress for battle with garlands of flowers on his helmet and laces on his breastplate. He enjoys fighting adorned as others will be adorned in triumph.

Thus, speak such stylish writers stylishly of their style, aught else they will not endure. If a composition be without what they call their conceits, it is as a face, **Cui gelasinus abest,** *(with no dimple)*[8] and they will not dignify it with so much as a glance. To their palate only what stings has a good taste, the remainder, **Melimela fatuaeque mariscae**, *(sweets of insipid figs)*[9] is food for children. In fine, they so idolize this quality, that they adore the hint of a conceit, wherever they

---

4 **Seneca, *Hercules Furens*,** 750/4:
> *In amne medio faucibus, siccis senex*
> *Sectatur undas. Abluit mentum latex,*
> *Fidemque cum in saepè decepto dedit,*
> *Fugit unda; in ore poma destituunt famem.*

5 **Gellius,** 15.8: *Dum libentissimè edis, tunc aufertur, et alia esca melior, atque amplior succenturiatur: Isque flos caenae habetur.*

6 **Suetonius, *Caesar*,** 6: *Etiam unguentati bene pugnare.* Perhaps this is proffered as a concession to the Tacitist, (1595-1654) Virgilio Malvezzi, to whom several approved Bologna editions of Bartoli's treatise are dedicated.

7 **Maximus of Tyre,** *Dissertations*, 29.

8 Martial, 7.25.

9 Martial, 7.7.

suspect they may find one. I might almost have said that they use them, like the lady, according to the mockery of Martial, used her pearls:

> *Not by the mystical mother goddess*
> *Nor by the Nile calves of Isis*
> *Nor by any other of the gods and goddesses of Heaven*
> *Does Gellia swear, but by her pearls.*[10]

The true modern style, others argue, is not this, but finds its vivid and veritable model is that ancient depiction bequeathed us by Quintilian in his *Institutes of Oratory*, 12.10, even if he was not the first to draw its portrait. Whether it be ancient or modern, there are those who hail this style with praise and applause. But this stylish style, if you inspect its nature and employ on the scales of good judgement, weighs nothing at all, for it is all surface without substance, the mere nothing of vanity, like the Indians of the New World who prize a piece of glass more than a pearl, a little copper bell more than a nugget of gold and take themselves for rich and pompous, "*every bit of nonsense they value as a prize.*"[11] The authors of this style, fantasizing away day and night, will wrack and spill their brains out, as spiders do, to weave from ingenious subtleties the webs of their disquisitions.

They sweat to produce conceits, which most often prove stillborn or unhealthy, baubles of glass annealed by a candle. When they are touched, not to say inspected, they break into pieces. Nonetheless with ever greater fragility their beauty is ever increased: "*In their very fragility consists their great value.*"[12]

A matter of most pleasant entertainment is to see their writings, like a sick man's dreams, shifting every sentence **de genere in genus.** *(from one genre to another).* Their words confirm exactly what they are saying, that their conceits are lightning flashes of Wit. They appear and disappear all at once. In the same instant they flit back and forth from east to west and mostly **sine medio** *(with nothing in between).* All their pages seem like the tail of a peacock spread against the sun,

---

10 **Martial,** 8, 81: *Non per mystica sacra Dindymenes,*
   *Nec per Niliacae bovem juvencae,*
   *Nullos denique per Deos Deasque,*
   *Jurat Gellia, sed per Uniones.*
11 **Seneca,** *Letter* 115.8: *et omne ludicrum ille in pretio est.*
12 **Pliny,** 33.2: *Imo quibus pretium faciat ipsa fragilitas.*

various in its colors, unsteady in its pace: *"Never the same, always different, ever itself as ever changing. A change comes with every movement."* [13]

And because they hold it for a maxim that this kind of writing weaves a garland of flowers, *"which only charm through variety,"* [14] they stuff in whatever does and does not fit. What you see will remind you not so much of the words, but the outrage of Pliny. He damns the superstitious medicine of the inventor of a certain counter-poison, a compound of fifty odd exotic ingredients, and some of them of infinitesimal quantities. *"The antidote of Mithridates is composed to fifty-four ingredients, all of different doses, one being the sixtieth part of a denarius. Which of the gods has come up with this monstrous trick? This is beyond the sophistication of mere mortals. It is an ostentation of art and a clear subterfuge of a science never penetrated by anyone."* [15]

For this comes their shrinking sentences, spliced into concision, and the effect of their multitudinous fine points, each one with an allusion of sense and a confusion of thought, *"And they end so fast, that their words are not brief but interrupted."* [16] Or rather, as elsewhere Seneca said, *"They don't end but jerk, just where you least expect a stop."* [17]

Finally, from not saying what they are saying, it is said a hundred times. Like those always with a new plan to begin life over, unable to live by living, said Manilius,

*We are always making plans to live, but we never do live.* [18]

As these Such, with their stylish speech, can as well finish at the beginning, as begin at the finish and about themselves they may say as sufficiently appropriate:

*We are always about to say something, but we never do speak.*

---

13 **Tertullian,** *De pallio,* **3**: *Nunquam ipsa, semper alia, etsi semper ipsa quando alia. Toties mutanda, quoties movenda.*
14 Pliny, 21.27: *quae varietate sola placent.*
15 **Pliny,** 29.8: *Mithridaticum antidotum, ex rebus quinquaginta quatuor componitur, interim nullo pondere equali, et quarundam rerum sexagesima denarii unius imperata. Quo Deorum perfidiam istam monstrante? Hominum enim subtilitas tanta esse non potuit. Ostentatio artis, et portentosa scientiae venditatio manifesta est, ac ne ipsi quidem illam noverunt.*
16 **Seneca the Elder,** *Controversiae 2,* preface: *et tam subito desinunt, ut non brevia sint, sed abrupta.*
17 **Seneca,** *Letter* 100.7 *Non desinunt sed cadunt, ubi maxime expectes relictura.*
18 **Manilius,** *Astronomica,* 5.899:
　　　*Victuros agimus semper, neque vivimus unquam.*
　　　*(Dicturos agimus semper, neque dicimus unquam.)*

Their discourse resembles the unhappy game which Seneca assigned to the emperor Claudius as a punishment in Hell, that he was always at the brink of casting the dice, but never had a go.

*Every time he would throw shaking them in the box*
*They both would fall out on the floor*
*And when he collected them and tried again*
*They would always fall through, every time he tried,*
*undoing his hope.*[19]

Where these Wits triumph is in their descriptions. When the occasion arises, they say to themselves, **Hic Rhodus, hic salta**. *(Now, the real challenge).*[20] And yet with such labor of art and Wit, and in such a hyperbolical and gigantic manner, what usually transpires is the more they want to say, the less they do say, equally distancing themselves from nature and verisimilitude. We may well say about their childish descriptions what Dorion said of a violent tempest at sea described by Timotheus of Miletus, *"He had seen a greater tempest in a teapot."*[21]

What would that ingenious Favorinus say today, after reading in Virgil, the description of Enceladus thundering under Etna:

*The molten rocks heaved forth*
*With a groan towards Heaven.*[22]

He judged this phrasing in a poet portraying a giant and an Aetna,

*Of all possible monsters, the greatest monstrosity of all.*[23]

What would he say, say I, if he heard, *to bloodlet roses in the cheeks, to construct arches of wonderment in the eyebrows to the triumph of others' virtues, to cross the fields of eternity with the footsteps of merit, etc.*, used as expressions

---

19 **Seneca,** *Apocolocyntosus*, 15.1/5:
   *Nam quoties missurus erat, resonante fritillo.*
   *Utraque subducto fugiebat tessera fundo.*
   *Cumque recollectos auderet mittere talos,*
   *Lusuro similis semper, semperque petenti;*
   *Decepere fidem.*
20 Aesop, Erasmus.
21 **Athenaeus,** *Deipnosophisti,* 8.19:
   *Majorem se in ferventi olla vidisse.*
22 *Aeneid* 3.576/7: *Liquefactaque saxa sub auras*
   *Cum gemitu glomerat.*
23 **Gellius,**17.10, copying Pindar:
   *Omnium quae monstra dicuntur, monstrosissimum:*

even for topics of common discourse, on matters they fail to aggrandize.

## 13.8 *Where it is the Fault of Poor Judgement to use a flowery and overly Ingenious Style*

But of conceits and the manner of using them, let everyone be his own judge following his own way and his taste for them. For my part, if I must say something in their regard in my presentation of these matters, I value them as jewels and take their worth from their nature and use. Let them be not false, but real and not wildly out of place, but set in proper context. First, there is the task of the Wit to find them, then the task of judgement to set them.

One's Wit should not take crystals for diamonds, one's judgement should not try to stick them where they do not belong, imitating the savages of America who make slits their faces to insert jewels there. They do not realize that they are more disfigured by the gashes, than embellished by the jewels. The face desires no ornament beyond its natural beauty. It is more spoiled and disfigured by a pearl, even of the rarest, encased in a cheek, than by the black blemish of a mole, placed there by nature. Likewise, for oratory, some things appear more beautiful for their simplicity, they resemble portraits, regarding which there are the very fine words of the younger Pliny about their painter: "*But he mustn't ruin it by adding improvements.*"[1]

Lysippus shaped the casting of a statue of Alexander so to the life, it seemed that into the bronze he cast the very soul of that great king. Nero, cruel even in his beneficence, brought harm even where his idea was to help. Among his other spoils from Greece, this statue came into his possession and he decided to gild it, judging that a statue of such excellent workmanship deserved to be of no other metal than gold. The fool could not see that warlike faces were better rendered by the roughness of bronze than by the sweetness of that feminine and lascivious ore. Therefore, the statue in Nero's gilt lost all of the noble part of Alexander, all of the masterfulness of Lysippus. Gilded, it was turned into a dead statue, when before it appeared a live image. So, to rectify Nero's stupid mistake, Alexander had to be flayed, scraping off

---

1 **Pliny the Younger**, *Letters* 4.28 *to Vibius Severus*:
*Ne errare quidem debet in melius. (ne in melius quidem sinas aberrare).*

with a file that skin of gold which had been fired on. Yet, stripped and manhandled, it was more beautiful than before with its coating of gold. *"With the gilding the artistry was ruined, (said the Naturtal Historian) so when the gold was removed, it was judged even more precious, despite the indentations on the work and the scars where there was some gold left."*[2] Embellishments, hence, are not always adornments; sometimes they are transformed into deformities,

> *Ornamentation can spoil the statement, if its meaning is clear.* [3]

where to be superfluously, and sometimes affectedly, conceited reveals in a great wealth of Wit, a great poverty of judgement.

With emotions then, either we should arouse them, or still them. This is the hardest part of the profession of rhetoric because the exquisite art of a most discerning judgement should be concealed under so natural a guise that what is being said not seem dictation of the Wit, but the heart's unburdening. It should not be belabored, but born of itself, not studied, but discovered in the very act of speaking. Of what use can a style be that is distilled drop by drop by the dim light of a candle? It has words wracked in their metaphors, double in their allusions, with spirited and lively meanings, capable more of titivating the brain, than of moving the heart. *"The dead require no funeral pipes, (Chrysologus said) simple emotion mourns them."*[4]

For myself, when I hear the emotions marshalled in such an unsuitable way it makes me feel more nauseous than someone suffering from seasickness. Itching my tongue is that saying of a sage emperor to his minister, stinking with musk, as he chased him from his chamber and his court, *"I'd rather you smelled of garlic."*[5]

How insufferable would it strike that great master of the stage Polus to employ the affectation of a childish style for the purpose of expressing emotion? So as to represent with greater realism the person of Hecuba, mourning the loss of her valorous son, the slain Hector, whose ashes she carried in an urn, the artist disinterred the bones of his own just buried son and filled the urn with them and went on stage

---

2 **Pliny, 34**.19. *detractum est aurum; pretiosiorque talis aestimatur, etiam cicatricibus operis, atque conscissuris, in quibus aurum haeserat, remanentibus.*
3 **Manilius**, *Astronomica* 3.39:
> *Ornari res ipsa negat, contenta doceri.*
4 **Peter Chrysologus** (406-450), *Sermon* 19: *Mortuum non artifex fistula sed simplex plangit affectio.*
5 *Mallem allium oleres.* See Seutonius, *Vespasian*, 8.3: *Malluissem allium oboluisses.*

bearing it in his arms. He. left the art of mourning to nature and conveyed imitation with reality, whilst under the mask of Hecuba, he acted as a bereaved father and under the name of Hector lamented the loss of his own son.[6] The expression of the emotions is truer, therefore, the more natural it is. And it is impossible, with one's thoughts focused on the movements of the soul, for the Wit to engage in belabored and ingenious devices. It is impossible, as a tempestuous and murky state of mind is beset by a thousand impulses and borne from the heart to the tongue, to have any time to select the words, to refashion them, and then, shifting from the natural to the figurative sense, to embellish them with flourishes and conceits. No, indeed. A writer with solid judgement, in dealing with any emotion, if he should feel importuned by an overactive Wit, with the suggestion of multiplying subtle meanings and clever ideas, let him use his hand to push them away with the words: **Non est hic locus.** *This is not the place.*"[7] He does with the eye of his mind, as the eyes of the body do when they see too much light. His pupils squint and shut out a part of it. And wisely so, like that famous Ariston,[8] whose task was to express in a statue of bronze the fury, shame, and grief of Athamas.[9] So, he mixed iron and bronze and relieved the brightness of the one, with the rustiness of the other. And a wonderful work it was, the poorer for its material, the more precious for its art, so that the rust, which is a fault in iron, became an asset in the bronze, and made it worth its weight in gold.

Finally, for one who must speak seriously to convince, to reprehend, to condemn action, vice, or person, a style that sings when it should thunder and instead of bolts of lightning, sends flashes of light, it becomes patently obvious when his sentences jump around like a fountain squirting, instead of running like a mighty stream, how far he is from his intended purpose. "*Therefore, not a broken and abbreviated display of oratory, but something broad and grand and sublime to thunder and flash upsetting and blending all the elements.*"[10] It needs to be full of nerve and

---

6 **Gellius**, 6.5. "*Historia de Polo histrione memoratu digna.*" Bartoli has replaced the Electra and Orestes of Gellius with Hecuba and Hector.
7 See Horace, *Ars poetica*, 14:
    *Sed nunc non est his locus.*
8 Pliny, 40.140.
9 Ovid, *Met.*, 4.512/5.
10 **Pliny the Younger, *Letters*** 1.20 **to Tacitus**: *Non enim amputata oratio et abscissa, sed lata, et magnifica, et excelsa tonat, fulgurat, omnia denique perturbat, ac miscet.*

masculine, not be feminine with seductive accoutrements and a cascade of charms. The orator should not assume a playful or jocund demeanor, but one majestic and severe, like the Pluto of the poet:

*With the countenance of Jove, but Jove the Thunderer.*[11]

"*What vanity,*" says Hippocrates, "*to busy oneself more in embroidering the bandages than in closing the wounds?*"[12] As if the beauty of the bindings were a balm to the bruise. Certain outworn, toothless grinds serve to burnish iron and smooth it out. But where it is rusty, then it will need something else, to scratch and to scrape. The closer it gets to the quick, the better it does. "*Why do you tickle my ears? Why are you playing around with me? Something different is called for. I must be disinfected, operated on and put on a regime for nourishment. That is why you were called in. Your job, doctor, is serious sickness, just as in a plague, and you waste my time with verbiage?*"[13]

The style we use to combat vice, is a warlike sword whose excellence and quality are not in its golden hilt, nor in its diamond studded pommel, but in its tempered steel. And the more bejeweled it is, and rich in inlay and decoration, the worse it grasps and the more clumsily it handles. Well spoke that brave Theban warrior, Epaminondas, to a young perfumed Athenian who laughed at the plain wooden hilt of his sword: *When we fight it's not the hilt you'll feel, but the blade: and the blade will make you weep, even if the hilt now makes you laugh.*[14] Says Tacitus, "*For the glitter of gold and silver can neither strike nor wound.*"[15]

Let the style therefore, we use to fight be no bridegroom, but a warrior. Where words must be arrows, the mouth should not issue forth flowers to glaze every sentence in a nimbus. It is not as if vices are like insects with an allergy to the smell of flowers as a deadly poison. No is it as if one may kill one's adversaries, as Heliogabalus did

---

11 **Seneca, *Hercules Furens*, 724/5:**
   *Vultus est illi Jovis; sed fulminantis.*
12 **Hippocrates, *On the Art of Medicine*, 1.5.**
13 **Seneca, *Letter* 75**.7: *Quid aures meas scalpis? quid oblectas? aliud igitur. Urendus, secandus, abstinendus sum. Ad haec adhibitus es. Tantum negotii habes quantum in pestilentia medicus circa verba occupatus es.*
14 **Synesius, *De Regno*,** (*On Imperial Rule*), 13.10: *Non igitur, inquit, in prelio periculum facies capuli, sed aciem ferri ne utiquam poteris culpare* (Latin: Camerarius, 1555).
15 Tacitus, *Agricola*, 22: *Auri enim fulgor, atque argenti neque tegit, neque vulnerate.*

his friends, suffocating them in roses.[16] It is an as yet unheard-of folly to fight a duel dancing, mixing assaults with somersaults, poems with parries. A bare arm brooks no pleasantries. Blows aiming for a heart wound should not to be drawn against an enemy breast, with the pleasant manner more of an embrace, than as one ready to strike a wound.

No one believes that the serious and severe style lacks its beauty, by lacking the embellishments of clever witticisms and of overblown conceits. Lions, for them to be beautiful, have no need of a brushed coat, gilded paws, rings on their ears, nor strings of pearls about the neck, with the look of allurements. The more fearsolme they are, the handsomer they are, the more matted and shaggier, the more striking they appear. As Seneca said, *"This (lion) has an untamed spirit, as nature ordains, impressively wild and he shows at his best when he cannot be eyed without fear, better than a lion who is languid and gilded."*[17]

## 13.9    *Examination and Correction of Our Writings*

The work of composing a book has an end. Here, I have undertaken to review only what concerns the invention and disposition of the subjects and consider questions of style in its expression and exposition, as the goal that I set for myself at the outset. What alone remains is to go over it with a finishing touch, and clean it up, examining minutely and passing severe judgement on each of its parts, to make sure it is, as Sidonius did inspecting the writing of his friend Remigius, *"Opportune in its examples, faithful in its testimony, suitable in its epithets, polished in its expression, substantive in its argument, with weight in its meaning, fluidity in its words, lightening in its clauses, etc."*[1] And experience will prove the observation of Seneca to be most true that the parts, ,that seemed most flawlessly lovely while they were being composed, on review no longer appear the same, nor can the author recognize

---

16 *Historia Augusta, Heliogabulus*, 2.
17 **Seneca, *Letter* 41**.6: *Hic spiritu acer qualem illum, esse natura voluit, speciosus ex horrido, cujus hic decor est, non sine timore aspici, praefertur illi languido, et bracteato.*

1 **Sidonius Apollinaris, *Opera*, 9, *Letter* 7**: *Opportunitas in exemplis, fides in testimoniis, proprietas in epithetis, urbanitas in figuris, pondus in sententibus, flumen in verbis, fulmen in clausulis, etc.*

them as his, "*he does not recognize himself in them.*"[2] This is because the ebullient spirits while the Wit is fervidly indicting, do not allow that tranquility, that limpid serenity of judgement, requisite to working in a balanced and deliberate fashion. Therefore, "*So often words will at first please, but they prove less impressive when studied more closely.*"[3] And Quintilian condemns the precipitous method of those who abandon themselves to a certain, more fury than fervor, of Wit. They write as an improvisation what comes into their heads; "*They take up and work the words they poured forth, but while they rework the words and the rhythms, the essential superficiality remains because of their haste.*"[4] Wherefore (he added) let them write, especially as beginners, with consideration and at a slow pace. They should put everything in its place and not throw words down, but select them judiciously, not place them haphazardly, not deem what comes quickly as good, "*For it is not quick writing that is good writing, but good writing that soon comes quickly.*"[5] Virgil was a man of most excellent judgement and in his writing **gradarius fuit,** *(was painstakingly slow.)* He would say that he gave birth to his verses, **more, atque ritu ursino,** *(in the manner of a bear)*[6] because not content with bringing them forth, he took them up, one by one, as the bear with her tongue cleans and shapes each part of her cubs, since she gives them birth, as not deformed, but still unformed.[7]

We should not, therefore, seek only to form the work, but to reform it also. And remember that others will use with them scornfully that severity in their condemnation, which we, through useless pity, spared in their correction. Let us in this take example from God himself. With this great lesson he has been ever since the beginning of the world our teacher, in that he made the world in one day, and was five in making it beautiful. First, he took darkness from Heaven, then sterility from the earth, adorning one with stars, the other with flowers,

---

2 Seneca, Letter 66.46: *Nec se agnoscit in illis.*

3 **Seneca, *Letter* 100**.3: *Fere quae impetu placent minus praestant ad manum relata.*

4 **Quintilian, *Institutiones oratoria* 10.3**.: *repetunt deinde, et componunt quae effuderant, sed verba emendantur, et numeri, manet in rebus temere congestis, quae fuit levitas.*

5 **Ibid**.: *Non enim citò scribendo fit, ut bene scribatur, sed bene scribendo sit ut citò.*

6 **Favorinus, in Gellius**, 17.10.

[7] Of this time-hallowed reference we may say, *Se non è vero, è ben trovato.*

until with His work completed, He praised it as worthy of his hand, *"And He rested from the work of the universe he had created."*[8] He could as well have made the world all at once and in a single moment made it perfect. But, as St. Ambrose finely observed, *"First, he laid the groundwork and built the physical universe, then he perfected it, gave it light and completed it. He wanted us to imitate him, so, in the first place we create something and then embellish it after, lest setting out to do both at the same time we are unable to bring it to any completion."*[9]

Nevertheless, I will not say that we should be so strangely cruel with our writings that we torment every word, every sentence and make them like the chords of the harp, *"the tighter they stretch, the more music they make."*[10] It was the ancient Controversialist, who said, *"They twist their writings into pieces by discussing every single word."*[11]

And we must know that in this particular the superstitious diligence of someone, like Protogenes, who *"won't take his brush off the painting,"*[12] is to be censured just as much as the negligence of the one who fails to make corrections. For while careless negligence does not excise the superfluous from writings, over-conscientious carefulness (which is worse) will excise the necessary. One, by not correcting, fails to change the bad into good; the other, by too much correcting, very often changes the good into bad. *"When a work is finished and completed, reworking it does not add but diminishes, and too much fussing does more harm than good."*[13] From wanting to placate their implacable genius, some are led to take up again a thousand times the same work, always weaving and re-weaving with Penelope the same piece, erasing today what they wrote yesterday. Theirs is like the torture of Sisyphus in hell. He never ceases to push up to the top of the incline his inconstant and deceitful stone when it falls back down to the bottom where he started, as it

---

8 *Genesis* 2.2: *Et requievit ab universo opere quod patrarat.*

9 **Ambrose, *Hexameron*, 1.7:** *Prius condit, et molitur res corporeas, deinde perficit, illuminat, absolvit. Imitatores enim suos nos esse voluit, ut prius faciamus aliqua, postea venustemus, ne, dum simul utrumque adorimur, neutrum possimus implere.*

10 **Sidonius, Apollinaris, Letters**. 8.9.4: *Quo plus torta, plus musica.*

11 **Seneca the Elder, *Controversiae* 1**, preface: *scripta enim sua torquent, qui de singulis verbis in consilium veniunt.*

12 Pliny, 35.80: *Nescit manum de tabula.*

13 **Pliny the Younger, *Letters*** 5.10 and 9.35: *Perfectum enim opus, absolutumque, non tam splendescit lima quam deteritur, et nimia cura deterit magis quàm emendat.*

deludes his pains and wearies his arms. They imitate the folly of the famous Apollodorus. He was unsatisfied with the statues he had taken great pains to make and in angry frustration smashed them to pieces with his hammer and was at the point of gnawing them with his teeth. So, he was called the Saturn of sculptors because he tore his children apart and wanted to eat them, though they were of stone. "*So now, you want to speak better than you can?*"[14] said an old master to a melancholy young man. He was incapable of the language he aspired to and he would not use the language that he had. He had unsuccessfully worked three long days on the opening of an oration. This is the way to learn not to speak well, but not to speak at all. Most susceptible to this are young men of Wit born with the seeds of lofty thoughts and elements of noble speech. They hate being ordinary, yet are not so extraordinary as they would like, "*Often it happens with adolescents gifted with Wit, that after studying diligently they fall into silence, from an excess of ambition for perfect eloquence.*"[15]

What man is there, even of most excellent judgement, to whom his works are so pleasing that as gold of twenty-four carats, there is nothing to be added of good or taken away of base alloy? A privilege granted to all things of this world is not being totally perfect. The sun has its smoke, the moon her spots; among the stars, some are overcast and some melancholy. And yet these are the most distinguished bodies in Heaven, nor should they be destroyed for not being so altogether beautiful as they might. Examine the books hailed as great works of art, celebrated for their great learning— their faces are of great beauty, but not without some blemish or defect. Not only is it true of the good Homer who **Quandoque dormitat**, *(betimes doth nod)*[16] but also for those, like Argus, who have a hundred eyes. For, if to reach complete satisfaction, they did not publish their works to the world before they had achieved total perfection, then farewell to books, there would not be even a single good one left in the world. But if our words can patiently suffer their defects to be outweighed by so many fine things,

---

14 **Petrarch** (1304-1374) *Epistolae Familiares:* 1.7: Letter to Tomaso Coloiro da Messina (1302-1341): *Nunquid in meliùs dicere vis quam potes?*
15 **Quintilian, *Institutiones oratoria* 10.3 in Petrarch, ibid.** *Accidit ingeniosis adolescentibus frequenter, ut labore consumantur, et in silentium usque descendant, nimia bene dicendi cupiditate.*
16 Horace, *Ars Poetica*, 359.

we need not despair that the best qualities found in our writings may garner more praise than their uncomely features find criticism.

Let us take for ourselves the mitigation offered by the astrologer to cripples as a consolation for their maimed, shriveled and disjointed limbs: See, said he, the Heavens and in them the constellations, one by one, not all of them are so beautiful that some are not deformed, maimed and lame. Scorpio has no claws; Pegasus and Taurus are only half there.

> *If you look with attention, in everything you will find,*
> *There is something missing in the stars*
> *Scorpio loses his arm in Libra, Taurus limps on a bad foot,*
> *Cancer has no eyes, the centaur has one but not the other,*
> *So, our lot in the world is linked to the stars*
> *And its order depends on the good influence of Heaven*
> *Where the constellations are even missing parts.*[17]

What will finally seal all the diligence we dedicate to our writings, is to submit them to the judgement, to the censure, to the correction of a faithful and knowledgeable friend. One eye of an outsider sees more in someone else's work than two do in one's own. Love of one's own creations brings a certain needful blindness, more deceptive, for being less suspected. Another's eyes see our things as they are in themselves, ours give judgement according to their capacity to see, not according to the reality of the object. "*We look at our own things from close up* (says the Stoic) *and always form a favorable opinion of them and we are much less prone to get in trouble from the flattering judgements of others than from our own.*"[18] A good friend should stand us in the same stead as his mirror did for Demosthenes. He used it as a corrector to mend the mistakes he made in his manner of delivery, customarily not

---

17 **Manilius, *Astronomica* 2.256/64:**
> *Quod si solerti circumspicis omnia cura.*
> *Fraudata invenies amissis sidera membris.*
> *Scorpius in Libra consumit brachia, Taurus*
> *Succidit incurvo claudus pede: Lumina Cancro*
> *Desunt, Centauro superest et quaeritur unum.*
> *Sic nostros casus solatur Mundus in astris,*
> *Omnis cum coelo fortunae pendeat ordo, Pŏ—*
> *Ipsaque debilibus formentur sidera membris.*

18 **Seneca, *De tranquillitate animi* 1:** *Familiariter domestica aspicimus, et semper judicio favor officit, nec est, quòd nos magis aliena judices adulatione perire quàm nostra.*

declaiming in public what he had not tried out in his mirror, **Quasi ante Magistrum** *(as before his teacher.)*[19]but be aware that to submit our writings to others to review them should not be a mere formality, calling forth for a valid critical opinion, not for commendation, but for emendation. Should it happen that, out of modesty or respect, our friend holds back from dealing with us freely and rigorously, we must act offended and urge him, as the orator Celio said to his confidante in this situation, that he should *"say something against it, so we have a difference between the two of us."* and not leave him *"angrieved because he found no faults to criticize."*[20]

But in our day, this has become quite difficult. There are few who are found to be knowledgeable and almost none of them who will, however much a friend, assume the role of assayer for another's writings. They are mindful of Philoxenus the poet, who used his pen freely to eliminate the better part of a tragedy by (a man who knew better how to create tragedies as a tyrant, than to write them as a poet) Dionysius of Syracuse. As a reward for his honest efforts, he was buried alive in a marble quarry.[21] We should not take offense when we learn what we want to know. Otherwise, among our friends we shall meet with the rapier stylus used by that ancient master Quintilius,

*If you wanted to defend the fault, rather than correct it,*
*Not another word or useless effort would he waste.*
*So that unrivaled you alone remain enamoured with your words.*[22]

\*     \*     \*     \*

19 **Apuleius, *Apologia* 1.**
20 **Seneca. *De Ira*,** 3.8.6*: Dic aliquid contra, ut duo simus, Quòd non irascatur, irati.*
21 **Plutarch, *On the Fortune of Alexander*, 2.**
22 Horace, *Ars poetica,* 442-4:
*Si defendere delictum, quam vertere malles:*
*Nullum ultra verbum, aut operam sumebat inanem,*
*Quin sine rivali teque, et tua solus amares.*

# *Obscurity*

But I have hitherto impersonated that Tiresias of antiquity. Blind himself, he opened the eyes of others. As he stumbled at every step, he showed the unsure the roads of safest travel. For this I should not be criticized, and if my style has a rusty edge, am I at fault because I used it to polish that of others? Who expects the hones which sharpen the blade of a sword to do the cutting? Who would have those mercury markers of stone, pointing the public roads to pilgrims, pick up and head for adventure themselves. The brain has no feeling, we hear from Cassiodorus, and this is true, yet the nerves are rooted there and from it they have the spirit for the noblest operations of the soul, as "it gives feeling to the rest of the body."[23]

If I have not the praise due a brush that can teach painting by painting, at least I may claim that of a piece of coal, to draw those first outlines that sketch out a drawing. If they then disappear under the painting their value is not wasted, for they have set the outlines for the colors and organized the composition.

## THE END

---

[23] **Cassiodorus, *De Anima*,** preface: *Sensum membris reliquis tradit.*

# EEN
# GELETTERD MAN
## VERDADIGD, en VERBETERD,

DOOR

## DANIEL BARTHOLI,

Priefter in de Maatfchappy *van* Jefus;

Uyt het Italiaanfch Vertaald,

DOOR

## L. BIDLOO.

### UNICUIQUE SUUM.

't AMSTERDAM,

By Hendrik Bosch, Boekverkoper over
't Meysjes Weeshuys, by de S. Lucyefteeg. 1722.

# ILLUSTRATIONS

*Cover, *Detail. Etching by James Neagle* (1807) *of* **Allegory of Study** *as the self-portrait of Salvator Rosa (Giovanni Battista Riccioli).*

*Back cover, *Mezzotint portrait of Daniello Bartoli as Rector of the Roman College,* 1671-1674.

*Half title, *identical in both the duodecimo editions of Rome and Florence,* 1645.

*Frontispiece, *Etching by James Neagle* (1807) *of* **Allegory of Study** *as the self-portrait of Salvator Rosa (Giovanni Battista Riccioli).*

*Preface, verso. *title page* **L'Huomo di Lettere difeso et emendato** (Rome, 1645), *editio princeps.*

*Preface, v, *Rosa's* **Allegoria della Menzogna** (*G.B. Riccioli*).

*Preface, xvii, *Frontispiece of editions printed by Giunti, Baba, and Hertz, Venice 1646, 1648, 1651, 1655, etc. An interesting clue to the artist's identity may be the outline of an angleic face on the right side of Jove that aeppears even more faintly above the pointing hand in the foliage on the canvas of Salvator Rosa's* **Alexander in the Studio of Apelles**, p. 73.

*P.10, *Title page of* **L'Huomo di Lettere** (Florence, 1645) *Girolamo Signoretti's edition, with his printer's letter of dedication to Salvator Rosa..*

*P.20, *Sixth octave of the Riccioli-Grimaldi Moon map, 1651, with* **Bartolus** *on the bottom left crater.*

*P.25, *Etching by Salvator Rosa,* **Alexander and Diogenes**, (1662).

*P.49, *Titlepage of the fifth edition of the French translation,* **La Guide des Beaux Esprit**, *by Thomas Le Blanc, S.J.* 1651 (Paris, 1669).

*P. 50 *Anonymous titelpagee, of German translation,* **Vertheidigung der Kunstliebenden und Gelehrten anständige Sitten** (Nůrnberg, 1654).

245

*P.73, *Etching by Salvator Rosa*, **Alexander in the Studio of Apelles**, (1662).

*PP. 78/79, *Fronispiece and title page of Thomas Salusbury's* **The Learned Man, Defended and Reform'd** (London, 1660). Taken from the Venetian frontispiece, [ xvi.]

*P.158, *Fronitspiece of German translation* **Vertheidigung der Kunstliebenden und Gelehrten anständige Sitten,** *by Graf Georg Adam von Kufstein, Der Kunstliebender* (Nűrnberg, 1654). D. BAR TOLI is on the scrool under the book on the table.

*P.166, *Etching by Salvator Rosa* **The Genius of Salvator Rosa**, (1662).

*P.184, *Frontispieice*, **L'Huomo di lettere** (Conzatti: Venice, 1665, 1670) *Plate with anonymous titlepage by Jacopo Picini*. Replacing the standard Venetian original in Giunti, etc. (by Rosa?), [end of preface, xvii].

*P.196, *Titlepage of Latin translation* **Character hominis literati** by Louis Janin, S.J. (Lyons, 1672). A second Latin translation: **Homo literatus difensus et emendatus** (Frankfurt an der Oder, 1693) by Prussian pastor, Georg Hoffman

*P.206, *Frontispiece for the Spanish tranlastion*, **El Hombre de Letras** *by Gaspar Sanz* (Madrid, 1678), *celebrated for his guitar textbook and music.*

*P.244., *Titlepage of the Dutch translation*, **Een Geletterd Man verdadigt, en verbeterd** *by Mennonite Lambert Bidloo* (Amsterdam, 1722).

*P.247, *Full Moon selenography of the Riccioli-Grimaldi Full Moon L'huomo di letterein octaves in* **Almagestum Novum** (Bologna, 1651).
*"Neither do Men inhabit the Moon, nor do Souls.migrate there"*

*P.248, *Fronitspeicee of the Dutch translation*, **Een Geletterd Man verdadigt, en verbeterd** *by Mennonite Lambert Bidloo* (Amsterdam, 1722).

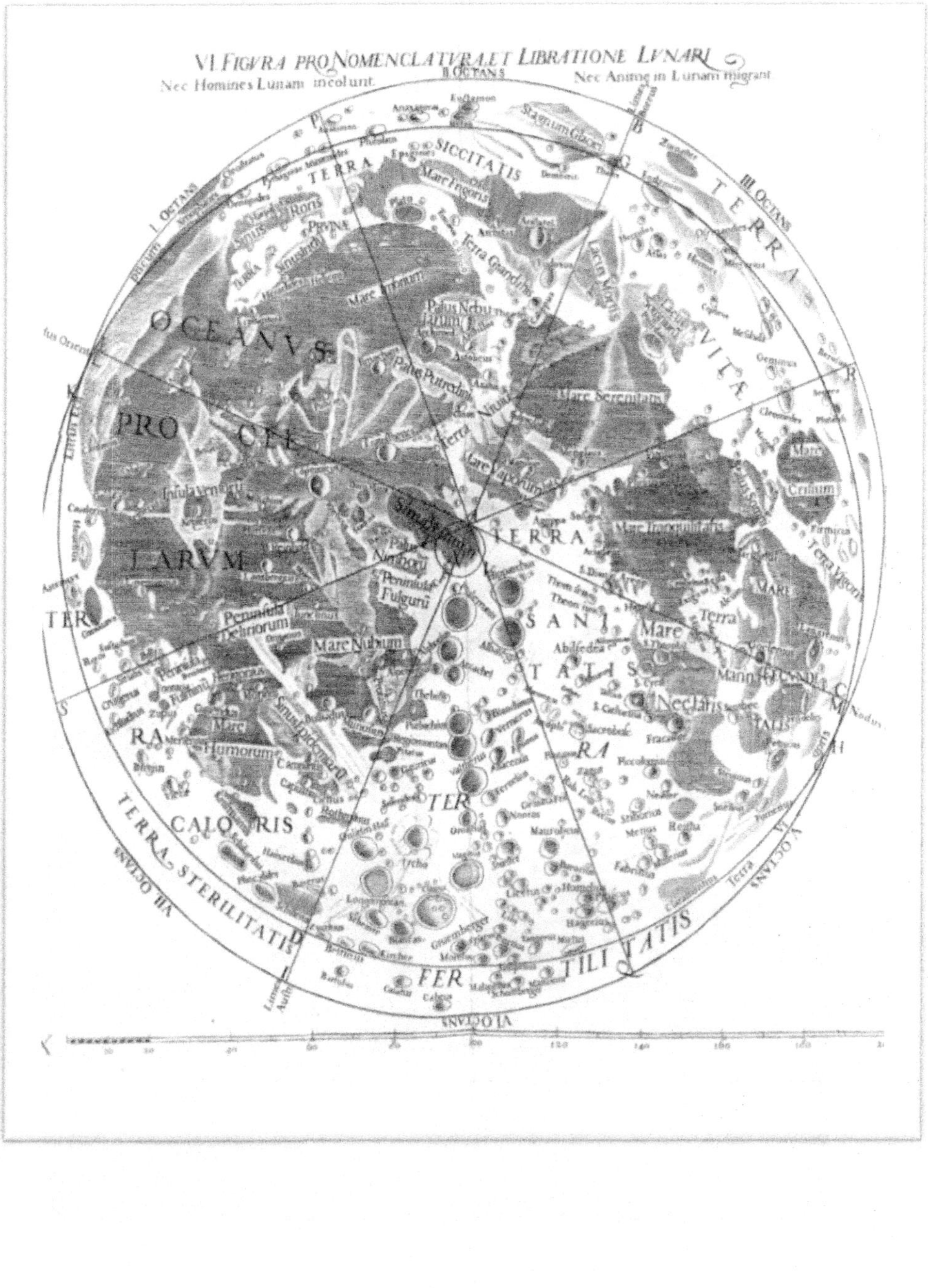
VI FIGVRA PRO NOMENCLATVRA ET LIBRATIONE LVNARI
Nec Homines Lunam incolunt
Nec Animae in Lunam migrant
II OCTANS
III OCTANS
V OCTANS
VI OCTANS
VII OCTANS
I OCTANS
TERRA SICCITATIS
Mare Frigoris
OCEANVS
PRO CEL LARVM
Mare Serenitatis
Mare Crisium
Mare Nubium
Mare Humorum
Nectaris
TERRA VITÆ
TERRA SANITATIS
TERRA CALORIS
TERRA STERILITATIS
TER FER TILITATIS

Printed in Great Britain
by Amazon